ALVCROMICON

15TH ANNIVERSARY – COLLECTOR'S EDITION

ALVAROMICON

— or —

SECRET TRADITIONS OF ELVES & FAERIES
THE BOOK OF ELVEN MAGICK & DRUID LORE

written by Joshua Free
with Foreword by David Zibert

Published underground as "Book of Elven-Faerie"
Revised and expanded to present this
15th Anniversary Edition.

© 2005 – 2020, JOSHUA FREE

ISBN : 978-0-578-54620-9

Come and enter the Enchanted Forest,
deep in the heart of the Green World,
and discover the greatest secrets of the
Ancient Mystery Tradition—
the hidden legacy of Elves & Faerie.

—TABLET OF CONTENTS—

GREENWOOD FOREST GRIMOIRE

THE ELVENOMICON--APPENDICES

FOREWORD TO THE 15TH ANNIVERSARY COLLECTOR'S EDITION

by David Zibert

THE ORIGINAL GUIDE TO THE ELVEN WAY! Come and enter the Enchanted Forest, deep in the heart of the Green World, and discover the greatest secrets of the Ancient Mystery Tradition—the hidden legacy and magick of Elves and Faerie.

Make your passage into Faerie as you discover the mysteries contained within this revolutionary and controversial underground classic by Joshua Free, revealing for the first time to the mortal world, a uniquely beautiful, authentic and complete guide to ancient Elven-Faerie Druidic Tradition, newly revised to commemorate the 15th Anniversary of the original *"Book of Elven-Faerie."*

The shinning path of the Elven Way grants any *Seeker* the key to unlock forbidden truths of esoteric archaeology including:

- How traditions of the Ancient Near East evolved into mythical, mystical and societal systems in Europe.
- How the forgotten arcane legacies of Elven-Faerie and even "Dragon" races on Earth have shaped the Western world and "Western magical tradition."
- How modern folk-magic and "New Age" revivals may be traced back to coincide with evolutions in Human civilization marked by specific ancient migrations.

"Elvenomicon" by Joshua Free offers an entire exploration into the Elven Way, Celtic Faerie Tradition and Danubian Druidism as never seen before. Drawing from hundreds of sources and underground groups, the "Elven-Faerie" tradition and system of magic is presented in its candid entirety, as applicable and alive today as it was thousands of years ago—and critically needed for our times and in our current environmental state.

The two complete "grimoires" included within the *"Elvenomicon"* bring an entirely new dimension of enchantment to the "New Age," allowing all dedicated initiates the opportunity to:

- Tap a vast otherworldly network of Elemental Power only alluded to elsewhere in "fairy" or "Druid" lore.
- Experience the vibrant energy of "Faerie magic" with over a dozen unique solitary rites and group liturgies.
- Access deep "Earth wisdom" known only to trees with a complete system of Elvish-Ogham "Forest Magick."

These long-lost teachings, traditions and techniques may even provide new historical foundations and credibility for modern magical revivals, resulting from *one seeker's* pursuits into the unspeakable origins of ancient Celtic Druidism...

"The normal world reflects a black magic spell designed to convince us that we are not Faerie Folk and that, in fact, Faerie does not exist. Once you see through the spell, a world of wonder unfolds before you."—The Silver Elves.[*]

Introducing the subject of the elves is always tricky business. Most, if not all, believes it impossible for such beings to actually exist, that they are contained only within the domain of imagination and fantasy. And yet, what is an "Elf" if not merely a word, a name? And names merely are *semantic* tools used for understanding an object (physical) or an idea (abstract).

"Semantics" are a language system, and like all systems it was created (programmed) and is gauged (updated) with some purpose or agenda in mind, not only by its original developer, but by those who eventually took control of said system

---

[*] The Silver Elves. *Elf Quotes*. Createspace, 2017. (p.70)

through time, as it is written: "Reality belongs to whomever holds the largest paradigm."[*] This is made particularly evident when looking up roots of the word "*reality*," as expressed in Joshua Free's major work, *The Complete Anunnaki Bible*:—

> *"This whole question of what is 'real' or 'not real' is a philosophical problem that affects not only the magickal world and metaphysics but all of science, religion and really any personal perception of 'truth.' The word 'reality' comes from an Indo-European root 'reg,' (as in 'regal,' 'region,' 'regular') which is related to a 'measuring device' or 'ruler' (and also as a 'ruler' as in 'king'). The word 'sane' relates to what is 'clean,' 'sanitary' or 'healthy' and functionally it was the purpose of the king or 'ruler' of the 'real world' or 'realm' to set boundaries for what is 'real' and 'not real'—and by which 'sanity' might be judged."[‡]*

It may be legitimately asked: who are these "Reality Engineers" behind our systems of perceptions and languages and, more importantly, what is their agenda concerning humanity —and everything else? Whatever the case might be, as per the "Hermetic teachings," everything in the universe follows the same course, coming from what might be called a singular, "divine breath." It thus logically follows that man-made systems—such as those of machines and computers—are based upon the same precept as the ordainment of the universe. This analogy offers great help when analyzing the reality program of the human life-wave.

Most human-made machines are programmed to think only in binary language—"1" and "0"—that computes as either of the terms "white" or "black," meaning "yes" or "no"—*Lux* or *Nox*. Humans, being some sort of "gods-made" machines,[§] are seemingly different. Indeed, we rather think through some kind of "grey zone," where lies notions such as 'maybe' or

---

[*]   Phil Brucato. *Mage: The Ascnesion (2nd Ed)*. White Wolf, 1995. (p. 42)
[‡]   Joshua Free. *The Complete Anunnaki Bible*. Joshua Free, 2019. (p. 19)
[§]   See *"The Complete Anunnaki Bible"* by Joshua Free.

'doubt', so that any "absolute" will appear "relative" from the perspective of the human program-paradigm. More appropriately, this zone is not "grey" but rather "rainbow," and it is within this zone that the games of semantic manipulation are played out as the "Reality Experiment." Names are used as a tool to define what lies in said grey zone (*i.e., reality*) with a common denominator so that humans may refer to them from the "I-not-I" perspective—shaping an "agreed upon reality," the wording themselves having no actual relation to what is named from a fundamental or "*Self-Honest*" perspective. Thus, names are applied to concepts defining reality, and it appears that an elite somewhere is controlling and tweaking which concepts and ideas are part of what is "real" and what is not, since what is created must always be somehow maintained, in one form or another—by some 'keepers,' or 'guardians'—or else disappear.

A clear demonstration of this erupted from a conversation I recently had with my circle—doing some translation work, I was looking for the French equivalent to the word "mind." Finding no satisfactory answer, I asked the opinion of friends and fellows—and while several alternatives were proposed— they each already possessed a more direct equivalent in English: i.e. "*esprit*" = "spirit"; "*conscience*" = "consciousness" or "*pensée*" = "thought," &tc; all of which are not the "mind." We concluded—although fully aware of what the "mind" is—that no exact word exists in French to express the idea. This is something very curious, since the "mind" is a rather important concept for humanity. Shouldn't an important concept, such as the mind, be readily and easily expressed in every tongue? What other important concepts are out there that have no word to express them? How purposefully so? What does this reveal about reality—and our perception thereof?

Elven tribes of yore fell victim not only to physical persecutions but also to the psychological semantic warfare methods previously alluded to in what can only be termed '*holocaust.*' This happened not only to the elves themselves but to all associated beings as well, now often relegated to fairy tales and fantasy role-playing games—beings such as *gnomes, faeries, dwarves, giants, trolls, &tc.*—we salute them!

Extending to the entire mythology of Pagan Europe—Elven Æurope—after the rise of Christianity: Indeed, the ancient gods and their tales are now seen as an integral of myths, which imply some kind of epic imagination, often interpreted through psychological lenses, as metaphors—more literal interpretations are seen as 'nonsense' or 'insane.' This process is, of course, not limited to Europe, but extends to all native spirituality, worldwide. It is also of interest to look upon the term "magic" in a similar light, also implying an act defying the rational—what is considered to be part of reality, being an act of the impossible or the miraculous. The word also refers to prestidigitation, or stage magic, which points to the use of 'deception,' or something 'false'—something that is "not real"—where true magic is actually concerned with practical applications for manipulating the "grey zone," allowing for a holistic, *Self-Honest*, reality experience.

As yet, the Elven Way is still well alive today, in some form or another, firmly rooted in our subconscious, for it is directly linked to our genetics. Elves not only marginally resurfaced, they are very popular today in pop culture—thanks to the work of fantasy pioneer J.R.R. Tolkien and role-playing games such as the ever-popular *Dungeons & Dragons*. Tolkien's influence regarding elves is now well known, and yet, while he is largely and rightfully recognized as the forefather of the fantasy genre, many believe that he created his world from scratch—when he actually "borrowed" much of it directly from ancient European pagan folklore. It thus happens that his work is, in some respects, a "revival"—or at least "survival"—of these lost traditions. Whether or not this reemergence occurred consciously seems irrelevant.

In *Dr. Leonid Korablev's* essay *"The True Elves of Europe"* he indicates that:

> "*Although Tolkien never made a secret of his sources, it is quite astounding how many of the folk and place-names in the 'Lord of the Rings' and 'Silmarillion' correspond precisely to ancient Norse-Icelandic, Anglo-Saxon and other ones that were actually used for things associated with elves. This seems to corroborate our hypothesis that in creating his elves, Tolkien might have been thinking of reconstructing the 'original' image that, should such an original exist, was reflected in various Elves of North-Western European mythologies.*"

In a manner similar to what has been remarked concerning the work of renowned author H.P. Lovecraft,[*] it appears that the forces behind Tolkien's inspiration—akin to the Greek "*dæmons*"—are using a human agent as a channel to resurface today. And we see this repeatedly in numerous instances at this dawn of a New Aeon.

Interesting parallels may also be drawn between the survival of the Elven Tradition through fantasy and that of the more commonly recognized Celtic Tradition and "Druidism," which stems from the same source and was kept preserved in the surviving writings of medieval Irish monks. This is demonstrated in another of Joshua Free's masterpieces, "*The Book of Pheryllt: A Complete Druid Source Book.*"[‡] It is curious to note how the Celtic Tradition and "Druidism" was absorbed by Christianity—thus any surviving texts are often viewed in the Neo-druid underground community as unauthentic, or else "corrupted," and yet it is this very commitment to writing which kept the tradition alive for us today.

Wherever we turn in the ancient world, we discover incredible testimonies that support the powerful ability of these archetypes to survive and adapt—an ability to adopt differing guises, often hidden in plain sight or else veiled as fantasy in the deceitful game of semantics. This is unsurprisingly quite

---

[*] Refer to "*Necronomicon Revelations -or- Crossing to the Abyss*" by Joshua Free. Joshua Free Publishing Imprint, 2019.

[‡] Published by Kima Global Books, South Africa, 2018.

typical of the Jovian-Mardukite energy current—the driving force behind all of the previously-mentioned aspects—accumulating and storing energy unnoticed, beneath the surface, only to bloom in full force when the conditions are gathered: just as a seed from a lone tree containing the potential of an eternal forest, waiting for millennia if necessary...

...finally to bloom against all odds when the stars are right.

—David Zibert
Mardukite Patesi of Canada
Council of Nabu-Tutu
Blue Room Office, Canada
Summer 2019

BOOK OF
ALVEN-FAERIE

—Ancient Eurasia—
Genesis of Elves & Faerie

Origins of the true "Elven-Ffayrie" legacy are prehistoric—relating back to distant roots in the *Ancient Near East*, lands of *Mesopotamia* and beings that Sumerians and Babylonians refer to as the "*Anunnaki.*" It is directly linked to the development of "agriculture"—a gift from "high minds" to nomadic cultures and a means to domesticate and systematize evolving societies. We see this present at the inception of our most recent "cradle of civilization"—and evidence of its migration as diverse "Elven," "Faerie" and "Druidic" traditions across ancient Eurasia—from Anatolia (Turkey) to Ireland.

Some readers will find this material shocking. Others will oppose the terminology used throughout this tome and even the stoic sincerity of its presentation—believing perhaps that this is an elaborate intellectual joke. However, the true esoteric legacy and lore of this subject not only compliments existing historical and anthropological data but also satisfactorily resolves many unanswered questions about origins of "humanity," development of cultural "systemology" and perhaps even the "human role" in the universe.

The legacy and lore explored herein is "occult" or "esoteric" for the fact that it remains hidden from public mainstream view—though hidden in plain sight—yet ever in the shadows. This process of bringing "what is hidden to light" may result in what some have called "enlightenment." Humans would seem to have lost a feeling, or a memory, linking them to the "Earth Ways," that perhaps was once "second nature" or "innate." Or, perhaps humans have not simply forgotten but have chosen—albeit subconsciously conditioned to choose by society—to ignore this inner calling; to deny it to the point where it is no longer heard and to even think about it is to be deemed "insane."

This book seeks to accomplish the impossible—for it contains a secret tradition in a concrete printed form that is not otherwise ever relayed as such by "Elves" themselves, those which do not actually record their histories and lore in this static manner. There is an innate reserve or cultural taboo regarding *fixed* writing of "sacred things"—called "light things" or "bright things"—including all history, "magic" and lore. The Druids later carried this in their tradition, believing that if one was no longer responsible to commit things to personal memory, then *"genetic memory"* attached to this legacy would become tainted or recessive and ultimately forgotten...

Cultural language and variegated regional semantics are all that separates the wisdom stream of the "Ancient Mystery School" as it evolved across time, alongside the systemology of the human condition. Spread of bloodlines, infiltration and development of diverse nations and their interpretations of a celestial-planetary religious pantheon all contributed toward further fragmentation of the original knowledge base. Once we move away from an evolving Egypto-Babylonian paradigm in the *"Ancient Near East"* paradigms, we can trace evolutions of its tradition by the "Light Folk" or "Star Folk" described elsewhere in Western Europe—generally as either of the High Elf (or "Dragon") "Sidhe Elves" of the "Faerie Courts," or else the Wood Elf or "Sylvan" varieties we find most often revived in modern "Neodruidism" and "Faerie Traditions."

According to the most ancient traditions, these "Elves" are the "firstborn" of Europe—separate and yet interconnected to the later "human" developments in the same region—and also direct descendants of the Anunnaki of E.DIN, or else the fertile cradle of systematized civilization and agriculture in Mesopotamia. Their existence is intermediary between what we classify as an "ancient god race" and "modern humans."

To those unfamiliar with this wide-angle scope of lore and the "generative" practices of the ancient Anunnaki, this data is in some ways misleading. When we examine the Anunnaki texts closely, we note that the "Elves" are indeed a part of the genetic "Eden experiments" but are not the same as what the same tablets refer to as the "first generation" of "human" life —or else *"Adamu"*—on these tablets. The "Elves" are created, and evolve, separately from the specific species, breed or "race" evolving as modern humans. Although lore suggests it is possible for them to interbreed, the "Elves" are specifically distinguishes as the "ninth Star race" (or "generation") of hybridized "half-gods" seeded on the Earth planet.

A popular modern derivative of this paradigm has become a mainstream household concept over the past few decades thanks to the wide revival interest in J.R.R. Tolkein's "Middle Earth." While it is easy to disregard all concepts related to a work of fiction—for the fact that it is relayed as "fiction"—an investigative seeker discovers inspiration is actually drawn from an author's own considerable interests or research into some aspect of history, esoterica or mythology. In Tolkein's version, the "Elves" are also the "first-born" race of "Middle Earth." He translates their name to link their genetic "star" ancestry as the *Children of Eru*"—with striking similarity to Celtic-Druid lore of the same as the "*Children of D'Anu.*"

"*Eru*" is "*Eurasian-Elvish*"—a feminine form of the name "Anu" in the earliest human language. Tolkein combined aspects of ancient language to base a "fictional" one for his own "Elves" and called it "*Quenya.*" It bares a resemblance in many ways to Mesopotamian, Nordic-Germanic, Irish and Gaelic-Welsh— elements of languages that are all attributed to "Elves" in their own respective historical mythologies.

The ancient "Elven Way" recognizes the name "Anu" or "Eru" as the Creative Force or "Source of All Being and Creation"— or essentially "God" in the most general "supreme" or "pro- genitive" sense. When we look to the Mesopotamian source traditions of the Babylonian "Mardukite" paradigm, the name "Eru" or "Erua" is given to "Sarpanit" (or "Zarpanitu")—the "hyridized-Elvish"* consort-wife of Marduk, the Anunnaki god of Babylon proper. By choosing an earthling spouse—and not the betrothed Inanna-Ishtar of the Anunnaki pantheon—Marduk relinquished "official rights" to reign in "Heaven." Babylon, in turn, became his medium to reign on "Earth" with assistance from his herald-heir-messenger-son "Nabu," who led a cult of cuneiform scribes and priest-magicians.

Even when the representative language and cultural icons change with time and geography, "*Elven Histories*" are aligned heavily with Sumerian and Babylonian lore—otherwise prehistoric and unrecorded—concerning an Anunnaki-governed Mesopotamia, from even a time before the "Flood." It alludes to a time "before humans"—something their loremasters insist is correctly interpreted. This memory does not, however, attempt to reconstruct fantastic stories by which to explain natural forces or even the cosmic genesis of the solar-system. For this knowledge is not maintained in memory by direct experience but was instead taught to them by the "stars."

Although it might seem more convenient to reflect only on the most recent examples of "Elves" and "Faerie" surviving in Western Europe, the truth is that this legacy is more wide-encompassing than the most familiar or popular stereotypes. It may be quite difficult for modern psyches to even grasp the existence of other terrestrial forms of evolved life in our past, interrelated yet separate from how we classify *homo sapiens*. Higher "forms" of life systematized and crossbred new forms of life in our distant histories—and while only fragmented knowledge remains of these events, it is an undeniable unanimous universal theme present in the backwaters of all lore regarding "Elven-Faerie" *and* "human" origins.

---

* *"Part-divine"*—of the seventh generation of Adapa, the original upgraded human, whose father was the Anunnaki god Enki and whose mother was a human. More details on the specifically Mesopotamian paradigm is found in modern "Mardukite" literature by Joshua Free.

If we take ancient lore at face value, a "higher class" of being essentially seeded this entire planet, then "Ascended," leaving the "Elves" and "Faerie" as Guardians responsible for it. Other "star-races" have since descended to the Earth, but we possess no reason to believe that all of these later appearances—or modern interactions with various interstellar or astral intelligences—are all directly linked to the same Anunnaki and Elven-Faerie races of our distant origins and/or of current relevance for this text. The faction or legacy we are presently concerned with relates specifically to the "Ancient Mystery School" and its genetic representation in the ancient world—primarily bloodlines of kingship and "royal families" that protected this genetic memory of the "Elven Courts" and "Fairy Princess" sort of archetypes in their DNA. Over time, the secret lore integrated more strongly with a "priest class," which shared in the same legacy, even if only intellectually. But, the secrets protected themselves as a myriad of cultural interpretations and languages transmutated its original form.

The following is one interpretation of the "Anunnaki genesis of the Elven-Faerie on Earth" derived from one tradition's "*Sylva D'Terrestai*"—roughly meaning "*Book of the Everlasting Forest*"—that bares a remarkable resemblance to the human version of the "Urantia Book"[*]:—

> The 'first generation' of Gaea is nameless. We know that it consisted of two people, twins, brought or sent here to be sure that Middle Earth was inhabitable in its physical form. Their lifespan was purposely short-lived, reaching full maturity with the passing of only 12 solar years. They were of such a nature that they were innately aware of the need to live for and with each other. Though the sexual gender is not mentioned, an aspect often obscure in matters of Elven-Ffayrie, "aliens" or any other interdimensional beings, we can

---

[*] "*Urantia Book*"—A literary contribution regarding higher spirituality, published in the 1950's of unknown "channeled" origins. It represents one possible evolving stage of an awakening understanding by human efforts over the past century.

be sure that they had the ability to reproduce. Thus, the planet was officially inhabited. [The vegetation and animals were here already, active and operating on their own 'genetic programs.']

At Eleven (Elven) years old, the 'Twins', as they are referred to, parented the firstborn of the 'second generation,' but truly it was the first Earth-born generation. In the act of love resulting in this conception (lust was not a part of the psyche yet) the genetic material really bloomed. With the birth of Andon and Fonta, it was clear that the abilities and genetic potential had actually increased as a result of the loving union of the "Twins." Yes, the whole is greater than the sum of the parts alone, and for whatever reason this evolution did happen and has never happened again. The cup being as full as possible with Andon and Fonta, could now only be emptied. For this reason there was a stress or pressure to maintain or preserve the purity and integrity of the Elven genetics and bloodline as time bore on...

As humans understand the social concepts, "genetics" and "race" are most frequently expressed in terms of skin color or pigment called "melanin." But this is not the strongest genetic indicator by itself—there are other cues, such as eye shape and color, hair type and color, skeletal structure and other facets anthropologists frequently use. According to the previous example, the descendents of Andon and Fonta are charged with possession of the true or original melanin of the "People of Earth," but they seem to have quickly relocated away from the "cradle of civilization." Andonites resembled closely to what we identify as Inuit Indians or "Eskimos" of "Elvish" decent that preserved a distinct genetics—as does another obscure evolving Elven race, the "Yezidi," which remained near Mesopotamia. But those "Elves" that left the "cradle" survived to evolve by first becoming "arboreal," else "living in the trees," using the forests for safety and shelter while honing their agricultural skills and herbal knowledge with the retreat of the last "Ice Age."

To continue from the previous text:—

Following the dispersion of Andonites across Europe, further generations and tribes emerged seemingly independent of one another. They continued first with the 'Foxhall Clan,' or 'Heidelberg Race,' who not only maintained some of their original Andonite genetics, but were also privileged to instruction of Onagar, the first 'Wise One.' With the ending of the Ice Age, folk culture emerged. Humans are adaptive, and modern day Hyperborean Inuits and Scandinavians seem to have mastered arctic living, yet have also had profound effects on the ecosystem of the North. With a focus shifting from keeping alive (or preservation) into expansion, more primitive and combative generations (races and factions) emerged. These others—such as the Badonan and Neanderthal—were not descendents from the Elves and did not survive...

For those races that did survive, a rainbow of genetic Melanin separated them by color. Each cousin race moved farther and farther from Mesopotamia but remained connected. The "red folk" became the Native American aboriginal shamans. The "orange folk" went to Africa for a while, but were later overrun by the "green folk." "Yellow folk" left Eurasia for East Asia. The "green folk" and "indigo folk" remained around North Africa, in Egypt and in their Mesopotamian homelands, which left the "blue folk" (or "light folk") who—according to this lore—represent the original strain back to the Source and are later known as the "*Fair Folk*" or "Faerie." From this point it is sometimes difficult to distinguish varying characteristics of "Faerie races"—"*dragons*," "*elves*" and "*fae*"—still present in some human genetics today, but it *is* there.

Celtic-Druid "Dragons" were eventually driven to Ireland, as were surviving vestiges of a "Dragon Priest-King" legacy that once even extended as far as the prehistoric Chinese empire. The Dragon-race carried very ancient and distinctive recessive traits: red hair, green eyes and fair or orange skin. It is the "Blue Race" of "Faerie," once residing in the Hyperborean

Germanic and Norse regions, that carry the more commonly attributed "Elven" traits we conjure to mind: blonde hair, blue eyes and fair or "albinic" complexion.

In addition to the "high" or "northern" Elven races that migrated throughout Eurasia, an additional Faerie emigration from the Ancient Near East stuck closer to Anatolia (Turkey), the Mediterranean and Danubian River Valley, spreading its prehistoric tradition from there. This included what evolved into the proto-Celtic and *La Tene* cultures; the "gypsy clans" throughout the Black Forests of Europe; the ancient Etruscan kingdom; Tartaria or Transylvania; even extending its reach to the Albigensian/Merovingian legacy of France.

Ancient tablets record all of the "wood elf" races as "dark headed"—marking them nearly indistinguishable from surrounding "human" populations. Much of our knowledge over time is an extension of our understanding—or rather, misunderstanding—of the ancient Anunnaki cuneiform tablets and other teachings from the "Ancient Mystery School." This information is fragmented and wholly disguised in the common "bedtime story" versions and reduced to fanciful religious "scriptures" that are little more than allegories in usefulness. They lead us to believe that all *homonids* on the planet are derived from a singular origin—Adam and Eve. While this would seem convenient in cataloging the descendants of a particular dynastic succession, it leaves many questions to be beheld.

The death of Abel—by Cain—alone would almost give reason to believe that everyone on the planet is the Son of Cain: of a lineage from Adam. The early Semitic *"Bible"* makes reference to other offspring begot by Adam and Eve, but these become mere background in the *Book of Genesis*. The *"Holy* Bible" omits Rabbinical lore of Adam taking a "wife" before Eve, named Lilith—lore mutated from early Sumerian *"lilitu"* demonology. The Vatican has removed these references believing that they know a "higher truth"—when in fact their own religion and "Bible" is completely based on Semitic texts.

We cannot tax the biblical Moses too heavily with fault—for he was roaming an endless desert charged with leading an up and coming nation of people. The story needed to start somewhere—and the Abrahamic tradition which first began in ancient Sumer (Mesopotamia) was no longer "clear." It all had to be simplified—reduced to something that the masses could remember, and simultaneously find motivation in. This legacy provided fuel sufficient to drive his people forward through their plight, resulting in an independent religion and Semitic race of "Hebrews."

The "Hebrews" and "Akkadians" (Babylonians) were once a part of the same Semitic cultural religion in Mesopotamia. It is only afterward that diverse peoples and languages spread out across the Ancient Near East—from Persia to Canaan. And while there is some scholarly debate about which early Anunnaki figure—or figures—is actually "Lord God Yahweh" of the *Old Testament*, there is little doubt that beneath the disguise of language and culture, the original ancient people once all shared a singular understanding of the "Celestial pantheon." And certainly this "Yahweh" or "Jehovah" of the *Old Testament* is a strikingly different persona than the "distant loving all-father" that Jesus is alluding to as "God" in the *New Testament*—a description which better fits the position and title of "Anu"—the *Heavenly King of the Anunnaki*."

As you reach for your handy copy of the *"Holy Bible"* to verify these things, a more intensive fifteen minutes of reading will also reveal to you that after Cain kills Abel, he leaves to lead a group of people occupying the land of Nod, even marrying a "cousin"—someone who is apparently born of something outside the *Eden Experiment*. Interestingly, Semitic texts reveal the strong possibly that Cain was not even Adam's son and was instead the result of an encounter between Eve and the "Serpent"—whoever or whatever that might be. It also seems clear that the Nodites did not originate in the Garden of Eden —so there was obviously something happening beyond what commoners are told in the standard *"Bible"* dilution.

Another example of the near-Eastern Elven legacy is the *Yezidi* people—a Mesopotamian sect found in northern Iraq that possess uniquely ancient genetics and culture that resembles a famous "lost tribe" that the Elves refer to. These folk are named for "God" in their language: who is *Yazdan*. According to their lore, this being is credited with creating (or naming) the Seven Chief Emissaries that we might best recognize as lore of the "Seven Anunnaki Zonei Gates." Most specifically for our purposes, the *Yezidi* claim to be descendants of "Adam but not Eve" and that the remainder of the world population exists independently of their own genetic legacy—a fact that is actually supported well with modern scientific DNA testing.

The biblical name Adam is derived from the "*Adamu*"—the class of Primitive Workers fashioned by the Anunnaki to ease the working toil of the ancient Igigi-Watchers, those developing the earliest prehistoric infrastructure in a time "before the Flood." If using the oldest writings as a base, the character we know as "Adam" is best related to "Adapa"—a name given to the "first man" of the newest race born of the "Eden Experiment" conducted by and personally begot by the Anunnaki god Enki—a son of Anu, and the father of Marduk.

Adapa's existence begins a new class of human being on Earth that is more advanced and intelligent than the original *Adamu* race. One branch of the Elven Way is actually named for "Adam-Adapa" which is also spelled "Edapa" and hence the "*Edaphic*" tradition. It emphasizes tending or "stewardship" of the ground or *Earth*. It is thought that Adam's long lifespan —as alluded to even in the "*Holy Bible*"—is the result of his purest genetic faculties, something lost with the breeding of later generations. At a later juncture, the Anunnaki instill a "program" into human DNA that restricts the "life-program" to 120 years. As suggested in my recension of the *Sylva D'Terrestai*:—

> *Outside the walls of Eden where things are not so sacred, the people began to get jealous about the 'supremacy' of those that*

resided within. Eve shared herself with one from the 'other races' because he had explained to her that it would 'help to spread the goodness and power' to the outland chaos. She had already been warned of this [by God]—not to mix the polarities of 'good' and 'bad.' The very moment Ffayrie mixed with Human, both Adam and Eve became aware of their mortality (prior they knew not death or suffering) because Eve's energy affected Adam when he shared himself with her thereafter. Adam and Eve lost their supreme graces. A new generation of Eve's offspring emerged that were quarter-breeds...

The man, Cain, was not the son of Adam. Cano,* the 'Serpent in the Garden' was responsible for the Degradation of Eden and jealousy between half-brothers (as Adam would clearly have had favoritism towards his own blood son.) After being tainted with the energy of lust, Eve laid with Adam and they shared the 'apple' and realized that now they were both impure and for the rest of their days. Cain went on to the Nodites and quarter-breeds, leaving Eves other children to carry the blood of Adam...

The "apple" or "cherry" remains an epitome of life and death as "decreed by the gods," or else divine fate or destiny. In the physical sense, it may even represent "life" via sexual union, or carry occult connotations to "blood." The "*Holy Bible*" even acknowledges the concept of two distinct opposing bloodlines quite frequently. Beginning with *Genesis 3:15*, we are told that there will be perpetual discord between the offspring of Cano ("the Serpent") against the remainder of Eve's children—presumably the "Sons of Adam." Then, Cain kills Abel from his jealousy of Abel being "so close" to Adam and leaves them all to pursue his own life. He does not actually carry the Adamic blood away with him; that all Humans have thought themselves to have been a part of since this story first spread.

Some translate the name "*Adapa*" as "found," and his wife—the biblical Eve—is found on ancient cuneiform tablets by the

---

* Sometimes written as *Kano*.

name *"Titi"* meaning "alive"—actually the compound double of the Sumerian word "TI" meaning "life." After being inspected by the Assembly of Anunnaki, Adapa returns to Earth to lead the life of a farmer-shepherd. The names "KA.IN" and "ABAEL" actually appear on Mesopotamian tablets as siblings. Ninurta—an emissary of the Anunnaki—instructs KA.IN in agriculture; while Marduk—another Anunnaki—is charged to teach ABAEL in shepherding. In this version, KA.IN also kills ABAEL and is exiled, requiring the Blessed Dynasty to be carried by further offspring of *Adapa* and *Titi*.

These same archetypal themes occur throughout history: the rivaling brothers; positions of royalty and supremacy; genetic integrity of a bloodline, *&tc.*—these are all very ancient and without a clear source or explanation without considering the mythic and prehistoric lore alluded to in Elven tradition. The same divisions and schisms of our ancestors are present with our own brothers and sisters—in family and community. We see the schismatic division in ancient Mesopotamian religions and followings split between legacies of Enlil and Enki. These two Anunnaki gods are also brothers—And in this instance, Enki represents the shepherd and Enlil is depicted as the farmer. Later in Babylon, Marduk assumes roles of both.

The Hebrew-Rabbinical *Book of Genesis*—and *Book of Enoch*—do contain some details regarding the Anunnaki or Igigi "Watchers"/*"Nephilim"*—referred to as *"Sons of God"*—those who took *"Daughters of Men"* as wives and begot children. Nearly all of these references—and remaining ones at the foundation of the entire Judeo-Christian paradigm—are dilutions from far more antiquated and complete cuneiform records, those we have since found and translated and others undoubtedly still waiting to be unearthed and added to our understanding.

According to ancient Anunnaki tablets, Enki was technically Adapa's father. And by successfully blending his "essence," he genetically advanced humanity and ensured his distinctive bloodline could be carried on Earth apart from himself.

After having several daughters, *Adapa* and *Titi* beget a child named SA.TI—the biblical "Seth." *Sati* and *Azura* have EN.SHI —the biblical "Enosh." *Enshi* and his sister-wife NO.AM beget KU.NIN—the biblical "Kenan." And on and on the generations go, the tablets closely matching common biblical scriptures— until we arrive at a special case: ENKI.ME, whose name means "By Enki, Understanding." This is the biblical "Enoch" that so greatly inspires mystic and occult lore. *Enkime*, of the seventh generation of *Adapa*, spent time with Enki and Marduk in "E.RI.DU"—the original proto-Sumerian home of Enki on the coast of the Persian Gulf in Mesopotamia. *Sarpanit*, a daughter of *Enkime*, was raised to goddess-status in Babylon after her marriage to Marduk, thereby launching a Mardukite legacy as an extension of Enki's original one.

It is important to remember that there are many semantic discrepancies between the stream of ancient esoteric lore and the Judeo-Christian or Gnostic interpretations that are more commonly known or simplified. To these scriptural scholars, the Anunnaki and Igigi are "angelic forces of God manifest on Earth." In another reference they might be considered "emis- saries" or "intermediaries between man and God." Whatever their nature, it is clear that these beings resided on the Earth in prehistoric times before present-day humans and this lore suggests that the rising human population (and its handling) caused—or continues to cause, depending on your beliefs— considerable conflict even among these "enlightened beings."

One commonly found primary facet of this ancient Elven lore relates back to the ability of these "ethereal," "godly," "an- gelic" or otherwise "faerie" beings to share consummate love with "mortals." In every ancient reference, this ability—even the thought of its physical action—was taboo in all respects among Anunnaki, Igigi, Elven-Faerie, &tc. In every instance "higher minds" considered humanity as still evolving "pets."

Close examination of cuneiform tablets records reveals that Enki conducted "genetic experiments" on humans. If we were to take ancient accounts literally, Enki is, in effect, the first to break the "Taboo of the Gods" by blending his own genetics with the Primitive Workers—a human female—resulting in the birth of Adapa. In the beginning, he attempts to hide the identity of Adapa from the Anunnaki, saying that he found the "*Adamu child*" as a baby floating abandoned on a river in a reed basket—*always a plethora of bastardized royal children being found in reed baskets on rivers in ancient times if you notice*. As a result, Enki maintained his Anunnaki position—as did his spouse Ninki. Although Enki broke the code of merging Anunnaki genetics directly with humans—or any indigenous planetary species—it is Marduk that is actually the first of the Anunnaki to take an Earthling spouse. Marduk justified *his* actions by explaining that his chosen mate—*Sarpanit*—was not simply of any Earth-blood, but a daughter of *Enkime*, and a descendant of Adapa—who was ultimately the son of Enki.

Rules of 'Kingship in Heaven' are very strict—Marduk was in-formed by both Enki and Ninki that he would forfeit all rights of "Kingship in Heaven" if he insisted on espousing any Earthling. As tablets record, Marduk is deliriously laughing when he responds that "such rights" have never been with his family and his time of rulership on Earth was already in danger of Enlilite usurpation. Marduk espouses Sarpanit and constructs Babylon—meanwhile *200 Igigi-Watchers* "descend to earth" and follow suit, taking females as wives. These are un-doubtedly the same beings recorded as "*Nephilim*" in *Genesis 6*. Lore even suggests that the *200* is a sum of *two-thirds* the total of the ranks: *300 Igigi-Watchers*—which follows perfectly with the later derived Semitic Judeo-Hebrew interpretation.

References to this lore are not only found in occult, esoteric and mystical sources—but also forgotten lore of the Gnostics and earliest Judeo-Christians. Consider the Dead Sea Scrolls, particularly the portion entitled: *Tales of the Patriarchs*. Within those pages we are made privy to a dialogue between *Enoch* and *Methuselah* where the natures of the "*Sons of God*" are re-vealed as "from a *star* origin." Elsewhere it suggests Noah was warned by a "mighty Watcher"—meaning a chief Anunnaki figure, and we know that since this "scripture" is based on a much older Mesopotamian version of the "Atra-Hasis" epic, this figure is undoubtedly Enki.

The *"Books of Enoch"*—which just so happens to include a work titled *"Book of the Watchers"*—describes the ability of "Enoch" to literally walk with "God" after being taken to "Heaven." The alleged author, Enoch, writes for posterity to preserve the "secrets of the Universe"—lore that was deemed too esoteric for acceptance by the orthodox Church. The "angels" instruct Enoch in the ways of magick and science, including a trip through the solar system—on his way to 'Heaven'—which is explicitly described in astronomical detail thousands of years ago, including a description of the earth as "round." In Gnostic and Semitic Judeo-Christian versions of this lore it is *Shamihaza* who leads "200 angels" down to earth—synchronous with older Mesopotamian sources mentioning *Shamgaz*, a leader among the "200 Igigi-Watchers" that did the same.

If we fast forward through the data, we arrive at a period of time after the initial corruption of Eden, when the *"Great Flood"* or *"Deluge"* occurred. Enlil held a strong inclination to allow the humans running rampant on Earth to simply perish unaided during a natural devastation. Out of all the Celestial pantheon, it was Enki and Marduk who sought to preserve their own legacy—and genetics—on earth: their personal domain. Some of this is described in contemporary versions of the Semitic "Noah," but far greater details are found on older cuneiform tablet writings—such as the *Atra-Asis* and *Epic of Gilgamesh*—predating the Hebrew scripture by thousands of years.

When we refer to specific races and bloodlines of a culture we are often singling out smaller sects from larger populations. Ancient Celtic culture is very Elven-Ffayrie oriented, but only the "Sidhe" and original "Drwyd" Wizards are considered a part of the actual "divine" bloodline or legacy themselves.

We find a similar situation again with the installation of the first "Dragon Kings" of "dragonblood" that appear in ancient Sumerian and Babylonian society; the Pharaohs of Egypt; the Scythians and original "Vampyres," the list goes on and on. Certain dynastic genealogies carry a long tradition of association with "royal sky-god lineages." It is is even likely that the Sidhe derived their name from Scythian anestry. The word is actually pronounced "*sithian*," and "sith" in Gaelic is "*sidth*" (singular) and "'*sidhe*" (plural) pronounced "shee." it is not difficult to see how "Anunnaki" lineages evolved into lore of "Devas" and "Sidhe" when each of these three names are varying regional titles for the same "Shinning Ones." These "Shinning Ones" emerge in a variety of forms in "New Age" mystical doctrine—typically as energies sought or connected with in ritual magick. Other lore indicates that the Anunnaki were similar to the Greek "Fates," a word based on lore of the European "*fata*"—yet another label for "Ffayrie."

Many stereotypes associated with "Elven Courts" and "Druid Councils" are rooted in the ancient proto-Sumerian Dragon Priesthood from a culture anthropologist classify as "*Ubaid*." Masses of these people expanded their civilization and knowledge beyond even the domain of Mesopotamia—they became known as Scythian and Dravidian folk that spread to Anatolia, India and Western Europe. In a region referred to as the *Gangetic*, the Aryans and Dravidians discovered one another and merged to form a race later many call the "*Tuatha De Dannan*" (*D'Anu*, or *Anu*.) This race—still considered Andite (or *Children of Andon*)—carried their culture along the Danube and Rhine Rivers, bringing Mediterranean and Mesopotamian systemology across mainland Europe, eventually reaching the British Isles. Along their travels they met the 'blue folk' who had continued to develop separately from the Eden project. These folk had developed the "*La Tene*" culture that we now call Celtic. Together this "Danubian" race established "Druidism," which dominated Europe until the rise of the Milesians and Roman populations—and the inception of "human history."

—The Age of Faerie—
Children of the Stars

Elven History—and the languages that preserve it—links directly with the cosmos. When we examine the words used to describe Elven-Ffayrie beings as *"Shinning Ones"* in any language, we find that they are really a reference to "shinning stars," including the hereditary Elven names "Eru" and "Anu" —as well as the common roots *"En-"*; *"El-"*; and *"Er-."* In some Elven traditions, the root *"Ela-"* is reserved exclusively to refer to "stars" specifically to avoid confusion. This then, by some interpretation, makes the Anunnaki (*"anu-nagi"* or *anu-naki*) the "star-dragons"—based purely on "Elvish" semantics. And a synonym for the same in Elven language is *"elaynor"*-- which can mean either "star-dragon" and "star-fire." Using this logic, the later "Children of Anu" become *"Children of the Stars,"* or "Star-born," which translates as *"elen"* and *"elan"* in Elven language.

"Eloya" translates in human tongue as either "Elven-heart" or "Star-heart." Ubaid Enki'ite proto-Sumerians are then: the descendents of a "star." We simply attribute differences in the terminology and semantics—as opposed to "Watchers" and "Nephilim" &tc.—to shifts in Eurasian cultural language and its ability to preserve the knowledge stream clearly. The "Watchers" appear in ancient times almost as intermediaries in form—between the physical plane of Gaea and the spiritual place of the Source. They are powerful when they appear in archaic lore, but are not "God," even when the names of the energies include: *En, Enlil, Enki, Ea, Yah, Iah, Jahovah, Iao,* and *Yahweh.* Traditional "scriptures" might have us believe that the whole lot of these earthborn intermediary beings were wiped away with the "Flood"—but they would be wrong.

Mesopotamian mythology mentions these intermediaries as "Dragon Kings"—humanoid, but not "human." These tablets give them names like Enlil and Enki—and refer to "Gaea" as Tiamat, their word for the *Primordial Dragon.** It is Enki who claimed the title "Lord of the Earth"—and he is credited with discovering and perfecting many bioengineering practices. When we consider the archaic *Near Eastern* lore of "fallen angels" and "genetic intervention," we better understand later Elven-attributed archetypes of "faerie lovers," "changelings" and even the idea of giving birth to "alien babies."

Contemporary society treats these subjects as "fantasy"—and nearly all humans hold the idea that the "Creatures of Faerie" are simply fictional beasties of "myth" and "legend." We are not only speaking of stereotypical Elven "fair-skinned forest dwelling gardeners"—but also the Sylphs, Sprytes, Dragons, Drakes, Dwarves, Gnomes, Merfolk (Undines), Nixes, Pixies and Leprechauns...among others. These are all "Children of Faerie"—misunderstood beings that now primarily exist only on the brink of Human imagination. And yet for those who dare to seek the underlying origins of this lore—we do find reason to "believe" that there is something very "real" here.

In our previous discourse [chapter] the idea of genetic intervention is approached—whether as a result of leading groups of humanoids on Earth, a Creator God, or some intermediary in between. Even "selective reproduction"—when used in the manner described in Elven-Ffayrie history—is a method of genetic intervention. Environmental adaptation also affects our genetics—and adaptation is necessary for the survival of any species. That means for a species to eventually overcome a barrier that affects its livelihood, it will have to change. This "genetic intervention" paradigm, at the very least, helps us resolve some unresolved issues regarding Human ancestry—since it is clear that all existence on earth is manipulated and controlled in some form or another of "authority."

---

* See also *"Draconomicon: The Book of Ancient Dragon Magick"* by Joshua Free.

As a science, *Anthropology* is unable to sufficiently answer the problems of Human origins. Originally, the field sought to find an answer that would correlate with the Judeo-Christian Genesis--but at the time these goals were established, religion and science were at war with one another. Instead of "God-creates-Man so man comes from a Supreme and beautiful being," it somehow developed into "Man is a primitive ape who just got lucky out of random chaos." Darwin and other evolutionary purists also failed to demonstrate how only some Cro-Magnon evolved into Human, when in fact, Cro-Magnons do not get "bred out" or evolve—they *go extinct*.

The real issue for our current purposes concerns the "star origins" of Elves and Faerie races. There is certainly enough literary support for this within a paradigm that allows for aliens, inter-dimensional or interstellar beings. If Humans were able to put aside pride long enough to see clearly, great wisdom might come from acceptance of an advanced civilization or aspects of prehistoric Man that exist beyond traditional knowledge of history. Without accepting the possibility of a particular 'scientific paradigm' or 'framework' you cannot expect to see it or prove it. Usually the expectations and rules of what we see and experience are programmed by the social culture to which we belong or are raised. Without looking beyond an existing boundary, achievements cannot be made.

The historical setting for the arrival of the *"Tuatha D'Anu"* is "officially confined" to the legacy of ancient Ireland—called *"Eire," "Erin,"* and *"Eriu."* They arrived there on Beltane (May Day or May's Eve) "concealed in a magical fog or mist." While the European mainland lay off to the East and South of Ireland, the Tuatha D'Anu arrived from the North and West of the Island, settling first in the mountains of Western Ireland. This led many to believe they were the "People of the North" or that they came from somewhere in the Atlantic Ocean. But, their ships, on the other hand, were said to be of a "sky-nature," which somehow caused an uncanny solar eclipse for the first three days of their arrival. This could otherwise be a reference to the thick fog that cloaked their ships—enveloping them as they reached harbor. In either case, the ancient Celtic manuscripts record that the Tuatha D'Anu intentionally destroyed their ships in flames upon landing.

When the Tuatha D'Anu arrived, Ireland was already inhabited by an Elven-Ffayrie race—another descendent from the "blue folk" called the "Nemed" or "Fir-Bolg," translated perhaps too literally as "Men of Bags." The Fir-Bolg were forced to take shelter as a result of the three days of smoke/fog/mist that affected Ireland. Needless to say they interpreted the Danubian arrival as an invasion of hostility—and a war ensued between the two Faerie races.

If we are to give European topics and semantics a treatment in this current volume, we must, of course, lend an ear to the Celtic-specific sources for literary verification. Unfortunately, medieval and modern writers have a habit of confusing membership in the Tuatha D'Anu with their adversaries, the Fir-Bolg. Why unschooled practitioners would call on both sides for reconstructionism or "magickal work" simultaneously in modern traditions is beyond the author's understanding. This occurs frequently in "New Age" interpretations of ancient mysteries—and is especially evident in revivals of Mesopotamian Neopaganism using the "Anunnaki" pantheon. More confusing still is the incorporation of the pre-Fir-Bolg Cthonic "Fomorian mythos." To be certain, we have compared our research for this volume with more antiquated cryptic Celtic manuscripts, especially: "The Book of Invasions," "The Book of Leinster," "The Book of Dun Cow," the Oghamist's "Book of Ballymote" (and "Scholar's Primer") and Pheryllt-Barddas material of the Welsh-Drwyds.

Some scholars and metaphysical writers are confused by the common spelling of the tribe—"Tuatha De Dannan"—and mistakenly align the Elven-Ffayrie tradition (origins) to "Dana," derived from 'Diana,' the Roman forest-huntress. The present author emphasizes the "D'Anu" spelling that is factually more accurate—as in the "*D'anube River*" and "*Children of Anu.*" To call them "Dannan" confuses them with the "Danes"—a separate Elven-Ffayrie legacy partly found among Scandinavians (Norse/Nordic), Vikings and "*Svei*" or "Swedes."

When the Romans encountered one Danubian clan in Scotland they called them "Picts" or "Pict-Sidhe"—or "pict-shees" —which is where one of the more popular titles developed. Where we are led to believe the word "pixie" means "small," its roots—"*Pict-*" and "*Pix-*"—relate specifically to etymology for the words "picture" and "pixels," which is why Elven lore refers to the same tribe as the "Painted Folk," those known for their use in tribal full-body art, reminiscent in many ways to certain "primitive" revivals today.

Tuatha D'Anu possessed a unique cultural magical tradition far surpassing any indigenous ones they encountered—making a tremendous impression on the proto-Celts—or *La Tene* culture. With the arrival of the Tuatha D'Anu, ritual and ceremonial "magick" practices began—aligned to the elements of nature, or else "Elementalism." The original Danubian tribe of Elven-Ffayrie carried with them the "Gifts of Faerie"—four objects or artifacts that proved their skill in the "Arts of Civilization" and crafts of magic—in fact, they viewed both "art" and "magic" as one and the same, a belief carried by most Elven and Faerie traditions. As such, "Western Æurope" saw the birth what we call the "Western Magical Tradition."

As some readers are undoubtedly familiar: Western ritual and "ceremonial magic" is based primarily on a four-fold alignment with the "Four Elements" and equally the four cardinal directions—or "four winds" if your prefer. These are the representations or embodiments of the four "Gates" to Beyond— or else "four corners" of the Universe—that bind together the parts we call "space and time." Using a paradigm such as the "Gifts of Faerie" allows a greater experiential understanding and handling of these energies—in ritual and consciousness, since they are both the same.

in Nature allowing for development of "Elemental Magick." Ceremonialists and modern Wizards of the O.T.O, Golden Dawn and such, have been unable to break away from the core and fundamental Elementalist paradigm for their ritualized magickal expressions. Though their 'higher' ceremonial and celestial practices are not the same as you might find among the naturalist shaman, the same correspondence charts of magick are as useful to them as to any Elf, Druid or Elemental Wizard.

According to tradition, the *"Gifts of Faerie"*—also known as the *"Gifts of Faeire"*—were brought to Ireland each from a different elementally-aligned city, by a surviving representative from that city. Many have believed these legendary cities existed on "Atlantis" or some other lost continent, meaning the Elven-Ffayrie—and specifically the Tuatha D'Anu—were the survivors of "Atlantis" or similar. Other lore suggests that their cities were of an "Otherworld" nature—perhaps "astral" and therefore, by definition, "stellar" or "celestial," meaning literally of a "star" nature. Another possibility is that these semantics are only a cultural paradigm and that the *Atlantis* described is really Mesopotamia—or similar—but *before* the "Great Flood."

THE GIFTS OF FAEIRE

"The 'Stone of Fal,' of the Northern city of Falias, came to us from Morfessa, High Wizard of the North. This stone was set at Tara, the 'Seat of the Kings' (literally "Dragons") where it would scream out whenever a true king set foot on it. Irish Druid history tells us that the only kings in Ireland during Celtic times were those who were made so on the 'Stone of Fal,' also called the 'Stone of Scone.' The true nature of the Element of Stone is Earth, and to the direction of North, Wizards have attributed it.

"The 'Spear of Lugh' emerged from the Eastern city of Gorias carried by Esras. Known also as the 'Spear of Destiny,' this tool never missed its target. Some say it was the implement used to pierce Christ's side at the Crucifixion and was also carried by Hitler's Nazi army. That the item never misses its target hints at the relationship between the Wizard and a tool. It is driven or activated by willpower (the art of directing energy to a target) and so it becomes the "wand" in the magickal tradition. Both the wand and the spear are attributed to the power and energies of Elemental Air, reserved to the direction of East.

"From the city of Finias the 'Sword of Nuada' came, carried from the South by Uscias. Here is the archetypal 'magic sword' archetype, for this blade carried with it other great names through history like "Albion," "Caliburn," and more famously, "Excalibur." It is connected to the Elven-Ffayrie tradition as the 'Sword of Greenwood Kings', carried by both Arthur Pendragon and Robin Hood. It is imbued with the ability to deal fatal blows with each strike, representing the surety of will, and the cutting, flaming, searing edge of willpower being properly directed. The sword or blade is always a symbol of Fire, dedicated to the Southern direction.

"The 'Cauldron of the Dagda,' or Kerridwen's 'Cauldron of Rebrith,' came to Ireland by Master Semias from the city of Murias to the West. In one legend, the cauldron acts as a 'horn o' plenty', refilling itself with an endless supply of food. Other lore suggests the artifact was used as a part of a healing ritual, reviving and curing the wounded. Some believe the 'Gundestrup Cauldron,' found in the swamps of Denmark is similar to the 'Cauldron of the Dagda.' As a symbol, the cauldron itself is a primary icon of magick and witchcraft. Most modern practitioners use a goblet or chalice, representing the 'Holy Grail,' as their representation of the Water Element. Ceremonially, the symbolism is almost identical. Some traditions incorporate both the cauldron and the chalice for different ritual purposes."

When the Tuatha D'Anu finally overcame the Fir-Bolg, they offered the remaining surrendering race—approximately 300 Elven-Ffayrie in all—their own region of Ireland to live and thrive, provided they could share the island in peace. The Tuatha D'Anu were clearly not as aggressive of a race as the Fir-Bolg or the Fomorians before them—or even their cousin-fey: the Danes, Scandinavian Vikings and Norse Wizards. The true Highborn-Elves enjoy long lifespans. They are not quick to throw that privilege away, nor is a scar or severe wound considered a battle trophy—since they would have to carry it with them perhaps hundreds of years. Yet, pacifist ideals of the Tuatha D'Anu did not keep them from eventually winning the battle with the Fir-Bolg, their own distant relations.

Danubians never came to Ireland seeking a fight. We are in some ways led to believe they were running from something themselves—had no doubt already seen countless battles and suffering and abandoned their ships on arrival to Ireland as if to say: "This is it! Here is our new home. We're sick of running." But existing populations viewed this as a malignant act of invasion—and battle was inevitable. Their intellectualism and few numbers did, however, keep them from fighting off the Milesians—the 'Sons of Mil,' or else, "mortal humans."

Around the year 500 BC—though some suggest earlier—the Milesian "Celts" invaded Ireland from Iberia—presumably Spain—intending to drive the Tuatha D'Anu out. They were "mortal Humans" using their strengths—overwhelming numbers and crude weapons—to take over Ireland. The Milesians possessed no "magical abilities" themselves and were immediately intrigued by the Tuatha D'Anu and their mysticism. Some of them thought to enslave the race and force them to use their magic for Humans. Of course, the Danubian Celts did not share this idea—so the Elven-Ffayrie simply left! A few remained—loving the land of Eriu so much that they somehow transitioned into its Underworld—and beneath the conscious surface of Human awareness. Invisible, they were later called "Daoine Sidhe"—dwellers of burial mounds or "fairy hills."

The Tuatha D'Anu that did not remain hidden in Ireland went on to become legendary "*Trooping Faerie-Sidhe*" of Scotland—the ones that Rev. Robert Kirk[*] encountered—those known elsewhere as the "*Seelie*" and "*Unseelie*" courts. Others went to Wales, joining their cousins—the "Pheryllt" Dragon Priests inhabiting mountainous regions there. In Wales, surviving members of the Tuatha D'Anu maintained their mystical ways and natural philosophy, called "*Druideachd*" or "*Derwyth*"—which is better known as "Druidism." Readers that may have previously believed that traditions of the Elven-Ffayrie have been handed down to European humans in the form of Celtic Druidry would be essentially correct. Yet, the largest misconception about Danubian Druidism and its later Celtic Faerie Tradition is that instead of a confinement to Ireland and the British Isles, it is actually found throughout Æurope/Eurasia. Before the world-wide destruction of the Drwyds by the Romans Empire, Keltia had extended from Ireland all the way to "Galatia,"—meaning Anatolia or modern day Turkey. In fact, Galatia was home to a "Drunemeton," a legendary and sacred place in Ancient Elven-Ffayrie Drwyd lore, where large convocations/gatherings took place annually.

The Sidhe shared a name and legacy with the bloodline of Scythian Kings. What's more: there may or may not be a connection between the "Scythians,"/"Sithians"/"Sidhe" and the iconic Scythe-Sickle blade of the Druids. This blade was used to cut sacred herbs—and is a symbol of the Fire Element. The "Golden Sickle" may actually be used in place of the sword or ritual blade as a tool of "Elemental Magick." Other traditions employ it specifically as an "herbalist dagger" or *boline*.

When we follow the trail of lore concerning the Sidhe, we can determine that they are the largest or rather the tallest descendents from the Tuatha D'Anu. With their adept mystical skill, it is difficult to judge size of full-blooded Elven-Ffayrie races because most of them have ability to alter it, "shapeshift," and "polymorph." The form that the Sidhe took after

---

*   *Rev. Robert Kirk*—explained later in the current volume.

the coming of the Milesians is considered ethereal or akashic-astral. This allowed them to transition easily into the Otherworld—an alternate "dimension." It could only be in such a form—spirit-like or invisible—beneath the surface of Human perception, that they would be able to remain in the same Green World, but in the "Hollow Hills" and the "Lands Beneath." Due to their ethereal nature, the Elvish Wizards and Drwyds (remaining in the physical world) said that "twilight" *threshold*—either dawn or dusk—is the best natural condition of *time* to see their "spirit-forms."

"Druidism" was never truly a "religion" to the Drwyds in the way we look at "religion" today. They may have viewed their own craft of knowledge as a philosophical art-form—or as a basic expression of "life." But—much like Moses and his own Abrahamic religion—ancient Drwyds were charged to lead a people with their wisdom, mysticism and natural philosophy, all of which reflected true teachings of the "Ancient Mystery School" and the legacy of "Dragon Kings" and Elven-Ffayrie wizards and priestesses. Just as we are able to witness in the Ancient Near East—cultural tradition developed as a result of "higher minds" mixing with indigenous populations. Keltia was a vast land occupied by many diverse tribes and clans. It is for this reason, giving credit to these wise "systematizers," that classical writers and historians refer to "Druidism" as the "Religion of the Celtic people."

Religious customs included water-elemental baptismal rites, representing an "Underworld Initiation." Baptism rituals are not exclusive to Christianity—especially since a Jew baptized Jesus himself. Funerary traditions involved a three-day wake, after which the actual funeral ceremony was observed. The *La Tene* culture seemed to cremate their dead at first, whereas the Ancient Ones preferred burial in mounds and tombs. The very idea of Elven-Ffayrie residing in burial mounds and Dragon Kings living in pyramidal tombs may have contributed to related traditions of "Vampyre" lore—another greatly misunderstood and misrepresented faction of esoterica.

Pliny the Elder speaks of an Elvish Drwyd custom of "cutting the Mistletoe"—a subject of minor controversy among some neodruid revival traditions. Everyone seems to have an opinion about how Mistletoe grows; the range of it in ancient times; and on what trees it can grow on (or not at all). It actually *does* grow on Oaks; just not very often. Mistletoe became associated with the Druidic *"Alban Arthuann"* festival—or Winter Solstice (Yule). Names for the Mistletoe in Gaelic languages translate to mean "all-heal" and "high branch." This sacred herb was considered the primary active ingredient in all herbal medicines and ritual incense—thus, it was incorporated in nearly all uses of "herbalism" and "tree magic" as the "supreme catalyst."

When the Milesian Celts finally equalized with the remaining Dragon heirs, Elvish Druids and Ffayrie Priestesses, they were no longer their own race isolated on a private island or mainland forest for the first time. To maintain and preserve their most sacred traditions, history and mystic rites—a part of which you hold in your hands right now—they had to form an "Order," "Mystery School" or "Secret Society." They reserved themselves to ancient and secret groves to learn and teach their way, independent of Human eyes. Yes, many of them were now a large part Human—but those still maintaining any part of this tradition remained separate from the 'herd.' The "Bardic College" and "Druid Order" were born—origins for the modern "Wizard School" archetype. And while some secret cabals had existed prior, the Druids maintained influence in the Celtic World ("Keltia") for one-thousand years.

Gaelic-Welsh was the official language or national language of the Elven-Ffayrie of the British Isles—first written publicly in Greek letters. There were other "characters" not used for common purposes, such as the Ogham Forest Alphabet. Today this system is considered primarily a divination tool in the "New Age," but it can more appropriately be used for "High Forest Magick" and communion (or communication) with the woodlands. The Ogham alphabet was even used for the construction of coded wood and stone signs spread all through-out Keltia readable only by the Elven Drwyds and members of their secret society.

Popularity of the Ogham system has grown in modern times alongside the Nordic Runes—and for similar purposes. While it was forbidden to write many of the sacred teachings down, lore was still maintained at hundreds of "sylvan libraries" formed from leaves and bark of trees to form characters and letters of the Ogham alphabet. The Romans destroyed many of these and St. Patrick reportedly burned (or overseen the destruction of) more than two hundred of them in Ireland. In a flash, the Romans and Christians became cardinal enemies of the Elves, Dragons, Faerie races, and the preservation of their most ancient tradition.

—The Dark Ages—
A Thousand-Year Elven Holocaust

The "Elven Holocaust"[*] is a period in world history synonymous with what we generally call the "Dark Ages." The Church of Rome controlled all maters of religion, science and state government during this era. Its suppressive influence caused the Secrets-of-the-Ages (the "Great Magical Arcanum") to be all but lost to human civilization forever—and this superior wisdom is only recently being reintroduced to mainstream awareness as it creeps out slowly from the underground.

Until the Dark Ages, the Dragon Kings were the noble class of Europe. Kingship or "Enlil-ship on Earth" is originally granted by "Divine Right" based on "royal blood" and "genetic integrity"—overseen by "dragon-priests," the true wizards of what is now considered "mythological history." In addition to Anunnaki-born, other related biblical figures carry this line, including Abraham and Moses, and even the Davidic House of Judah. More seeded dynasties were maintained in Egypt and elsewhere throughout Europe, especially after the migration of the Tuatha D'Anu. Parts of this original tradition have seeped into many surviving systems of Hebrew mysticism, the Edaphic Tradition and preserved lore and histories of the Ancient Near Eastern *Holy Lands* held by secret societies.

The Judeo-Christian system forsakes Anunnaki lore for later Semitic visions of monotheism held where Enki is the "wrathful God" of the *Old Testament* who worked with his "angels" (or names eventually passed on to Marduk when he attempts

---

[*]   *"Thousand-Year Elven Holocaust"*—a term coined by the late Nicholas de Vere von Drakenberg of the "Imperial Sovereign Dragon Court and Society" to describe the period of Dark Ages illustrated in this chapter.

succession for "Enlil-ship") on Earth to perform remarkable feats. Immediate descendents of Enki are primarily the Babylonian "Elder Gods" of Mesopotamian Tablets—the Mardukite Pantheon of Babylon—and cousin to the Nephilim or Watcher races—specifically dedicated to Anu and Enlil—as mentioned in some translations of accepted scripture. This same bloodline went on to manifest throughout Europe as the Elf Kings and Faerie Queens of legendary renown.

The term "Elven Holocaust" refers specifically to the chaotic period of intellectual and spiritual "Dark Ages" on the Earth between 751 AD and 1736 AD. After this point, Fraudulent Medium Laws & Anti-Witchcraft Acts still made participation and/or adherence to the esoteric legacy illegal. In similar fashion to how Romans eradicated Druidry, the new Church now feared any remaining true remnants of the esoteric past that might threaten their own self-given totalitarian "divine right to rule." As a result, they moved to eliminate all traces of "magic," and anyone in possession of its knowledge could be punished by death—including those naturally of Elven and Faerie "witch" ancestry. We use the word "holocaust" to describe these events due its parallels with World War II. True "royal blood" maintained by Dragon Kings until 751 AD now ceased to reside in the royal households. The Roman Church began distributing conquered lands and rights of Kingship for their own political and administrative ends.

Curiously, up until the Dark Ages, the Dragon Kings and Elves were actually cooperatively coexisting with the Church. They even carried truths about Jesus, the "Holy Lands" and the Old Testament—which they mistakenly shared with the Church. The Merovingian legacy descended directly from the knights of Solomon's Temple. Elements of their tradition and genetic memory is maintained later by some exclusive orders of Freemasons, Cathars and Templar Knights—all of which originally required a family lineage of membership to be considered for admission/initiation. Today we see a different kind of "accepted" membership that is not nearly as strict in its criteria.

The "Merovingians" were "Knights of the Temple" protecting the mysteries of Rome until they were brutally "dispatched" in 751 AD—or even earlier, as some suggest that executions may have begun in the year 664—and replaced by the group known as the Carolingians, those with no affiliation with the original Elves and Dragon Kings.

A document appeared in 751 AD allegedly signed during the 4th Century reign of Emperor Constantine. This is what made enforcement of an "Elven Holocaust" possible—and justifiable in the eyes of the Church. When Pope Sylvester cured him of leprosy, Constantine supposedly donated the entire wealth and power of the Roman Empire to the Church...and yet this was not invoked until several centuries later, leaving many to believe this document—*The Donation of Constantine*"—is not even authentic, but purely a forgery used for political ends. With activation of this "trust," the Roman Church assumed control over the "known world," thrusting civilization into the Dark Ages. Certainly this could not be the original and true vision of Jesus Christ for his "church." Consequently, all Dragon Kings were replaced by those crowned by the Vatican.

After the "Age of Faerie" was forgotten, Danubian Druids became mythological and legendary deities of the Celtic people: they believed the Sidhe always resided in the invisible world; and the era of "magic" ended, giving way to a false lineage ruling Æurope under the banner of "Holy Mother Church." Although Gnostic and Essene sects of early Christianity inspired the now "secret" gospels, as well as Christ himself, those in control during the Dark Ages ruled under the name of Jesus, but developed propaganda for a religion of genocide.

While surviving members of the Elven-Ffayrie may hold a lingering resentment against ignorant members of Christian Tradition in history, they do not find contradiction between Christ's actual teachings and their own. The misuse of a "Religious Empire" by the Church, however, marked the beginning of the "Dark Ages," a time when even Christians were leaving

Catholicism to start their own protestant religions. In breaking with the original Church, however, these new religions continued propagating fundamentalist misconceptions about the Bible and its history—and no longer connected to Rome, they also lost access to Vatican records—even if most of them remained off limits. During these Dark Ages, a new version of the "*Bible*" emerged eliminating all esoteric references to the Elven-Ffayrie Histories, mysticism, reincarnation, *Old Testament* interactions with the Anunnaki, and several full books. By this time, all of the former traditions and lore relating to the Elven-Ffayrie, Druids and Dragon folk were condemned as "demonology" and "devil-worship" by the Church, and were equally considered off-limits "for the safety of your soul."

It is clear the Church viewed the Elven-Ffayrie as a threat. No longer would they be recorded in history as the true "Sons of God"—no longer would they be acknowledged as the true ruling class of Æurope. A time for "Elves, Magic and Gods" gave way to the "Time of Men" and their ways. In time, the Elven Histories were construed as little more than fictitious mythology or cultural embellishments of diverse pagan pantheons.

For example—in one myth "God" comes to Lilith while she is bathing her children and asks her to present them all to Him. Embarrassed by those who were already clean for God's arrival, she hid away the unwashed. Already knowing full well the truth, God asks her if she has presented all of them. She replies, saying, "Yes"—and those children hidden away from God's sight were then cursed to live out their lives as Elven-Ffayrie. Hidden from God's sight, they would live hidden and invisible from the eyes of Men. Other disturbing Elven genesis lore may be found in the Nordic Elven-Ffayrie tradition. Their version describes all Elven-Ffayrie as emerging or born from maggots feeding on the corpse of an ancient Wizard and Giant—"Ymir." Many other legends from the Dark Ages depict Elven-Ffayrie as fallen angels; and regarding "pixies"— the Church clergy explained that they were human souls of children that died before receiving a "true" baptism.

History-keeping is a very dangerous business. Entire traditions, races and people have been threshed out of existence due to personal biases and retention errors. Once things are written, they are rewritten, re-recorded, then changed again. With each new discovery one must alter what was previously accepted as fact, or be a victim to ignorance. But nations take over one another and then rewrite history. This was the case when the Romans finally conquered the Celts and annihilated Elvish Druidism—forcing most survivors "underground," beneath the "exoteric" surface world and out of public sight.

Druids handled all matters of authentic kingship in ancient times. They designated specific rulers—and no Celtic King was completely "official" without a ceremony overseen by a Druid Elf, and one of their representatives to "advise him" during his reign. Coexisting with Celtic society, the "royal line" again preserved Elven-Ffayrie Tradition—they installed their own blood into that of Kings and Druids to ensure a continuation of the legacy, albeit separate from the general Celtic population. For this reason, modern practitioners must differentiate between what is general "Celtic" from what is purely "Druidic," "Alferic" or "Elven" if their intention is to maintain authenticity of any modern Elven-Faerie tradition.

Before the Dark Ages, all kings and mystic priests were Elven-Ffayrie. We might assume—given chronology—that the 5th Century King Arthur is essentially the last of the great Pagan Celtic Kings. Emerging new leadership thrust civilization into ignorance and "Dark Ages." These were not the legendary mystic seers and sages of the prior age—now known to the people as "pagan" or "heathen." All magic from the prior age was dubbed "evil" with few exceptions: the god-given powers employed by Moses and Jesus. Such were not classified within a domain of "magic" and were instead "miracles" conducted by "God's hand" alone. Then, after the Roman Church starts governing coronation of Kings, all existing claims to former Dragon legacies and soverignty are denounced and its Elven-Ffayrie bloodlines annihilated—and forced underground.

The original legacy of Dragon Kings spans many regions and eras following the development of human culture in Mesopotamia. Historical references to *dragons* often confuse many novice students, and potentially even the current reader. The Elves, faerie races and dragons we speak of here do not resemble the "stereotypical" fantasy appearances a person is likely to conjure to mind. Certainly there are many forms and types of energy manifesting all around us, but for our current purposes of historical analysis, we are restricting our view to the "humanoids" derived from a "star race"—whether we wish to attach other labels like "astral," "inter-dimensional" or "extra-terrestrial" to this is a matter of personal taste, because such details are only alluded to on the ancient tablets.

Despite common popular beliefs about all things "fairy," the noble Elves are actually "tall"—not dwarfed and some Anunnaki races may have had scaled skin, but they weren't little green men or "winged-serpents." Our descriptions of the Anunnaki demonstrate that they were also tall—in fact, in addition to being "Watchers," the biblical "Nephilim" are often translated by scholars to mean "giant." Where many Humans have rounded facial features, the Elves generally carry more narrow, angular, sharper traits and pale skin that tans very quickly in the sun—which can given them a very Near Eastern appearance.

Sumerian and Babylonian cuneiform tablets—and secret lore maintained by the Dragon King legacy—suggest that specific dynastic bloodlines were seeded by the Anunnaki in Mesopotamia—but also elsewhere, in Egypt, the Indus Valley and so forth. This spread across the planet in tow of a developing human systemology as a caste of "priests and kings." From the time of prehistory until the rising power of the Romans and later Church, priest-kings historically maintained global power for thousands of years. This "higher," "winged" class of "Sky Gods"—the "Elder Race"—found representations in the art, culture, religion and government of all of these ancient civilizations and the heavenly pantheons they observed.

Angelic lore—and battles between angels—originates here, specifically derived from the genetic memory of an ancient "War in Heaven," then extended in human consciousness to disputes between Enki (the "Lord of the Earth") and Enlil (the "Bull of Heaven") over the handling of human populations. Other commonly held angelic lore was later adopted from the Persian Zoroastrian tradition, but the moral dualism reflecting in these "dogmas" is dependent on the idea of Lucifer or Satan. And in orthodox interpretations of ancient history, it is Enki—the Lord of this Earth—that is demonized as Satan or Lucifer. Some of these same properties even fell into our classic understanding of his heir-son Marduk. But, the image of the Dragon—as attached to this class of Anunnaki or Star-beings and their Elven-Faerie descendents—was demonized by the Church and used as a symbol of effigy for all evil in the world. In one account, even Enlil refers to Marduk as "the evil serpent in Babylon that the world needs to be rid of." Among medieval secret societies this "angelic rogue" energy current materialized as "Baphomet"—the goat-headed swan-winged "dragon"—and another representation of the "devil" for the Church to demonize.

It is obvious that the true and faithful rendering of ancient history—and our clear understanding of it—became so convoluted over two millenniums of world governance outside of true Dragon sovereignty that it is now reduced to mythology, and even more recently as a subject of controversy and conspiracy in the "New Age" over the past several decades—and now we have many claims of dragon societies and courts in operation today.

Perhaps the most impressive and original modern institution of the "Dragon Court" links back to the late esoteric researcher, Nicholas de Vere, whose work went on to inspire many similar "copy-cat" organizations. But the real "Dragon Court" is not an open-admission correspondence school—and it is not very concerned with the rest of humanity insofar as they would prefer a reinstatement of pre-Vatican caste systems.

The concept of Dragon sovereignty is lost to modern systems —although we might like to think of it as a backbone to some current *Illuminati,* none of the current conspiracy theories comes close to the true realization that those in charge are not sovereign, nor have they been for a very long time, since the decision to ultimate destroy this planet, and its inhabitants, yet again. This is not happening all at once—but it *is* happening—and no true "Lords of the Earth" would be allowing this. The fate charted for humanity is nothing short of utter self-destruction and self-annihilation in the crudest sense—for we have not truly evolved so far from our ignorant days of spiritual handicapping during the Dark Ages. You may interpret this message however you please, but these events —the suppression of the Children of Faerie—blatantly caused the destruction of our Earth Planet.

Today, remnants of the Anunnaki tradition and Faerie faith of Æurope are concentrated into such specific locations and elements of archaic culture that it is sometimes difficult for a modern *seeker* to truly relate to the wide scope and sweeping influences that our current study touches upon. It is very important to understand, especially as pertaining to the subject of Druidism, that this tradition was not always restricted to the westernmost tips of modern-day Europe. The original "Danubian" cultural influence of the Tuatha D'Anu stretched all the way back to ancient Mesopotamia as we have seen, and even from those roots, had expanded in other directions as well, like a star-burst. When we consider, for example, the "Drunemeton" of Galatia/Anatolia/Turkey, it is a very peculiar location for the Arch Druids ("Arch Dragons") of Western Europe to share convocation, if indeed the tradition was only restricted to Western Europe.

Semantic connections between "Druids" and "oaks" are practically cliché—what is less known is the relationship between the "*drui*" or "*draoi*" and the serpent or dragon. This is why Arch-Drui and Ban-Draoi carry translated titles, like "Grand Dragon," "Imperial Dragon" or even "Pen-Dragons" in Keltia.

We are told St. Patrick drove the last "serpent-dragons" from Ireland and once removed from society, dragons were later associated with caves *they hid in.** Since then, genetic integrity of the Dragon Kings and Elves is under constant scrutiny as "racism." This is not so surprising in a world of blind acceptance and diversity celebration. That is not to say ignorant people have not used this lore in the past to support racism. This has unfortunately already occurred and will probably continue to—that cannot be helped. But this is not the focus of our present volume.

We find an emphasis of concentration on specific genealogies and bloodlines everywhere we turn in the ancient world and in every culture—this is nothing new. Each emphasized this aspect specifically over the higher spiritual ideals—which is something the present author will not allow to run rampant in this text. Nonetheless, this concept of preserving royal bloodlines and dynastic traditions has a familiar presence in history—particularly concerning the descent of rulers, kings, monarchs, pharaohs and any other claims to "Enlil-ship" on this planet. One example: the Ancient Near Eastern Semtic "Chosen People" of "Yahweh"—a group that even to this day prefers to exercise a degree of genetic separatism in marriage (sexual and breeding) practices, instinctively preserving their cultural genetic memory.

Overtly, the global legacy of the Dragon Kings fell during the Elven Holocaust. This was an effort—quite successful—by the Roman Church to exercise all religious and political control of the known world, ultimately throwing Western Civilization into the Dark Ages. With establishment of Anti-Witchcraft and Magick Acts, the Elves, faerie folk and Dragon Kings were considered witches by heredity—criminals of both state and religion. Such events forced any surviving "Elves" into the underground—and the "Dragons" to their caves. All occult interests from this point were confined to "secret societies."

---

* See also *"Draconomicon: The Book of Ancient Dragon Magick"* by Joshua Free.

In 751 AD, the last of the Elven Mergovians—the *"Keepers and Guardians of the Holy Temple"*—said to be descendents from Solomon's own ancient occult temple-builders, are disbanded and excommunicated from Rome and "separated from the blessing" of *"Holy Mother Church,"* to be replaced by a new group of Vatican-selected "Carologians." Up until the 6th and 7th centuries, Gnostic Wizards and Drwyds actually worked closely with the Catholic Church. They saw Jesus as a figure of each of their own traditions. This disturbed the later heirs of the Church that saw the Elven-Ffayrie as a threat to the "Seat of Rome" and the Vatican's new authority to select kings and rulers, where once this privilege rested with Drwyds and the Elven (and Dragon) lineages.

The Wheel of Time turns but the cycles of history repeat. Yet again, the *"Sons of Man"* feared the *"Sons of God"* would rebel and thus the "New Church" was formed independent of them, with only a shred of the original Gnostic vision remaining. The focus of the Church now: to take control of Æurope and eradicate "paganism." The church installed leaders that could be easily controlled by its own inclinations. Under religious pressure, royalty was coerced to uphold Church law above all —meaning also to outlaw all witchcraft and "magic." Even as the Church openly borrowed many ancient customs in order to ease the conversion of pagans, the laws were put forth to quickly suppress any *real* folk practice of these traditions.

Pope Gregory IX launched the historically famous Inquisition in the 13th Century. This later received more fuel with the publication of a ridiculous text—the "Malleus Maleficarum" or "Witches' Hammer"—a completely useless witch-hunter's manual. In England, King Henry VIII was among the first to outlaw witchcraft as a significant "state" offense, authorizing "burning at the stake" as capital punishment as early as 1542. In 1563, Queen-Elizabeth-I increased strictness of these laws —a peculiar move by someone personally fascinated by the occult and who had, in her employment, a "royal court magician," the famous John Dee—co-founder of the *Enochian*

Magic system. She obviously protected Dee from the same mandates she herself installed (or upheld), but referred to him often as her *"astrologer royale."* Throughout Europe, various laws were in place allowing persecution and capital punishment of witches until an English repeal in 1736—after the public revival of Freemasonry and neodruidism in 1717. Strict laws were replaced with "Fraudulent Mediums Acts," which *could* imprison those guilty of claims to witchcraft or performing spellcraft—but no longer authorized executions.

Magical spiritual traditions once constituted the entire systemology of life and government in the ancient world; then it was entirely demonized as Satanism by the Church. Once the original practices and practitioners were sufficiently "out of the picture" long enough to be nearly forgotten, both church and state finally dictated that witchcraft and "magic" was an illusion—was not real—as enforceable by the Fraudulent Mediums Acts (or similar). Even prior to the union of Rome and the Church, Rome had handled their politics this way, as seen in their encounters with early Celtic Druids and Elven races.

When the darker overloads of the Church finally left—or died out—they left not only the Church, but also all it had affected, in a shambles. Many practitioners became confused with conflicting aspects of Christianity's evolution, and those now left in charge had little more to offer than to say: "Have faith." However, the Vatican still possessed the wealth and records of the Roman Empire and some of the Elven Kings it had usurped. Works once attributed to legend are now resurfacing—like the *Dead Seas Scrolls, Apocrypha,* the *Book of Enoch* and the *Gospel of Thomas,* to name a few. Yet, only the initiates of the Inner Vatican Circle once knew of this lore.

When we consider all of this in light of the Elven-Ffayrie specifically—as is the subject of our volume—the people of the Renaissance era, and even modern society today, can usually distinguish their beliefs regarding "Elves and Faeries" into one of the following categories:

MAJOR BELIEFS CONCERNING ELVES & FAERIES

1. The Sidhe-Sylvans are a distant genetic relation to Mortal Humans.

2. Ffayrie beings are "Nature Spirits" which inhabit the Green World Forest—where *magical* things happen.

3. Elven-Ffayrie races are descendents from the "Fallen Angels" or are the "Children of Lilith"—but essentially "vampyres," "demons" or "Christian-devils."

4. Fey creatures are ancient ancestral spirits (genetic relatives)—particularly Eurasian—who were so attached to the land that they remained after the rise of Humans, albeit beneath the surface—or "invisible"—upholding their pledge as "Gaea's Guardians" even in death.

During the Dark Ages, the persecution of "magic" drove its beliefs, practices and practitioners out of public sight. The remaining "wizarding blood"—its legacy and direct lineage—was split in two: one group went into the deep woods where Nature-oriented more shamanic-like traditions developed. The Faerie legacy was also carried by another faction—an elitist group descending from the Dragon race that maintains a large chain of secret societies coexisting with mortal society even to this day—and of which does play an important role in our global events and affairs, while simultaneously operating almost independently and "above" society.

The "secret societies" and "Elven Councils" of the Dark Ages did not exist to the same social degree as in the Age of Faerie —just as modern Druids do not, by that trade alone, have a position in society today as they once did in ancient Keltia. The knowledge stream and lineage has also fallen along the way and continues to cycle out from our world and our consciousness—apart from a select few *Seekers*.

All branches of the "Ancient Mystery School" have endured their own evolution across time and space—all of its members today, are in effect, reconstructionists—distant descendants with "mystical inclinations." Many of the elitist organizations still existent today moved further and further away from the true legacy and lineages that once guarded these societies thousands of years ago—and many of these organizations are granting "outsiders" membership "on commitment," which only occurs when esoteric membership is on the decline—and as a result, we have witnessed a surge of interest in these matters in the new millennium. Between the Ancient Drwyds and neodruids of today, there stands a long lineage of Masonic, Rosicrucian and Illumiinati organizations—and each has its own claims to "secret knowledge" about human history, in addition to a flavor of practical metaphysical lore. Nearly all secret sects, mystical cabals and magical orders have at one time shared their roots with this legacy.

We might assume—from the Elven Histories—that after its prehistoric "star origins," the original root tradition mainly emerged in the Mediterranean/Mesopotamian region, forming a "delta" of Sumerian/Babylonian, Greek and Egyptian wisdom traditions that now share the same umbrella: Hermetic. "Hermetic Tradition" is a later synthesis of the three, of which Mesopotamia is the oldest, but it is *here* that many modern occultists are successfully able to trace their varying "secret traditions" back to. Where the classical world is quite familiar and we have long experienced the colorful revival of Egyptology, only recently has the more antiquated Mesopotamian mythos received public attention. This foreign wider encompassing paradigm has brought with it a whole new set of cultural language and vocabulary semantics to consider in developing a true holistic understanding of our origins.

Elitist practitioners of Modern Hermetics trace some of their lore and tradition to the Gnostics. Gnosticism was the highest religion of the Hermetic-Delta until the arrival of the Roman Empire. In Ærope we find remnants of the same tradition as maintained by the Celtic Druids and the La Tene culture until it too is finally pushed to the very shores of the ocean and its islands and northern most "Hyperborean" reaches before it is completely forced underground—but it is not obliterated. The tradition split in two: some mystics taking to the woods and others becoming Holy Knights, that surfaced during the Crusades—among them the "Cathars" and "Knights Templar" —"Knights of the Temple"—that pledged to uphold the legacy the "True Church," that was no longer present in Rome.

Something very curious occurred in the year 1717: both the Knight-Rangers and Mystics rose again—and in public view. The neodruids and neo-masons—or Freemasons—emerged in England. On paper, many of the current long-standing orders and lodges of the same may actually trace their origins to this event—taking place in England, at the Apple Tree Tavern.[*] Only after the end of the Dark Ages does both the "Ancient Order of Druids" and "Ancient Order of Freemasonry" enter society in plain sight. From there it spread across the world in some revival form or another. Many scholars and skeptics viewed—and continue to view—these reconstructions and revivals as completely without merit. This continued through most of the 1900s as well, and is only beginning to change as more and more people take interest in "alternative paths."

The "knight-ranger" lineage became the "Illuminoids" that inspired the modern Masonic Traditions today with their neodruidic ideals. The other arm—the Mystics—became the Rosicrucians—Mystics of the Rose-Cross and other similar branches of active esoteric practice. Illuminoid Masons and Rosicrucians with interests in more "magickal" aspects of the Hermetic tradition formed the "Hermetic Order of the Golden Dawn"—or "GD"—and other lesser known occult fraternities and underground groups. The Golden Dawn was originally a very elitist and secret organization up until the publication of a large portion of its "graded" materials as interpreted by

---

[*] See also *"The Druid's Handbook: Ancient Magick for a New Age"* by Joshua Free.

Aleister Crowley for his version of the GD—called Argentium
Astrum, or "AA"--the "Order of the Silver Star." This was
later clarified officially by Israel Regardie, known famous for
his presentation of a complete system of Golden Dawn magic
in a more "authentic" form. Clearly, Crowley was something
of a protestant mystic and a bit of rogue—not unlike Edward
Kelley, the assistant to Dr. John Dee during the development
of *Enochian Magic*—a subject of serious interest to Crowley, as
introduced among the highest grades of GD material. Another
group—the "Ordo Templi Orientis" or "OTO"—also emerged
and was even handed down to Crowley at one juncture, later
contributed to heavily by his secretary, Kenneth Grant. The
mystical forces that these organizations made contract with
were—and continue to be—astral, inter-dimensional or extra-
terrestrial in nature, and Anunnaki in origin—which is dealt
with at more length in a subsequent Mardukite publication.[*]

The other more rural family, solitary mystic and folk traditions did not often share ties with larger organized revivals,
both during the Dark Ages and after. Many of these "hereditary" and "country" traditions developed in isolation and so,
it has been the past century of time where the two have been
able to openly blend—which has certainly happened when we
analyze the actual core roots of modern "Wicca" movements,
which are the same. These "simplified" methodologies began
rising in popularity toward the end of the 20th century and
continue to attract a large following today.

For the first time in over a thousand years, mystical Nature-
oriented "religions" exist in the public eye. New versions of
Keltoi-Norse Neopaganism and eclectic Faery Wicca seem to
sprout up every day now. What's more: many of them earn
some degree of actual "religious" validation. And while the
"Ancient Mystery School" was once exclusive to a specific
legacy of practitioners—either by mystic ability or lineage/

---

[*] Since released as *"Necronomicon: The Anunnaki Bible"* or *"The
Complete Anunnaki Bible: A Source Book of Esoteric Archaeology"*
by Joshua Free.

and heredity—access to the "secret traditions" is now accessible independent of an instructor and from wherever books
are sold for the mere price of only forty bucks. For some, this
could be interpreted as somewhat dangerous in itself.

—Elves & Druids—
The Secret World of Faerie

Long ago, in the far and distant past, the "gods" once roamed the Earth—figures of legendary renown—that passed "divine right to rule" or "*Enlil-ship*" to their chosen messengers as intermediaries between "gods" and "men." As time bore on and human populations grew, the "gods" left Earth, leaving their systemology in the hands of "priest-kings," "priestesses" and "mystics" that brought the tradition into recorded history. The "blue race" of "Fair Folk" moved westward from the Ancient Near East. These "higher minds" carried influential lore of this "Ancient Mystery School" in their migrations across Æurope, and a new highborn priestly class of Dragon Courts, Elf Kings and Faerie Queens of legend emerged.

Previous lesson-chapters in this series adequately introduce a wide-spanning legacy of Elven royalty and Dragon courts that lend us their traditions for this current tome. The Elves—as "Children of Eru/Anu" or "Children of the Stars" inherited the planet as long-distant descendants of Enki—"Lord of the Earth." Enki—an Anunnaki god residing in the proto-Sumerian capital of Eridu—was first to introduce traditions of magic and science on Earth—which directly sprung up the "Ancient Mystery School" spreading throughout the ancient Mesopotamia/Mediterranean region—a region referred to in some lore as (*yes, you guessed it*) "Middle Earth," the "mid-branch" place of "meetings" and "crossings" between "worlds"—or between the heavens and the Earth. This Elven race descended from the "Shinning Ones," the "star race," "angels" or "Sons of God"—connected with all of the original global "religions." Eventually, they become avatars of "wizarding" blood, "Earth deities" and "Tuatha d'Anu" heroes of "Celtic Myth."

Following the rise of the Sons of Mil—the rise of human populations in Keltia—most mystically inclined members of Elven
and Faerie races "transitioned" into the Otherworld, though
the legacy of Druidism continued on in public forms until the
time of Saint Patrick and the "Elven Holocaust" or Dark Ages.
After focused persecution lifted and many diabolical laws
were repealed, the possession of "wizarding blood" —and the
practice of magic—no longer carried a death sentence. Yet, by
this new era of "enlightenment," dilution of Elven lore and
Faerie ancestry dissolved contemporary human understanding of the subject, reducing it to the best that remains from
the Grimm family collection as "fable" and "fantasy."

The Elven Way and Faerie Faith were not altogether lost. As
the world revival of druidry or "neodruidism" emerged, more
remnants of the ancient way started receiving attention, and
even documentation. The original of these pertain mainly to
daily magical rural living—the traditions that earth-oriented
and Nature-based druids and "neopagans" frequently follow
today. And this "Edaphic" tradition is, indeed, an original and
innate form of "practical magick" in honor of the Ancient and
"Shinning Ones." Elves and Faerie races traditionally practice
what we consider "green magic," however, the other type—
called "ceremonial high magick"—is also present in the legacy of the Dragon Kings, those first in possession of grimoires
like the "*Sacred Book of Magic of Abramelin the Magic*" and other
Rosicrucian documents, or journals of *Enochian magic,* long
before the inception of the Golden Dawn System.

In contemporary lore, and even in some New Age interpretations, the term "Elven" is applied as a catch-all category for a
host of ancestral spirits, Nature-spirits and elemental spirits
aligned to a combination of earth and air forces. Some types
occur in cultural traditions including the *Dark Elves* of the *Unseelie Court,* misunderstood "devas," the "*Sidhe*" or *High Elves*
of the *Seelie Court,* the *Linchetto* of Etruscan-Italy, the *Quendi* of
Sumerian *Eridu* and finally, the *Silvani/Sylph* woodland inhabiting Nature guardians—sometimes called *Wood Elves.*

Modern ritual and "practical magick" systems are aligned to "elemental magick" and elemental currents of energy that share affinity with specific "elementals"—the spiritual forms taken by "transitioned" Elves and Faerie Folk. These entities —appropriated to the "astral plane"—are called in ceremonial and ritual magick at the appropriate corners of the nemeton or ritual circle. In the Edaphic tradition influencing this current book, "Elves" usually replace the traditional gnomes as "guardians of the north." In a similar fashion, "Dragons" or "Fire-Drakes" may replace the djinn. There are other types of elemental entities that may be incorporated with ritual magic and/or daily magical living, as described within this chapter.

Lore of "Changelings" appear frequently in connection to traditional Elven-Ffayrie history—and although we do not know its definitive source, it is carried in worldwide belief systems. "Changelings" are fundamentally human replacements, often newborns, which are switched with an "elf-child." That the Faerie races share a "low reproductive rate" is one driving theory behind this lore—therefore maintaining their populations and/or evolving their genetic diversity by occasionally "stealing humans." It is also possible that this lore applies to phenomenon attributed to many "Otherworldly beings" even in alternative culture today, although we choose contemporary semantics reflecting our technological knowledge, such as:"alien babies," "cloning" and "DNA harvesting." However, throughout the Dark Ages of the Church, religious beliefs maintained that sickly children and infant deaths were all consequences of faerie—or demonic—assault.

"Changeling Theory" is not restricted only to newborns and children—although the archetype of the "stolen child" is the most iconic. Direct interactions between Elven-Ffayrie and Humans are not common—sexual unions between them even less so. The only instance of "fairy theft" in the current Edaphic tradition is the lore of "transignation"—when someone may not be willing or even aware of themselves being used as a simulacrum host for a "walk-in" entity.

In the anthropological examination of Elven-Ffayrie by *W.Y. Wentz,*[*] another theory regarding "fairy theft" is put forth. It is possible—as he suggests—that after the Milesian human invasion, and the attempts at entrapping the Danubian race before their flight for hills and caves, that they occasionally kidnapped the unattended off-spring of the people who had conquered them. It is also theoretically possible that the later Elvish Drwyds themselves, after being driven underground to hide in the dense forests and old groves, may have kidnapped potential apprentices to raise and pass down their knowledge and wisdom to, before returning them to Human society.

When we examine other more recent historical cases like that of *Rev. Robert Kirk*—and perhaps *Thomas Rhymer* and others— we know that select mortals (perhaps even of Elven-Ffayrie lineage) have been taken to the "Otherworld Faerieland." Our primary examples of Faerie-lore, when Otherworld beings interact with mortals, all take place in a surreal yet vividly tangible manner. We know that the Elementals are capable of imbuing all types of life with their spirit. There is also lore regarding their ability to use simulacra from birth or "walk-in" at some point during the person's "more able" years, such as puberty. Either of these abilities—"transition" or "transignation"—requires, what we would consider, incredibly powerful magical abilities to perform, especially for permanent effects.

Elves and Ffayrie have abilities to disorient wanderers that happen upon enchanted fey woods. This belief inspired an old saying: *"Faerie folk live in old oaks."* Surviving superstition inspires warned travelers passing through such forests to wear their cloaks backwards, or inside out (reversed) to ward against enchantments and glamours that might get a person lost. It is even possible that doing so subconsciously increases one's "awareness." Clouds, heavy mist and dense fog are all natural threshold conditions related to the Otherworld and Elven-Ffayrie. Just as many unsuspecting travelers might get lost, there is a long-standing magical tradition of using fog to

---

[*] W.Y. Wentz—*"Fairy-Faith in Celtic Countries."*

aid physical access the Otherworld. It is assumed that these twilight misty creates a conduit between worlds that may be employed from either side. And while misleading wanderers through a forest might at first seem malicious, it is possible that Elven-Ffayrie beings make efforts to keep people away from certain locales, powerful thresholds or even dimensional portals and "star-gates" between worlds.

Elven-Ffayrie beings are often described as peculiarly restless. This is historically displayed in their nomadic lifestyle, undoubtedly running deep in genetic memory from being "on the move" for thousands of years. However, the *Seelie* "Sidhe Court" of the ancient Danubian race does not constantly shift their living circumstances because of some mundane dissatisfaction. On the contrary, regular movement of the Court is traditional—e.g. "it has always been that way"—and partly to "normalize" underlying "compulsions," (for lack of finer terminology). While the tradition may not be recognized by more solitary Faerie beings, the Danubian Sidhe relocate to a new dwelling space at the beginning of each "quarter." These times of movement were marked by ceremonial observations by the Druids—the *"Four Albans"*—which is to say the annual equinoxes and solstices.

Dwelling places for Elven-Ffayrie are constructed in a manner unlike that of Humans. The Elvish style is "natural"—it is set into the land; built in harmony with the energies of the land; not standing apart from it. Case in point: Elves will come to a large tree and say, "Hm...I could live in this." A Human would come by and say, "Hm...let me cut this down to make a home to live in." For example, homes of other woodland animals do not disrupt Nature, yet the upgraded Human species does not resonate any equilibrium with its natural environment—existing almost as its direct *"antithesis."* As such, Humans carry a false sense of elitism on the planet—and unable to naturally survive in its environment, they operate as an exception to all other life on Earth, when they are, in fact, the most recent guests to this Green World.

According to the accounts of *Rev. Robert Kirk*, the Sidhe Court resided in a particular faerie "mound," "hill" or "*howe*" at that time. When describing the space/time of the Otherworld Faerieland, Kirk found that, in his experience of it, the Otherworld was far too vast to have been contained within a single hill—providing early examples of "hyperspace" or a "fourth spatial dimension." Interestingly, many of these "Hollowed Hills" were ancient burial sites of Elven-Ffayrie ancestors once residing on the surface world. The "*Tuatha D'Anu*" and other royal-fey bloodlines would preserve the remains of their ancestors in "tomb-hills." And although not used for burial, funerary rites of the "Ancient Mystery School" were practiced in "pyramids" and "ziggurats"—artificial "hills" or mountains with cave-like chambers built in places that did not have these naturally occurring landforms. This motif also lends some "Gothic" overtones, inspiring other related mystical traditions emphasizing the more "vampyric" semantics.

Since Elven-Ffayrie dwellings are natural, many are intended only for temporary use as a result of their frequent migration and the fact that they spend little of their time actually home. Of course, when we speak of the nomadic life of the "Trooping Faerie" and the *Seelie Sidhe Court*, we are not including all solitary sylvan folk that do not participate in these "*Rades.*" These Rade-times are traditionally significant in Druidism because they are the most optimum annual threshold periods for mystics to actually see movement of nature-bound Otherworldly beings. These experiences provide us with cultural "memory" of elemental beings. Also—the *Unseelie Court* does not share in the *Seelie Court's* celebrations—like the solitaries —or "*Rades.*" Solitaries and sylvan folk also represent more "earthy" types, giving rise to our idea of dressing in leaves and wearing acorn-shaped hats; whereas the Sidhe Court and "High Elves" actually dress in more grandiose attire.

Elven Tradition is revived in Druidism, but it is not the same as the magic practiced by Humans—which employs these other beings to lend their Otherworldly powers to Human ritual.

It is from Human lore *about* Elves—based on Human perception and vocabulary of "other" worlds—that we find terms like "Middle Earth" ("M.E."), "Mid-branch," and "Middle-world"—all of which imply the third-dimensional plane. Each "point" in Middle Earth (physical space) has a center, called "*midhe.*" This center is connected to an ethereal "Recursive Spiral" of cosmic energy where space/time ascends and descends, coiling into upper and lower frequencies/dimensions, ultimately unifying all things—but at different perceptual or semantic levels of understanding or classification. But they are connected *All-as-One*. Make no mistakes here in thinking of the spiral-like Multiverse in terms of absolute "upper" and "lower" worlds. We use this terminology as only an abstract differentiation to describe the effect or relationship we perceive as one plane or level of existence with another—but they are all connected together. If we apply modern science vocabulary and hyper-geometry in our view of an "Infinite" Universe or Multiverse, than we must accept that there are infinite "smaller/lower" or "larger/upper" levels of existence or dimensions. Elven lore even suggests a type of hyperspace existence that is subjective to experience—particularly as Humans define "time."

The "Lands Below"—as Robert Kirk experienced them—possessed its own moon, stars, and even a sun similar to Earth's. He explained that by appearance, everything seemed more vividly real than even the physical world. *So... the "Hollow Hills" have their own sky..?* Remember that the Otherworld—that which is unseen from our view of reality or has not collapsed or condensed into our reality—is indeed without limit. While there is some perceived separation between the Middle World and the Otherworld, the iconic idea of Faerieland as some exclusively "Subterranean" or "Underground" realm is not clearly relayed in any of Kirk's experiences—or the lore of others—except as pertaining to portals and entrances. This generalization expressly shows they exist, again, beneath the surface of perceptions—as if simply behind a door or "gate" that we are unable to simply peer through in day-to-day life.

When we confine our semantics to the mortal view of reality, the limitlessness of existence is collapsed in "our" dimension as various natural conditions that we can observe within our range of "awareness." Some of these are considered "portals" or "thresholds" because they allow for a more fluid exchange of energies between "worlds"—else, between degrees of the same singular "world." Specific conditions promote specific types of inter-dimensional energetic activity, which affects both the "external" world we are experiencing and the "internal" mental set doing the experiencing—a further example that these "two" facets are really one and the same spectrum of energy: that our "internal" and "external" worlds are One.

The cross-quarter thresholds—the equinoxes and solstices—share qualities from other "degrees" of reality experience semantics, such as astronomical alignment, or electromagnetic fields around earth, but they are most often distinguished in Druidic tradition as the "Four Albans"—or *Four Lights*—which compose at least half of the Celtic "Grove Festivals" revived in modern "neopaganism" today. Springtime—between the Spring Equinox and Summer Solstice—is traditionally the most active period of the year for elemental Nature-spirits. Beltane (May's Eve) and Midsummer's Eve are particularly famous times for "Faerie Rade." Note that *Beltane* (May's Eve) and *Samhain* (ancient "Halloween") also mark periods of peak inter-dimensional activity—times that correspond to the setting and rise of the Pleiades (respectively).

Another facet of inter-dimensional "fairy lore" is called the "fairy ring"—naturally occurring circles or rings found on the ground in Nature that are set apart from its natural surrounding. Often this manifests as a bit of grass that grows higher or darker, forming a ring—usually only a few feet in diameter—or it may be a ring of mushrooms. Traditionally, "Faerie-Rings" are signs of not only Elven-Ffayrie activity in an area, but also places in which a transition into—or from—the "Otherworld" is likely or has already occurred. Other degrees of semantics may be applied to this phenomenon too.

Conventional scientists that have studied this growth tell us that—at a physical and biological degree of understanding—there is a "mycelium" or "fungus" that grows beneath the ground that can cause abnormal growth and/or mushrooms. Terrence McKenna—in *Archaic Revival*—suggests that these original spores are probably not even indigenous to planet Earth. The physical appearance—and explanation—of "Faerie-Rings" and other natural phenomenon does not eliminate the existence of energetic activity that may be "perturbing" what we can see from beneath the surface of our awareness and understanding. It is also curious to note that Humans have experienced "alien" and "fairy" encounters under psychoactive effects of mushrooms, DMT and other hallucinogenic substances. It is possible that some of the receptors activated in the brain as a result of their use do allow for a "wider range" of perceptual experience of reality—but there are no guarantees that these "external" methods will result in Self-Honest experiences. Wizards suggest that falling asleep in a Faerie-Ring or on an Elven-Mound will increase your chances of Otherworld contact—possibly due to a presence of spores, *who knows?* Other folklore suggests that if you run around one nine times you will do the same—*kicking up more spores?*

One of the main issues—for Humans—regarding physically transitioning into the Otherworld, relates to inept faculties to not only sense "portal frequencies," but also adjust personal vibrations to successfully "transition" into other existential states. Most Humans do not carry an awareness of the energetic matrix we occupy, then alone possess an understanding of its influence—such is, and always has been, the main focus of the "wizarding ways" and high mystical arts. In other instances and occult practices, similar results may be obtained using "astral projection" and other experimental practices—frequency shifts in consciousness where the physical body is not transported, yet we can mentally experience it because everything is connected—our consciousness is already connected to the ALL. Our sensory faculties are simply limited to a specific range of an infinite spectrum of energies.

The cosmic spectrum of infinite potentiality includes many possible frequencies in existence "above" and "below" what Humans are normally capable of sensing. While these various degrees might be perceived and classified as separate "levels" in exclusion to one another, the separation exists only in consciousness—there is no actual separation between a subject and the individual doing the observing; there is only one singular reality. Each "degree" of vision—each magnification of the microscope—yields only one "degree" of awareness, data and knowledge, but it is not the only "degree" of possible understanding, nor is it likely to be the true holistic totality of a "thing"—since we are always going to classify "things" in exclusion to all other "things."

One degree of observation in 1925 led the British antiquarian, Alfred Watkins, to discover the existence of "Ley Lines" or "Dragon Lines"—naturally occurring lines running across the surface of the Earth Planet. These lines or "fields" vibrate a more significant magnitude of energy than its surrounding area—similar to the appearance of "Faerie Rings," but larger and in a "line." The lines sometimes link ancient sacred sites and other energetic "thresholds" or "portals." Some have put forth theories regarding underground water sources or mineral veins contributing to the visible surface appearance, but modern science suggests that the core of the Earth produces an electromagnetic field that interacts with other environmental systems and conditions.

The Ley Lines are now a basic facet of modern Earth-oriented traditions. Even sensitive mystics have learned how to trace or follow the lines of power using dowsing techniques.[*] In our present Edaphic Tradition—and some neodruid systems—the lines are called "Dragon Lines," named for the "flight path" of "dragons" as they moved between sacred sites—places where higher concentrations of natural forces collect or condense, even forming significant notable "vortex" energy spots.

---

[*] See also *"Draconomicon: The Book of Ancient Dragon Magick"* by Joshua Free.

Wizards and mystics throughout the ages are renown for their abilities to recognize the true power of Nature—particularly when there is a large concentration of these energies in a particular area. Over time, these places become recognizably "magical" locales frequently visited for "magical work" by those sensitive enough to be aware. When such locations are identified, practitioners may even intentionally consecrate a "grove" of trees or "henge" of stones to mark the "*nemeton*"—or "sacred space"—specifically for personal "magical work" or even gatherings. Specific types of energy tend to concentrate relative to the region or terrain involved—the water element is sparse in the desert, just as those same dry-heat energies are quite absent in the jungle. Energies may also be amplified by other neutral catalysts, such as a presence of quartz crystal or other conductive minerals beneath the ground. A person could just as cleverly bury appropriate crystal clusters beneath a sacred space to increase resonance within the "*nemeton*."

Another energetic interaction taking place between worlds is called an "Elf-Shot." If someone—typically a Human—is hit by an arrowhead from an Elf or Faerie being, we call them "Elf-Shot." This lore is the subject of some controversy in the New Age and as a result is not frequently discussed. The tradition holds, however, that one of the consequences of being struck by such an arrow is some degree of "Faerie-Sight"—or, at the very least, the ability to see the fey that shot you.

Rarer, but more serious, consequences of "Elf-Shot" include permanent "transitions" to the Otherworld or "Faerieland"—which other Humans, in many instances, would only see as "death," because the "body" often remains in the physical world. This may not even occur overnight and might first be recognized as an illness that purges impurities of the physical body so that its spirit can be free. Keep in mind: this is not something that may be self-induced. In fact, it usually only happens unintentionally—because Elven Courts seldom assist Humans in "seeing them" or "inviting" them to their world.

Sometimes an "Elf-Shot" occurs when a Human just happens to be in the line of fire between rivaling courts—such as the *Seelie* and *Unseelie*. It is also possible that an "Elf-Shot" victim is struck without knowing it has occurred—so if they are not perceptive, they may not see the fey that shot them. Even if it does not produce an illness, it has been known to inadvertently have other unpleasant side-effects—such as promoting discord between friends and neighbors.

"Foison" is a common game where members of the fey will "steal" Human food. This should not to be misinterpreted as an act of malevolence—it *is* a "game." Lore suggests that they only eat the essence of Human food and not the foods themselves—possibly lending to the "thin" "angelic" "ethereal" descriptions carried by many of the types. As a result, they will absorb only what is necessary from foodstuff—leaving the remains often without nutrients. There are reports from farmers in Celtic Countries where the insides of their stalks are carefully eaten while leaving outsides intact and whole. Modern folk might just think it is a result of some pests, but often it does not seem eaten, rotted, infested or touched.

According to lore, foods prepared in Faerieland are the most exquisite—pure natural and organic essences drawn from the sweetest life-giving nectar of the Green World. One popular belief is that if you eat any foods during your stay in the Otherworld, you may find yourself trapped there. Although *Rev. Robert Kirk* was eventually trapped in Faerieland, it was not a result of eating the food there. He had tasted it and still continued to "transition" back and forth between worlds several times. However, he reports that the "want" or "memory" of it lingered perpetually and could not be equaled in the physical world. Cuneiform Tablets describe an exchange between Enki and Adapa—where Enki instructs Adapa on the dangers of eating the "Food of Death" when visiting the "Otherworld," though Anu eventually offers Adapa the "Food of Life" and it is refused because of Enki's instructions. Had he eaten of it, the Human race would have been "as like the gods."

Long-standing metaphysical connections exist between faerie beings and foodstuffs. Wizards and mystics traditionally use food offerings in their workings and ritual magic to entice the Elven-Ffayrie, other Elemental Beings and helpful energies to their magic circles. They will also leave milk and sweat-bread cookies out to invite them into their home—something retained in the modern "Santa Claus" mythology today. Often, energy currents of these Otherworld beings may be extended to a Druid—or anyone calling on them or another ancestral energy current—without a "physical apparition."

The "Geirt Coimitheth" or "Just-Halver" is an anomaly of the Otherworld. Its titles are references to its abilities and function—called a "joint-eater" or "marrow-eater"—a reference to it feeding on energy or essences of humans; possibly even a human Elven-Ffayrie Simulacra. Humans will "live-to-eat" or eat for pleasure, while the fey generally just eat-to-live and take only what essences and nutrients are necessary for survival. A "Geirt Coimitheth" is really a shadow—or the shadow of a person—a "co-walker" that feeds on what the host eats.

With a lack of substance in ethereal/astral planes, there is a shortage of food-stuff—but memory of such remains. Those who maintain food and drug addictions in the physical world find great difficulty satisfying these cravings in a spiritual dimension. Addictions conditioned on the mind and spirit can actually remain in tact after one's physical lifetime, but are not ever satisfied. While truly ethereal beings have no need to eat physical substances, Elven-Faerie beings are not indigenous to the Astral World and once ate regularly as we do.

"Co-walkers" are Elven-Ffayrie creatures that walk invisibly in the Middle World of humans in disguise. They take on human form—"Simulacrum Transignation"—or they can simply take the appearance of a human. Like all elementals, they reserve a right to remain invisible—yet present—or to mimic surrounding and camouflage themselves. These abilities may also be used to assume animal forms.

The "Giert Coimitheth" is just one example of a co-walker that shadows a human form. Others exist as well—some not so clearly classified—that simply shadow Elvish descendents or assume a full "transignation" or "walk-in" using physical simulacra. There is still a lot of debate about the semantics and vocabulary that should be used for this spiritual phenomenon. Other lore suggests that the co-walker may act as a "spirit-guide," guardian "*ang-elf*" or "co-magician." They may also be of any elemental type.

Elves of the Unseelie Court share many of the same attributes as their relatives of the Light. Their appearance is tall and slender like the Sylvan Elves, with long angular and hardened faces set in humorless stoic expressions. Their eyes appear small, squinted, and hollow—yet burning and piercing. They are used to residing in a Realm of Darkness and make habitats in larger underground subterranean labyrinths and caves. "Dark Elves" typically lead solitary lives, but there is large capital city for the Unseelie Court, as reported by *Rev. Robert Kirk* in his journals and secret writings.

"Dark Elves" are so-called because they are no longer one-to-one with the "Tribe of Starlight." They are set apart—exiled from the Seelie Court—taking their lives to even further "underground crevices." They are still "fey-folk," but submission to anger and brooding has left many of them blinded to pursuits of harmony and ascension. There are modern references to Dark Elves, calling them "*Drow*"—as rhymes with "cow"—yet this word does not appear in ancient Elvish languages. But, there is, however, the ancient word "*Daetenin*"—meaning "Dark-Dragon folk"—and the unseelie word "*Ishmaen,*" which is an Elven slur towards Wizards and Druids that have perverted their magical birthright. "Dark Elves" are not inherently evil—they simply remain perpetually bitter about their conditions of existence as a result of the "Rise of Humans." It is this very subject that drew a dividing line between Seelie and Unseelie Courts—which were originally the same race before the Rise of Humans and the Underground "transition."

The Elven-Druid Histories studied in previous chaper-lessons have focused on varying lineages existent on the surface world, such as the migrating "royal bloodline" of the Sidhe or High Elves and Drwyds. There is another sect of Elven-Ffayrie that are forest-oriented—called the "Wood Elves." These are the "Elven" spirits that make frequent contact during "Green Magic" and other earth-oriented mystical systems. "Sylvanus Folk" actually resided in the Otherworld prior to the "transitioning" of the *Tuatha D'Anu-Sidhe* and were not a part of that lineage—though they could interbreed—but maintained their own distinct woodland tradition. The "Sylves"/"Sylphs" or "Wood Elves" are also known as the "Keepers of the Trees," though not necessarily inhabitants of trees—which is recorded in lore as a *"Dryad."* The "Sylves," then, tend to the trees housing Dryads—and their cousins, the "Sylphs," are "Keepers of Flowers and Herbs" and "Guardians of the Wind."

Sylvan Folk are essentially caretakers for the Green World of Nature. Traditionally, Sylves or Elves (masculine) are keepers of the "Elven Garden"—which is to say the forests. The Sylphs or Ffayrie (feminine) are the keepers of the "Ffayrie Garden" or ground flowers. By "keeping" we of course mean "tending to" the life from the perspective of another dimension, as a tree's living spirit is interdimensional—as is all life. The life of a tree—and its spirit—both exists and affects other planes of existence. Care-taking is not a mundane act—it is a conscious acknowledgment of a holistic interdimensional relationship with all life. *They don't do it just to make the yard "look nice."*

Sylphs and Sylves tend to their gardens as a parent would a child—imbuing and charging it with love and energy. This is an important practice in such magical traditions—as the code states: all intentional acts are "magical." For them, tending the Earth is not performed out of idleness or "passing the time"—they take great pride in their work and are able to move tremendous amounts of energy through it. Sylvan Folk believe that their "life purpose"—or lesson of "dharma" required for their Ascension, or return to the Source-of-All—is to achieve a state of "Perfect Love." This is far from the same state experienced by Humans in carnal, lustful or purely pro-creative relationships—and better reflects the pure love that a "gardener" might feel toward the beautiful flowers planted and tended to. Maybe the term "gardener" is too passive in the English language, which is why J.R.R. Tolkein probably chose the term "tree-herder"—implying a more active role.

Otherworldly Elves do not have facial, arm, hand, chest, back, pubic, leg, foot, toe or orifice hair. This also matches descrip-tions of other inter-dimensional beings—even the genetics of "aliens," particularly those described as "Grays." Modern Hu-mans society has become increasingly interested in removing unnecessary body-hair—even if only for aesthetics. As for the other stereotypical "Elvish" appearances—they match the tall slender forms that we have spoken of previously.

Sylvanus Folk carry a strong dislike for hardened steel and iron. According to their ancient traditions—and those of the Watchers throughout history—these metals have only been associated with destructive ends. In fact, before the period of "Dark Ages" imposed by Romans and the Church, the ancient world had "fallen" once before, when at the apex of a new age of spiritual technology—c. 12th Century B.C.—these intellec-tual pursuits were stopped short by the Iron Age, leading to a cruder Dark Age and even more disgusting Industrial Age.

All Elves and fey hold some feelings against Humans that do not maintain the "Faerie-Code" or "Sylva Forest Code," par-ticularly those Human responsibilities of ecological planetary protection, land stewardship and animal care-taking that are inherited by any global dominating species. There is no deny-ing that Humans have—as a collective species—utterly failed in properly upholding these responsibilities. Forests and nat-ural wilds are both the home and children of Elementals—and deserving of our respect. Many of these spiritual beings are exclusively found in the most remote woodland and virgin untouched soils—and even what some might consider desolate wastelands and deserts—where all physical and/or sub-conscious thresholds and veils between the surface world and the Elven Otherworld are thinnest and most accessible.

Those of the Seelie Court, along with the highborn Sidhe, are particularly civil towards mortals—except where the destruction of the environment, Nature and life is concerned. The mystical practices of both the Danubian Sidhe and the Wood Elves comprises the mystical tradition of "Elvish Wizardry"—what Humans have experienced as "Druidism"—which is explored at length in later portions of the current book.

True Elves are slow to make friends and even slower to allow disharmonic relationships or enemies. In their relationships with humans, human Druids and human Wizards—as we will explore in our next chapter-lesson—Elves are known to first test those who might be potential allies. As a general stereotype they may be whimsical, but they are also quite serious, stoic and carry a genetic knowledge that far surpasses Human book-learning. They carry a youthful charm and enthusiasm, yet reflect an old soul that is wise beyond their visible physical years. Of the many elemental types, species, entities and spiritual forms throughout the history of magic, it is the Elves that are the closest in connectivity to Humans, bonded since an ancient crossings—ever changing the shape of history, lore, magic, tradition and wisdom on the planet Earth.

—Mortals & Elves—
& The Life of Robert Kirk

Previous chapter-lessons in the current volume mainly concern information and lore regarding phenomenon of Elven-fey "transitions" and encounters in the "physical world" or "surface world" of mortal Humans. The legacy of Reverend Robert Kirk is amazing—and unique—because it chronicles Elven lore from the *other side*—from a man who physically entered the Otherworld, became an initiate of the Elven-Ffayrie Tradition and returned to *our side* able to share it—at least, for a time and in some guise or another. We are not referring here to "mental/astral travel" or the type of "guided meditations" that run rampant in "New Age" How-To books for "entering the faerieland." Records and accounts of Robert Kirk's experiences are unparalleled in recent history.

Robert Kirk gained admittance to the "Otherworld," accessing the "Elven Libraries" on repeated occasions—not simply by happenstance or coincidence. He was even allowed to keep a sketch-diary journal to account for his experiences—which have now been widely circulated in various editions. The legacy of Robert Kirk's life and work is so monumental for our modern pursuits and studies of Elven-Ffayrie tradition that we shall bring this portion of the "Book of Elven-Faerie" to a close with a close examination of its lore—before turning the *Seeker* loose on the "grimoire" portions of *The Elvenomicon*.

Elemental and/or mortal "transitions"—or any contact with "nature spirits"—requires appropriate conditions or natural circumstances in addition to skills in directing or channeling currents of energy. During appropriate times, Robert Kirk was able to return to the same "Faerie Howe," or Hollow Hill and gain entrance at will. We make mention of these things here to entice you—but the story of Robert Kirk truly should begin, well, at the beginning...

Born in the year 1644, Robert Kirk was the *seventh son* of an Episcopalian minister and later even became a minister himself, in his home parish of Aberfoyle—Perthshire, Scotland. Although a devout Christian, Kirk spent his life interested and influenced by Elven-Faerie lore—though his religion did not permit him to accept the "magical" and "occult" aspects of the actual tradition. He did, however, see the importance in preserving Celtic lore and the ancient Gaelic-Welsh language—even overseeing a Gaelic translation of the *Holy Bible*, personally translating the *Psalms* and *Proverbs*. Kirk's missionary life reflected *Bardic Culdee* in the past who preserved the Celtic and Druidic symbolism in the *Book of Kells*, an "illuminated" manuscript of the Four Gospels in the Gaelic language.

It is evident that Robert Kirk never intended on becoming a monumental "New Age" figure—or advocate for the "occult" and active "mystery traditions" revived today in favor of the Elven Way. His writings do, however, display a personal familiarity with archaic Hermetic-Gnostic lore and Rosicrucian doctrines—making a direct reference to several in his most popularly known treatise: "*The Secret Commonwealth of Elves, Fauns and Faeries.*" The precise nature of Kirk's personal background is unclear—but he likely had access to many obscure Celtic manuscripts and other esoteric documents as an esteemed member of the Christian Clergy. It is likely that his strict religious upbringing resulted in a reluctance to delve into metaphysical matters—and it comes as no surprise that his "pagan" interests were of noted concern to his father.

The infamous "Faerie Howe"—where Robert Kirk's body was eventually found—was a location that he visited frequently throughout his life. But, one day, Kirk actually discovered, or rather, had revealed to him, the entrance to the "Faerieland Otherworld." By means of a special knock at the right times of month and day, Kirk would be granted repeated access to an alternate dimension—called many names throughout lore: the *Elflands*, the *Faerieland*, the *Faerieworld*, the *Otherworld*, just to name a few. In his published accounts, he does not always refer to these matters—especially concerning the Otherworld —in first person. He prefers instead to attribute the accounts, lore and traditions to those seers and mystics interviewed as part of his research. No doubt there were many political and esoteric reasons for such anonymity, especially during this time in history. His work was based on journals from 1688-1692, implying four years of practical "Otherworld Initiation" to compliment his research in folklore—at a time when, just across the pond in newly founded puritan America, people were burned at the stake for even speaking of such things.

Robert Kirk's "*Secret Commonwealth of Elves*" was never published in its complete state—and never at all during Kirk's lifetime. Some scholars believe that all of the first person references concerning mysticism, the Otherworld Tradition and Elven-Ffayrie encounters, were replaced as "accounts from seers"—or edited out of the "official" manuscript altogether— before its eventually distribution to a 17th century predominantly Christian society as authored by a Christian minister. In spite of this, Kirk emphasizes and insists that there is no real conflict between his own religious beliefs and what he learns concerning the Elven-Ffayrie tradition. The only real contradiction emerges from the minds of Fundamentalist Christians that see these beings as demons and devils. Kirk even goes as far as to say that he feels that it is his God-given mission in life to clarify misconceptions concerning the fey among his human Christian brethren.

It may be that Antiquarian writers of Robert Kirk's time—and the Brothers' Grimm, John Aubrey and Iolo Morganwg, just to mention a few—all felt that there was a very real part of folklore and Elven-Faerie Tradition hidden within the secret folds of Nature—and that it was quickly disappearing from contemporary society and required advocates for its preservation.

After one disturbing encounter in Faerieland—concerning a chance episode with a solitary *Dark Elf*—Robert Kirk took it upon himself to seek out the city of the *Unseelie Court* and attempt to apologize for the rise in tension resulting from his appearance in the Otherworld. Apparently, he had not yet realized that by even setting foot on the grounds of the *Dark Elves*, he was in violation of the most severe *Unseelie* laws. The *Unseelie Court* immediately sentenced him to death—but the *Seelie Court* intervened, altering their judgment, ultimately deciding that Kirk should remain forever a "prisoner" in the Otherworld, and this permanent "transition" would still leave his physical body dead in the "Middle World." He is then allowed only one night to return to the "Lands Above" to set his affairs in order—being allowed to leave in good faith—then during this time he leaves his journals behind for his son and returns to the "Lands Below" to serve out his sentence.

Some time after Kirk's death, he makes a spiritual appearance to a relative—claiming he will again appear at the Christening of her daughter. He states that at that time, her husband is to throw an iron dagger at his apparition—if he does so, then the enchantment of the Faerieland would be broken and he could return to the "Middle World." According to accounts that followed—when the Christening came and Kirk's spirit did appear, those who were present were so astounded that they did not move to throw a dagger and so Kirk remained in the Otherworld.

Years later, Kirk makes his second attempt to communicate—this time with a different family occupying the house Kirk once resided in. His apparition informs them that they are to baptize their child in his writing room and stab a dagger in the seat of the chair Kirk sat in to write—still in the room. If they did this, he said he would be free again. But, again, this is not even attempted and Kirk is never freed. Although easy to dismiss, these accounts do reflect behaviors that we might actually expect from the population at that time—or it may be that an eternity in the Otherworld was Kirk's destiny.

Mortals seeking encounters with nature-bound spirits—such as the Elven-Ffayrie—should first start by immersing themselves in natural valleys, untouched woodlands and virgin forests. By this, we mean those places where Humans are not falling trees and houses are not being developed—or even in view. Also avoid places overrun by electromagnetic transmission through power lines and satellite dishes which can cause mystic-interference. While smaller and urban parks are nice for walks, picnics, or maybe even studying, meditation or working with a specific tree current—most of these have been planned, planted and are arranged and maintained with little left to grow wild. They are also usually host to too much Human foot traffic and activity to make for the best places to meditate or connect with Nature—and especially those spirits that inhabit it.

Make certain your own foot traffic is light and quiet—walking slow and deliberately—being sure not to disturb the natural vibrations of the environment. Your energy must be in alignment with Nature—so take care that you are not disrupting the "natural flow" and wildlife with fast movement, ruckus or chatter. If the visible "Green World" you *can* see is disrupted by your presence, then you can rest assure that the same sentiment is shared by the "Nature-spirits." They really do carry a disdain for Human noise—so stop, sit and *shut up* often—perhaps with your back against a tree. Be patient. You may wish to practice certain breathing exercises or any meditations that will calm your vibrations and put you in tune with frequencies matching your surroundings. Calm your body; still your mind—activate your "light body" and "light shield" if you are proficient in such esoterica—but the key here, no matter the technique involved—is to *increase awareness.*

During the course of your personal ventures, experiments and experiences—should you happen upon a natural physical entrance to the Otherworld, lore suggests that you should not disturb it, or do anything immediately at first. Stop and wait. Watch and be patient, again. If nothing changes, try encircling it nine times and then waiting some more at the "door-way." You might then try knocking three times—making certain it will not disturb anything loose. Another secret knock sequence that is applicable here is: 1-2-3 or /-//-///.

If an initiate is not given a "portal key" by direct personal apprenticeship with Elven-Ffayrie folk, the only other available option is trial and error. Do not, however, be a menace—this will only work against your efforts. After three passive attempts, an alternative is to set up a "Circle of Power" to help meditate and calm your mind—and if you desire, practice Elemental magick rites—"opening thresholds" or "calling the quarters"—whatever your preferred means of summoning Elemental powers or currents of energy with ritual applications. Fey folk are commonly attracted to Elemental Magick because it specifically acknowledges their existence, asks for their assistance and utilizes energy streams they are akin to.

While selecting areas of exploration in the forest, keep in mind that some Elven-Ffayrie types are especially attracted to places where land meets water. These might be ponds, streams, waterfalls, or the archetypal "babbling brook." Lore suggests that these places carry intensive connectivity that links the physical world with the astral plane or Otherworld—making them very common places of spiritual encounter.

The element of water is among the most sacred in Elven tradition—for its "life-giving" qualities—as is the air we breathe. Running water is specifically related to irrigation—which is an essential aspect of agricultural work and gardening—a skill mastered famously in the Ancient Near East and carried across Europe as the populations transformed from nomadic hunter-gathers into settled farmers. "Nature-spirits" and agriculture carry a long-standing tradition together. Naturally, living closer to the natural Elemental world allowed early "pagan" cultures to experience more significant encounters with the Elemental beings and "Nature-spirits" sharing an affinity with the planet Earth.

Elemental Spirits and Nature-beings encountered in magical practices are typically neutral in polarity and crystalline in nature. This means that they are generally charged with an energy type that mirrors the polarity of willpower, intention and emotional energy discharged by a Mystic, Druid, or Wizard, &tc. This is essentially how the power of thoughtforms operates and how the psyche divides oneness into polarities of "good" and "evil." Hence, rituals "of the light" will attract spirits of a like nature—and those dark sacrificial ceremonies of cult abuse, that we often hear about in horror stories, will generate intense emotional resonance with "evil" polarities. Energy—as the Wizard understands it—is basically a catalyst of "attraction" operating on the "principle of like-forces." A ritual, rite or meditation will attract the same type of energy that is radiated from its conductance—if successful.

Nature-Wizards and Shamans often use sages and sweetgrass as an incense smoke to clear an area of unwanted, static or negatively charged energies. Another "Faerie" formula is ash, elder and hawthorne—burned in equal parts. This also aids in charging an area with a vibrational resonance that is more likely to attract the Sylvanus Folk—if that is your desire. The fey folk are attracted to small shiny objects, mirrors and trinkets. They are also partial to the colors: green, red, blue and yellow. Natural folk-style acoustic music is sure to entice them. Remember that the Elven-Ffayrie are traditionally interested in celebrations of life and love—so you must invite them to bright shinning places that are not somber or negative in any way. Only once you have made your own *life* a place that is fit to include such experiences, will it be possible to make it your *reality*.

ELVEN-DRUID GRIMOIRE

—Elven-Faerie Grimoire—
An Introduction to Elven Magick

The "Elven-Faerie Grimiore" or "Faerie-Druid Grimoire" is the result of many years of experimentation, deliberation and contemplation spent in personal dedication to the Elven Tradition before attempting to set this version of it in down in print. It does possess a deep underground source—one that has never been revealed by any of its initiates, but which is frequently drawn from by the same—as obvious from a composition of many popular New Age titles that emerged during the 1990's—and which provided many of the original New Age "covens," "groups" and "groves" with inspiration to outline a *"Book of Enchantment, Shadows & Light"* independent of more traditional British Wiccan manuals authored by Gerald Gardner and Alesiter Crowley with scattered influences by Charles Leland and Margaret Murray.

Until a blatant presence of published Elven-Faerie and Druid Traditions in 1980's and 1990's esoteric occultism, there were few readily available alternatives to the "traditional witchcraft" scene for neopagan revivals. It is evident by an iconic resurgence of "elven," "druidic," "dragon" and "faerie" motifs that this other covert underground movement to increase human awareness has proven, in part, quite effective. The Elven Way and Faerie Tradition are now a part of nearly all relevant 21st century "new consciousness," "new thought" or otherwise "earth-oriented" forms of "nature mysticism." As such, *this* work—as a *"living grimoire"*—has been reevaluated several times before arriving in its currently refined state. And this happens frequently when one is working to solidify the Elven "words of light" to the printed page—for they are fluid and dynamic, shimmering in the waves of a cosmic sea.

It is quite difficult to fully bring the full essence of the "Elven Way" to life using "books." The Elven Way is experienced in Nature—as a part of everyday life, a life that some are drawn to innately, and others are not so inclined. First and foremost it is a "mystical system," by human standards—one closely aligned to what we might consider "green magic"—or "green magick" if you prefer. Where *all* magic is tied to nature and the Cosmos—"*green magic*" specifically emphasizes the energy of the woodlands—trees, green wilderness, forests and valleys. Only Druidry and indigenous shamanism reflect the same kinds of "pathway" for Human Ascension that is alluded to in Elven Tradition. Although most New Age texts equate Elves and other elemental faerie beings exclusively with the Otherworld or Astral Plane, more experienced practitioners understand the connection between these races and a "very real" legacy of Elven-Dragon traditions and the *Tuatha d'Anu* that migrated westward across Europe from Mesopotamia and Anatolia, carrying with them a vast tradition and repository of knowledge from the "Ancient Mystery School." These matters have been discussed at length in our previous "Elven-Faerie" discourse within the present volume.

The term "Elven magic" ("Elven magick") is used to distinguish this "Elven-Ffayrie" system—also called the "*Edaphic Tradition*"—from others in the New Age. However, to the Elves themselves, magic is simply "magic" and it comes from an innate faculty—not some "supernatural" facet of life. Once again: Magic is *not* a "supernatural" power. On the contrary, "magick" is quite "natural" and follows principles of "natural law" or "cosmic law." When Humans refer to "magick," they are simply referring to an esoteric study and use of creative forces in the Universe to manifest reality. It is the practical application of the true knowledge and lore in everyday life.

True "magick" in the Elves Tradition is innate—they do not require years of study and training that the Wizard Schools of Humans and "Fey-Touched" must resort to. The Elven-Ffayrie simply do not see "magick" as something "outside" of themselves. It is developed and refined as part of their everyday natural life—over a period of progressive self-discovery, just as Humans might choose to refine their own personal tastes and skills through muscle memory. Wisdom of experience—and these must be Self-Honest experiences from a point of true knowledge—only develops with time, and this is something that Elven-Ffayrie races are not short on while residing in the Lands Beyond. Elves and faerie folk also view magick as a part of art. When something created or changed becomes charged or imbued with energy as a result of intention, it becomes art—and they learned to use this art to shape the natural world that we see all around us—our "reality." And magick—in all of its forms—will create, transform or even destroy some reflection of our global "reality."

"Magickal feats"—as conceived and purported by Humans—are accomplished via the activation of the mind's subconscious faculties—which then becomes "potential power." It may be activated with specific use of symbolism and imagery or focal aids that help an individual direct or channel energy. We are always actively participating in this *game*—but it is only with our *conscious* participation that we have the power to create. Many customs and methods of raising energy for this very purpose exist—ritual movements, breathing exercises, ceremonial dances—all of which entice the awareness of the total *Self* to become actively involved in bringing about desired results. All intentional acts are "magical"—even when it is cyclic self-talk of defeatism—and we put our awareness and attention-energies into wherever our focus lies. All acts, whether mundane or esoteric—are magical because they are movements of energy that create change—in accordance with will—and following natural laws and cosmic principles that may or may not be widely understood. The Human condition is easily distracted, and so rituals and ceremonial drama; the use of music and vocalized intentions; the alternative attire and altar dressings; the fragrance of sweet and musty incense and flickering firelight—all are effectively used to bring the *Self* into full awareness and control of the *Self* alone.

It is important to realize—especially if you desire a true understanding of "Elven magick"—that it is not the rituals and incantations themselves that hold the "power" in magic. A catalyst only represents potential until properly used—and that use is based on ability. "Magickal abilities" come from within—first and foremost—from the part of the "individual" that is not "separated" from the All—but is interconnected and linked absolutely to the fundamental Oneness of reality. Elven-Druid Wizards and Mystics channel energy currents tied to the Elemental Forces. These energies are considered external "higher powers" when present ceremonially. They are called by "will"—but often they are simply energetically attracted to the use of the magic conducted naturally. Since we know they are always present, the Wizard or Druid uses a form of long-standing etiquette when calling and dismissing any external—or thoughtformed—energies and entities.

The "Elven-Druid Grimoire" provides a practical application of Elven-Faerie lore and Druidic magic that has stood the test of time now for over two decades and which will continue to inspire aligned realizations of the Elven Way in perpetuity.

—The Elven Way—
Elements of the Tradition

Elven-Faerie tradition alludes to a singular unifying Oneness —an ALL interconnected with All life and energy in the Cosmos. However, the energy that manifests the world of forms that we experience within the parameters of physical reality (within a Human range) is filtered down and condensed into a series of perceived "levels," "degrees," "vibrations" and "frequencies" which are constantly in motion in accord with the Cosmic Law of ALL. There are—in reality—no actual separations between these varying degrees although we experience them that way subjectively as individuals perceiving a "world around us"—not always realizing that it is *us* that projects the separation of "things" from other "things." This holistic type of "*systemology*" is "meta-thinking" for most Humans.

Some elemental schema that follow in this chapter-lesson do relate directly to traditional—or more familiar—"Fourfold Elemental" paradigms aligned to the *Tuatha d'Anu* lore. However, Elven-Ffayrie traditions often record their Elemental schema in other methods that are not restricted to the cross-quarter symmetry that many *Seekers* are undoubtedly used to encountering in other sources of western magical tradition. They may more commonly appear as threefold, sixfold and ninefold "aspects" or "elements"—called "*duile*" by Gaelic-Welsh fey traditions. Neodruids and other New Age Wizards have also called the same: "*aires*"—so named after the "Four Winds." Sometimes the classification of elements are misunderstood—for example, because "*Nwyvre*" may be interpreted as both "*Akasha*" and "*Fire*," but as you will see, Elvish Wizards interpret the traditional "Fire Element" a bit differently when experienced in the "Otherworld."

THE THREEFOLD ELEMENTAL SCHEMA

Element of Land: bone, tissue, muscle, skin, soil, ground, minerals, crystals, plant life, vegetation, and mainland ecosystem.

Element of Sky: oxygen, lungs, voice, circulatory system, winds, upper atmosphere, clouds, vapor, and winged life.

Element of Sea: blood, fluids, hormones, neurochemicals, natural bodies of water, running water and marine life.

THE SIXFOLD ELEMENTAL SCHEMA

Element of Stone: "brown magick"—animals, business, gems, metals and soil.

Element of Earth: "green magick"—agriculture, ecology, fertility, forests, herbalism and trees.

Element of Vapor & Cloud: "indigo magick"—quantum physics, Otherworld magick, psychic powers, spirits and time travel.

Element of Wind: "yellow magick"—alertness, books, communication, confidence, knowledge, study, reading and writing.

Element of Sun: "red magick" & "orange magick"— alchemy, art, courage, healing, love, passion, strength, success and attraction.

Element of Sea: "blue magick"—creativity, dreams, love, emotion, glamour, the moon, enchantment, mysticism, peace, tranquility, understanding and visions.

THE NINEFOLD ELEMENTAL SCHEMA

Element of Salt—Land: nighttime, northwest, white, consecration ceremonies and purification.

Element of Earth—Land: midnight, north, green, trees/forest growth magick and fertility.

Element of Stone—Land: evening, northeast, brown, crystal magick, charging and protection.

Element of Wind—Sky: morning twilight, east, yellow, new beginnings, insight and summoning.

Element of Star(fire)—Sky: dawn, southeast, white, dreams, wish magick and awareness.

Element of Sun—Sky: noon, south, gold, insight, willpower, strength and leadership.

Element of Vapor & Cloud—Sea: twilight, southwest, astral magick, Otherworld work and enchantments.

Element of Sea—Sea: sunset, west, blue, subconscious magick, dreams, healing and love.

Element of Rain—Sea: dust, west-northwest, purple, emotions, emotional healing, cleansing, love and beauty.

Practice of Elemental Magick in Elvish Wizardry is typically composed of three main levels of progression—or degrees of experience. They relate not only to the development of one's abilities, but are also the same steps taken for ritualized exercises in meditation for effective physical magick:—

1. Dedication: study and initiation.
2. Purification: grounding and creating sacred space.
3. Invocation: calling forth and dismissing Elementals.

When utilizing rites of "Elemental Magick," a Wizard gains astral, spiritual and subconscious experience with a specific element. While all normal ritual observations will employ the four Elemental Quarters of the Middle World, Elvish Wizards often focus on a single element during personal meditations —working intensely with a particular aspect of the Elemental Kingdoms. By encountering each single element individually, an Apprentice Wizard to gains experience and "authority" with a each specific element before calling its powers directly in a ceremonial/ritual setting. However, when an affinity to a particular element emerges be warned that you will begin to assimilate attributes specific to that elemental type. For example—a Wizard who works with the Air Element most of the time may begin to develop a more *flighty*, *spacey* and *imaginative* personality. A "Fire Wizard" might develop an increased sense of personal *courage* and/or *passion*, but also *irritability* when untempered, &tc.

Elven Tradition observes four main styles or types of magickal practice. They are the ceremonial/ritualisitic (*Air*); energy and/or light work (*Fire*); use of astral or spirit vision to access the Otherworld (*Water*); and tree/forest magick (*Earth*). The "grimoires" within the current *Elvenomicon* anthology make a collective use of all these practices as specific to the observance of a modern "Elven-Druid Faerie Tradition." This book does not, however, claim to substitute the material of a full "magickal primer" for the novice.* In additional to elemental schema provided previously, the following are the "Elemental Keys" of the four primary "*duile*" as more commonly used in Elemental Magick by various Wizards, Druids and Mystics of the "Lands Above." Elsewhere in Druidic lore they are referred to as the "Elven Keys" or "Faerie Keys"—relating quite succinctly with lore introduced in a previous chapter-lesson as the "*Gifts of Faeire*"—which inspired the original Elemental "magic" correspondences of the *Tuatha D'Anu*.

---

* For a more generalized magickal primer, see also *"The Sorcerer's Handbook"* by Joshua Free (writing as Merlyn Stone) or his more recently composed *"Arcanum: The Great Magical Arcanum."*

THE FOURFOLD ELEMENTAL SCHEMA

Element of Earth: Elven Key to foundation and fertility, Kingdom of Stone, North, midnight and winter, ruled by King Ghobas, pentacles and holed stones are indicative of the Stone of Fal.

Element of Air: Elven Key to communication and intellect, Kingdom of Wind, East, dawn and spring, ruled by King Paraldas, wands and feathers represent the Spear of Lugh.

Element of Fire: Elven Key to transformation and protection, Kingdom of Flame, South, noon and summer, ruled by King Djin, the blade, staff & 'golden sickle' are representations of the Sword of Nuada.

Element of Water: Elven Key to inner wisdom and well-being, Kingdoms of Sea, West, dusk and autumn, ruled by King Niksas, the goblet, chalice, cup, mirrors and pools follow the tradition of the Cauldron of Dagda and Kerridwen.

—The Remetona—
Casting the Circle of Power

Meditation is a common and effective practice, but there is a subconscious desire inherent in wizardry—and those called to its orders—that seeks a uniform physical ritualization or ceremony to represent energetic action of "Natural Law." For these reasons, all ritual and ceremonial observations should occur within the "Circle of Power." Here, the Elvish Wizard creates a microcosm—or fractal miniaturization—of the Universe. Currents of Elemental energy are represented in ritual with symbolic catalysts or tools.

The "Circle of Power" is really the atomic *sphere*—fractal in nature, duplicating itself in "smaller" and "larger" dimensions or degrees, "above" and "below" frequency vibrations of what Humans separate as the "physical world." It may help to envision it not as a circle, but as a multi-dimensional "sphere." In eastern traditions, this is called a "mandala," but in the Elven-Druid traditions, sacred space is frequently referred to as a *"nemeton."* This "Magick Sphere" is not only a *microcosm* of the cosmos but simultaneously is a *macrocosm*—an expanded or enlarged view—of the subatomic and cellular worlds existing "beyond" mortal perceptual vision. All these varying worlds or dimensions are connected in the "Absolute Reality" or unified field—what ancient Druids called *"Ceugent,"* where exists only the Source of All Being and Creation.

Preliminary ceremonial methods for casting the "Circle of Power" or "Magick Sphere" vary between known systems of practical occultism. More variations probably exist in the "New Age" concerning "Rites of the Magick Circle" than any other aspect of practical metaphysics. The "Magick Sphere" or "*Nemeton*" is a sacred place of power. It is suggested that you should bring this "magic" to the wilderness and forests—find a clearing, or if possible, a "grove of trees." There you may even call on "Earth" and "Stone" as you erect your own "stone circle" or "henge of stones." The size of your "*kirc*" or physical "sacred circle" will vary based on the location used and the number of participants expected to be present at a given time. Understand that when you bring magick to the same place repeatedly—especially when you are permitted to leave your circle in place—the woodlands will become reminiscent of an ancient archetypal "Enchanted Forest" as the land takes on an increased "charge" over time.

According to classical accounts, the "*Nemeton*" is a "sacred space" when using terminology of ancient Druids and Elves—the same vocabulary appears regarding groves and henges. The famous "*Drunemeton*"—an annual gathering place of ancient Druids, Dragon-kind and Elves—existed somewhere in ancient Anatolia/Galatia (modern-day Turkey), revealing to us the true extent of geographic expansion once maintained by the Druids. There is even an ancient Druidic deity named as a patron of sacred space—Nemetona—the "Goddess of the Grove," closely identifying with a feminine form of the Dagda or Kernunnos as the male "Lord of the Forest" or Green Man. Stonehenge and Woodhenge are two basic examples in Britain of ancient structures built to mark a "*nemeton.*" Groves and henges can easily be "artificially" planted or manufactured—and later consecrated—so long as they are "left open to the sky."

The "Nemeton"—sacred space—is a critical component of practical "ritual magick" energy-work. A wizard must be free of physical, emotional and mental restraints, or bonds to the "material" degrees of existence, during "magical" operations. Creating and distinguishing "sacred space" allows both the conscious and subconscious mind to synchronize the salient belief that "something magical is about to happen."

In the past, Druids and Elves have followed the energetic vibrations or currents ("*ley lines*") of Nature to reach certain "power spots" and distinguished locations that even an only partially sensitive Human might describe as "enchanted" or "magical." Modern Wizards and Mystics dedicated to "green magic" continue to do this today, seeking out places for personal and overt "Earth power" to work their magick from. A *Seeker* is encouraged to research the vibrations and energetic currents of local trees and find natural representations that reflect the stream-current or ray that best reflects your own energies and/or the function of a ritual. Additional lore to assist this is provided in the "*Greenwood Forest Grimoire*"—also within the current *Elvenomicon* volume. New Age practitioners frequently consider the astrophysical qualities of celestial bodies—such as the Sun and Moon—during selection of the ritual area and timing of ceremonies—especially those linked to annual seasonal cycles, *e.g.* solstices and equinoxes.

A "*Nemeton*" for a solitary practitioner does not obviously carry the same space requirements as one intended for group (or even "coven") use. The center of the *Nemeton* is typically marked with an Altar. The same rules apply to the altar: the size and shape are dependent on your needs. Be sure to leave enough space to to move around the altar within the circle without affecting boundaries of the *Nemeton*. For group magick—practitioners will likely require much more space to move around freely. Here, you might reflect on energetic tension differences between times when you are alone and when you are in a crowded room. If movement is restricted in close quarters, the energy does not have the freedom to expand—and those gathered together will be more likely to draw their energies and auras in rather than properly project them out.

When you are ready to perform your magick, go to your "altar." For projective magick, it is customary to call forth and visualize a white field of light to surround yourself with—or another relevant ray-vibration of light—and ask your "Higher Self"—or interconnected consciousness—to guide and protect you in your magickal endeavors. After this an Elvish Wizard asks for peace, grace and acknowledgment from the elemental spirits in the Universe—and then the ritual can begin:—

Take a "goblet of water," holding it up to the west and say:

May the Spirits of Water bestow their blessing and remember.

Take up the "bowl of salt," and hold it up to the northern direction and say:

May the Spirits of Earth bestow their blessing and remember.

Sprinkle a portion of the "salt" into the "water," hold it up, facing north and affirm:

By this alchemical expression do I transform and purify my being—consecrating my spirit to the Source of All Light and the Children of Light, the Ancient and Shinning Ones.

Take up the "incense resin" (or stick) and hold it up to the east, saying:

May the Spirits of Air bestow their blessing and remember.

Hold up the "incense burner" to the south and say:

May the Spirits of Fire bestow their blessing and remember.

If you are using an incense stick, light it—otherwise the coals you should be prepared within the burner. Then add some of the incense resin to it and affirm:

By this alchemical expression do I hereby transform and purify my being, stripping away old skin, leaving my mortal body, affirming my Elven (Ffayrie) soul, consecrated to the Source of All Light and Starfire.

Allow the incense to burn. Take the chalice of salt-water and go to the north, working clockwise around the circle, sprinkling the water lightly as you walk. Be sure to ration your use so that some remains. Once you have moved about full circle, returning again to the north, go to your altar or 'work space' and take up the incense burner—adding some more if necessary—and go to the east, moving again around the entire boundary of the circle, slowly and deliberately. Your actions should express that you are walking or testing the boundaries of the "ends of the Universe"—represented by the Nemeton.

Go to the north with your "magick wand,"—carrying it in your projective hand (the one you write with) and begin to inscribe your circle, tracing or defining it on a metaphysical level—where before, you were only testing and sensing it. When using a wand in this way, your projective arm usually crosses the body as you walk clockwise in your initial conjuring of the "Circle of Power." Empower and/or envision your arm as an extension of your will, and the "magick wand" as a further extension—representing where your will meets that of the external energies that your will has summoned and attracted. See bluish-white energy projecting from your wand and imprinting the horizon of your circle at waist height. You may wish, if you are adept in visualization, to see this band of energy extending both above and below to form a "sphere."

Once you circumnavigate the "kirc," return to the central altar and address the Universe:

> Here I stand at the Entrance of the Golden Threshold. Between the Finite and Infinite Universe do I stand. The mortal spark burns deep within my being and I am flawed. The Divine spark burns deep within my being and I am flawless. Once I acknowledge the connectedness I share with the Source of All, I am complete and at one with all life in the Universe. I am a "Child of Starlight."

Feel the presence of the "Forces of Nature" surrounding your

"*Nemeton*," attracted to the "Circle of Light," that you have conjured. Acknowledge them by calling out:

> *I feel many varieties of energy imbued with Light and Life from the Otherworld coming to the edge of my Circle of Power. I hereby invite you in, all friendly spirits who aid in the positive magick of Nature. Witness and defend my ritual. Shield and protect this Sacred Nemeton, the Holy Mandala consecrated to the Light, the Children of Light, the Ancient and Shinning Ones. Being a Child of Starlight, I stand here to recognize and honor my ancestors and preserve the Elven Ways. May the Universal Spirit burn deep within my spirit.*

Take the "pentacle" or "holed-stone" from the altar and go to the north. Trace your "Sign of Earth"* with the tool and see it green. As the portal opens, visualize a Sylvan Tree Elf emerge from the Otherworld (from the north) to join your ritual circle. It does not matter that you must at first envision or imagine these energetic events in your mind's eye. They are present even when we do not see them—just as much as there is electricity in the air and gravity accompanying condensed masses, we do not have to always "see" this unseen power to tap its potential. The energy is summoned in ritual by personally generating a like energy which is projected and will attract and exchange with other similar energies in kind. See the "Sign of Earth" blazing bright as you speak the Earth Key:

> *Moh-ar Dee-ah-el Heh-keh-teh-gah. Ahd-hoo-ee Glee-im Awe-guhs Foil-chah nah Speer-ohd-dee deh Cah-reeg en-duil-yah Awe-guhs Tah-lave See-uh ar aye-it sho. In the names of the Northern Quadrangle, I call thee spirits and powers of stone, leaf, land and the pentacle, to witness and defend this rite, shield and protect this "Magick Sphere." King and Queen of the Gnomes and Sylves, on this side of the Sacred Circle are you invited.*

Go to the east and trace the "Sign of Air" with the wand, envi-

---

* A personal symbol, glyph or *"Sign of Portal"* aligned with the element.

sioning it yellow or purple. With the Air threshold veil lifted, envision an emergence of a Sylphen fey coming to your circle from the (eastern) Otherworld as you intone the Air Key:

> *Oh-roh Ee-bah Ah-oh-zodpee. Ahd-hoo-ee Glee-im Awe-guhs Foil-chah nah Speer-ohd-dee deh Spay-er en-ghee-huh Awe-guhs Nay-all See-uh ar aye-it sho. In the names of the Eastern Quadrangle, I call thee spirits and powers of the sky, wind, air and wand. Shield and protect this "Magick Sphere." King and Queen of the Sylphs and Sprytes of the breeze and flowers, on this side of the Sacred Circle are you invited now.*

Bring with you to the south your "sword," 'sickle' or 'blade,' and trace your "Sigil of Fire" in the air with the tool, seeing it red. As you open the portal of the south, you see a draconian figure emerge from the Otherworld, coming forth to join your magickal rite as you speak the Fire Key:

> *Oh-ee-peh Teh-ah-ah Peh-doh-keh. Ah-nahsh Glee-im Awe-gu-hs Foil-chah nah Speer-ohd-dee deh Gree-uhn Awe-guhs chin-nuh See-uh ar aye-it sho. In the names of the Southern Quadrangle, I call thee spirits and powers of the skystar, sun, flame and sword. Shield and protect this "Magick Sphere." King and Queen of the Fire-Drakes and Dragons, on this side of the Sacred Circle are you invited now.*

Take the "goblet," 'chalice' or 'cup' to the western direction and use it to trace the "Water Sign' and see it blue. From the west you can imagine merfolk, or 'undine,' appear from the Otherworld mists, as you intone the Water Key:

> *Em-peh-heh Are-es-el Gah-ee-oh-leh. Ah-neer Glee-im Awe-gu-hs Foil-chah nah Speer-ohd-dee deh Gah-lahk En-oo-esh-ka Awe-guhs mwir-uh See-uh ar aye-it sho. In the names of the Western Quadrangle, I call thee spirits and powers of the moon, sea, water and grail. Shield and protect this "Magick Sphere." King and Queen of the Merfolk of the wave, on this side of the Sacred Circle are you invited now.*

Leave each of your representations of the "Gifts of Faeire"—the "Elemental tools"—at their respective directions. After all of these "keys" are activated, return to the altar/workspace and affirm:

> *Guh Renv-en en-na Too-huh deh Dahn-non Bahn-ahk-tree or-een. Cos-eent en Nuh-dee-huh doh are aye-it show. Etz-are-peh. Heh-coh-mah. Nah-en-tah. Bee-toh-em. In the names of Akasha, Nyu, Spirit of the Quintessenal Fifth Element, I call the Spirits of the Tuatha D'Anu, the Danubian Sidhe, the Ancient and Shinning Ones. High Elves of the Otherworld, shield and protect this "Magick Sphere." Spirits of the Wood Elves, you too are invited to my Circle of Power.*

Visualize the boundary of the sphere clearly, as it descends into the ground beneath you and into the sky above. See its auric shield as a bright "force field" of light and energy complete with your "Sigils of Elemental Portals" burning brightly in each cardinal direction. Each of the Elementals called to the circle stand guard near their respective seals. Meditate on what is happening and hold the images clearly in your mind. Finally intone:

> *Elemental Spirits of the Otherworld shield and protect this "Magick Sphere." Be a witness now and co-magician in the magick I summon here in this Sacred Space. Guardians of the Universe, Watchers and Portal Messengers, come now to witness and aid in the celebration of Light and Love enacted here in my ceremony. May the grace and blessing of the Source of All Being and Creation pervade in my spirit forever and always.*

The "Circle of Power" or "*Nemeton*" is now ready for magickal work. Remember to "Extinguish the Powers of the Magick Sphere" before completing your ceremony and departing from your Sacred Space—as given in the next section.

—The Nemetona—
Extinguishing the Circle

In every tradition that casts or summons a "Circle of Power," there is a similar concluding rite where all energies called *in* during the ritual are thanked and dismissed. Elemental energies used for crafting or casting the "Circle of Power" must be extinguished too. This is an important formality maintained by Elvish Wizards and Druids. Without a ceremonial manner of etiquette for opening a circle so closed, there is nothing to distinguish the Sacred Space or *Nemeton* from the ordinary surrounding space. The "Magick Sphere" exists as a psychological and spiritual thought-formed boundary to confine and focus the energy channeled by the Wizard. It has a second purpose—as a "Circle of Protection" for Wizards when they are channeling raw energy currents. And finally, it represents the fractal reality, which has been discussed in prior sections.

To open a circle sealed by magick—or otherwise extinguish the powers of the circle so cast—move around the boundary of the circle counter-clockwise, thanking and dismissing the Elementals while retrieving the tools left there. If you have traced any sigils, lore suggests that you retrace them in reverse—"erasing" them and sealing/closing the portals that they access—even if they are mental doorways for a novice—you don't want to leave these "open." If you began (or oriented) your *Nemeton* to the north (Earth Element), then you will want to finish there—so begin in the west. If you started in the east, begin your extinguishing in the north—always working backwards, counter-clockwise—or *"tuathal"*—when opening the circle at the end of a rite. Use the following formal incantations in the order most appropriate to your needs.

WEST: *Slahn Ah-we-leh Speer-ohd-dee deh Gah-lahk En-oo-eesh-kah Awe-guhs Mwir-uh. Guh-rehv Mee-luh mah Ah-guhv. Depart in peace Western spirits of moon, sea, water and grail. May the energies of the Water Element return to your place of dwelling until you are again called.*

SOUTH: *Slahn Ah-we-leh Speer-ohd-dee deh Ghree-uhn Awe-guhs Chin-Nuh. Guh rehv Mee-luh mah Ah-guhv. Depart in peace Southern spirits of skystar, flame, sun and blade. May the energies of the Fire Element return to your place of dwelling until you are again called.*

EAST: *Slahn Ah-we-leh Speer-ohd-dee deh Spay-ir En-ghee-huh Awe-guhs Nay-ahl. Guh rehv Mee-luh mah Ah- guhv. Depart in peace Eastern spirits of sky, wind, air and wand. May the energies of the Air Element return to your place of dwelling until you are again called.*

NORTH: *Slahn Ah-we-leh Speer-ohd-dee deh Cah-reeg En-duil-yuh Awe-guhs Taw-luhv. Guh rehv Mee-luh mah Ah-guhv. Depart in peace Northern spirits of leaf, land, stone and pentacle. May the energies of the Earth Element return to your place of dwelling until you are again called.*

When the final ritual tools are retrieved, bring them back to your central working space and address the Universe with:

Slahn Ah-we-luh En-too-huh deh Dahn-non Awe-guhs. Guh rehv Mee-luh mah Ah-guhv. Skee-uh deh Dree-uckt Show. Many thanks and blessings to the spirits who have gathered here. Depart in peace spirits of the Tuatha D'Anu, Wood Elves, Sidhe, and all Ancient and Shinning Ones who have blessed me with your mystical presence. Return to the Sidhe Hills and Faerie Dwellings until you are again called forth. May the grace of the rays of the Source of All Being and Creation go with all who have come to join in this magickal work. I depart in peace to my place of dwelling until I return here again in magick's hour. The "Magick Sphere" stands open now, but is never broken. Awen (Ah-oo-een).

With these last words, the energies of the circle itself are extinguished. You may raise your arms and see the bluish-white energy of the "magick sphere" burn brightly—and then as you quickly lower your arms, see these energies of the *Nemeton* ground and fade.

—The Gifts of Faerie—
Consecrating Symbols of Power

This rite may be used for "charging" or "consecrating" ritual tools—particularly "Elemental tools" representing the "Gifts of Faeire." It may also be used to ceremonially charge amulets and talismans for other magical purposes. Essentially, all implements or "tools" of magic must be consecrated—dedicated and "charged" for "magickal" purposes—prior to their incorporation into ritual and ceremony. Otherwise they are simply mundane physical objects. A "Magickal tool" is so considered because a Wizard is able to use it to connect to the energy that the tool represents—or is a catalyst for. Remember: *like forces attract like forces* in magic.

Conjure your "Circle of Power"—then say:

> *May peace and love fill my spirit so I may be a beacon of light and life projecting such energy outward in all directions of the Universe. May the Ancient and Shinning Ones hear my call. I ask the spirits of the Earth who are friendly to the Elven Ways to join me in consecrating this sacred icon to thy tradition. Come now and bless this [name(s) of talisman(s) to be consecrated], so that you will more easily recognize it when I present it to you in the future.*

You will need your item(s) available when you conduct the ritual. This simplified rite should be used only for "Elemental tools" or if not, an item that is used for more than a single-use "spell." For example, you might charge a runic pendant to attract love energy into your life, but Elven Wizardry is not used to gain the specific love of so-and-so, such as you might find in a targeted love-spell. True "Elvish Magick" is timeless and not restricted to a specific event or person (usually) and therefore the construction of general talismans that attract love would are more appropriate for this rite than a "love spell." Other examples may just as easily be applied here.

When the tool is "ready"—assuming it is constructed during this operation—say:

> Hail to the Sidhe, the High Ones, and to the Sylvanus, the Sylphs and Sylves and the Wood Elves themselves. Hail to the Lords and Ladies of the Land, Sky, and Sea. Greetings to all Creatures of Faerie—all ye welcomed here. Mark well what you witnessed this day/eve and remember. May the Eternal Source of Everpresent Light, look favorably on the magick I conceive.

In order for this consecration to be effective, you must charge the item with your intentions. This requires some proficiency in the ability of energy channeling. [For those eyes falling upon this with no prior experience, you are now bidden by these words read here to never misuse what is discovered in our grimoire of rites and secret spells. By *this oath* between us I will offer the clue needed to make this work.] You will need to feel and see your thought-form, goal or Elemental current clearly outside of yourself. Breathe this energy—or aetheric matter—in and feel it completely wash through your body as you absorb it through your every pore. Feel it run through your entire circulatory system. You are Assimilating this energy in total—so it had better be positive—and focus it on your arms and hands, projecting it from within and releasing or pushing it into the item.

Take your "symbol of power" to the north with the "bowl of salt." Set the bowl on the "pentacle"—or Earth-stone (unless this ritual is used to consecrate your Earth-tool for the first time, then the ground will work) and set the item in the bowl of salt and/or sprinkling some of the salt on it saying:

Look here and witness ye Spirits of the North. By sprinkling this [n.] with the Salt of the Earth do I consecrate it by the names and Seals of the Earth Element.

Take your "symbol of power" to the southeast, bringing your "incense burner" with, and if there is not already sufficient smoke, add more incense resin. For this rite you will want to select an essence to burn that correlates with the talisman or purpose of the rite. Pass it through the smoke and say:

Look here and witness ye Spirits of the East and South. I pass this [n.] through the burning herbal resins that waft through the air. In doing so I now consecrate it by the ancient names and seals of the elements Air and Fire.

Continue your clockwise movement to the western direction, and use your "bowl of water"—or *'sacred vessel'*—to sprinkle some of the water onto the "symbol of power" saying:

Look here and witness ye Spirits of the West. I pass this [n.] through your realm by sprinkling it with your water of life and renewal. By the secret names of the Sea do I consecrate this symbol as witnessed by the Water Element.

If consecrating symbols representing "Gifts of Faeire" using this rite, it is customary to call on—and charge the tool—with energies appropriate to the original *Tuatha d'Anu* artifacts.

> Stone of Fal—North/Earth, Master Morfessas
> Spear of Lugh—East/Air, Master Esras
> Sword of Nuada—South/Fire, Master Uscias
> Cauldron of Dagda—West/Water, Master Semias

A tool is ritually consecrated prior to its use as a sacred tool—but, there are no arcane rules concerning how long a tool will hold a charge—or how often it should be recharged. They do take on a charge over time with regular use. Gem/metal objects hold a charge the longest; followed by wood; then liquid.

—Children of Faerie—
Rites of Calling

The "Children of Faerie" do not submit themselves to the will of Wizards like those spirits conjured and encountered from medieval grimoires—which are in actuality thought-formed ancestral and cosmic extensions of ourselves and our own consciousness as One with the ALL. "Children of Faerie" will certainly not so easily cater to Human whims. Thus, there is no ritual or ceremony that will ensure "conjuration" of the "Elven-Ffayrie" beings. However, various methods are hidden in esoteric lore of Druidism and surviving remnants of those teachings of the Elven Wizards and Mystics once restricted to initiates of the "Ancient Mystery School." Therefore, what we may include here are "suggestions" to entice, gain favor or otherwise develop working relationships with nature-bound spirits. This is a prerequisite for any ceremonial or "at will" contact in Elven Wizard traditions. Of course, magical work of this nature will require access to the physical "Green World" —where you believe the "nature spirits" reside. You need not even bother with this in a purely urban setting where you are almost guaranteed to find disappointment.

Once initial contact is made, initiating it in the future is increasingly easier—and more innate—with each success. When a relationship has commenced, be sure to ask the spirit(s) their names (and signs) and their preferred method of future contact. This is the only manner by which Fey-Touched Humans become privy to a true mystical apprenticeship with the Elven-Ffayrie far surpassing what has been considered "acceptable" by *them* for me to print in this tome. I am permitted only inclusion of "Outer Court" or "Outer Circle" lore that will be used by *them* to test *you* as a potential initiate.

We should expect that they will certainly screen potential "Elf-Friends" and "Ffayrie-Allies." It is true that even the current author has had a great many things withheld until we are no longer rewriting and reissuing new editions of this information to the public. Instead, and so as to safeguard our own existent Oaths, the *Elvenomicon* is prepared as an objective mystical guide—relaying to potential initiates Nature's own "recruiting manual" for an awakening available to those truly enlightened folk that have not fully forgotten who they are in a world of depersonalization and disenchantment.

If you are reading these words in the dark half of the year, you may still have time to prepare an initial rite of contact on a forthcoming Beltane or Midsummer. For this you will need a "Silver Wand"—an apple-wood wand with three silver bells hanging from white ribbon. It should be consecrated prior to this rite. Use this wand to conjure your circle. Then, starting in the northeast, sprinkle "Primrose flower petals"—moving *deosil* around the boundary of your circle, As you say:—

> *Under stone, under sea, under every blade of grass. In the winds, in the flames, in the circle that I cast. Elf and Ffayrie, come to me. Grant me favor and be blest.*

Ignite your incense coals in your sand-filled "cauldron" or "burner" at the south-west. Heap on some incense—an herb-and-twig mixture followed by sweet-smelling resins—and feel the smoke radiating from your "Magick Sphere" and into the Otherworld dimension, acting as a beacon to your call:—

> *I have studied the way of Sidhe. I shall awaken every tree. I have called to share my home, with Undina, Sylpha, Elf and Gnome. I emerge from a world of mortal strife, here to partake in Faerie life.*

Prepare three small "shot glasses" in the northwest with "elderberry wine" or "milk and honey." Set out 'sweetbreads' or "cookies" alongside this. Then, take up your "bowl of salt" and sprinkle a circular boundary around the food offering as you speak:

> *Gifts of Faeire granted me, Elemental tools here on display.*
> *Now a gift I give to thee, to ignite a bond 'tween you and me.*
> *Overnight I'll leave this food, in hopes we'll meet here some day.*

Remains of the food may be removed the next day. Essences of the offering will already have been taken—or not. The physical food itself may or may not. "Nature spirits" also send their animal allies to feast on the physical foodstuff once they have accepted the sentiment of the gift. Typically, Elvish Wizards will make regular food offerings to the Otherworld Fey—and a particular location and at regular intervals.

"Circles of Power" for the sole intention of calling the Elven-Ffayrie spirits may be consecrated or conjured differently. Elemental callings may even be modified to meet the needs of contacting members of the Sylvanus Folk—those maintain their own Elemental hierarchy. The following are the suggestions listed in the original Elven-Faerie Grimoire:

THE SYLVANUS FOLK—CORRESPONDENCES

EAST: Air Element—"Tree Elves"
South: Fire Element—"Sprytes" ("Pixies")
West: Water Element—"Mushroom Fey"
North: Earth Element—"Woodland Gnomes"
Elf King: "Lord Oberon" (Auberon)
Faerie Queen: "Lady Titania"

In your woodland travels or spiritual walks in the forests, valleys and mountain ranges throughout the Middle World, you may very well find something in Nature that your inner voice tells you is a gateway threshold to the Otherworld. At these places you can conjure a circle for the purposes of Faerie-calling but be advised: do not disturb the physical environment; do not make a lot of noise; and keep ritual incantations to a minimal and lighthearted—which is why many of those included in this book seem so whimsical. Keep them directed specifically toward "nature spirits." You might speak something like:—

> I am a spirit of peace. Let peace ring throughout the entire Universe. May my energy and vibration be that only of peace, love and harmony that I extend to the Creatures of Elphame. Know that I [your magickal name] come to you in admiration and respect. I seek contact and initiation to your Otherworld, in grace and goodness. I shall not disturb, trespass or break the solemn vows shared between us. I seek to be your companion and will adhere to the boundaries of that friendship. By the grace of the All-Source, please come forth and make thyself known.

Elven-Ffayrie lore suggests that animals as messengers of the Otherworld. Some are considered "more sacred" or more iconic to specific aspects of the tradition than others—but *all* woodland, marine and flying creatures are sacred as representing interconnection of All life as "One" in the Universe with ALL life—meaning that all life is one and equal at the Source of All Being. Animals maintain a role, almost as if ambassadors, negotiators or again, "messengers" between the "World of Men" and the "World of Nature"—or the physical visible world and the unseen Otherworld. As a general species the Humans have not treated their stewardship of Earth with due respect—nor is it it shown to our animal brethren as it should be. Working with animals in both the physical world and in the spirit realm (or astral) may even grant favorable attitudes toward you from the fey.

—Elven Wizardry—
Rites of Faerie Spellcraft

Elven Wizards create their own unique types of "prayer," which others might just as easily call "spells"—and still others refer to as "creative visualization therapy." Our minds, the *Self* and its interconnection to All may go by many names, but we are most concerned here with the techniques that do yield results—regardless of various forms of methodology and semantics applied to the same use of "Cosmic Law" for thousands of years.

"Faerie spells" may be created by an individual for any particular need or occasion. Remember: "magick" to Elves is a creative art—one that the Masters take great pride in. In order to "write your own magick," however, you will need to be acquainted and proficient with traditional rites and the rules of spellcraft. To those uninitiated, a "spell" is a short magickal working performed in a "Circle of Power" in order to bring about a desired result or movement of energy toward a certain direction. This does not necessarily occur immediately and may take days, weeks, months and even years (in some instances) to manifest—depending on the situation.

Most common uses of "Faerie Spellcraft" include protection, fertility & abundance, prosperity & wealth, and the banishment of negativity and/or warding away of unwanted energy. There are many other uses of magick—such as the ever popular "single use love spell," which is not dealt with in this tradition of magick. According to lore, the most popular days for magical work in the Elven tradition are "Elf Day"or "Tree Day" (*Tuesday*) and "Fey Day" (*Saturday*).

Every day is *magical*. Each of the planet-oriented days of the week represent attributes connected to a "ray" of the "Elven Star"—which allows us to glean the Sevenfold Schema of the original source tradition in the *Ancient Near East*. Note here: there are seven days—thus seven colors, seven notes of music and naturally seven (6+1) points on the "Elven Star" are all correlated within the paradigm of Elven Tradition.

THE SEVENFOLD SCHEMA—or—ELVEN STAR

Monday: Moonday; blue; "G" note; pearl stone; silver.
Tuesday: Elf Day/Tree Day; red; "C"; ruby; iron.
Wednesday: Woden's Day; orange; "D"; opal; mercury.
Thursday: Thor's Day; indigo; "A"; sapphire; tin.
Friday: Freya's Day; green; "F"; emerald; copper.
Saturday: Fey Day; violet; "B"; onyx; lead.
Sunday: Sun Day; yellow; "E"; diamond; gold.

Herbs sometimes appear in lore as "Elf Amulets." Acorns aid in fertility rites—and acorns found by moonlight are symbols of prosperity and abundance. They are the fruit and seed of the oak tree and carry a long history of traditional use for fertility, love, and protective purposes. They should, unless otherwise advised, always be gathered in daylight hours, preferably at noon. Keep your chosen intention for the amulet in the mind while collecting them. In ceremonial magick, wands made from oak are often capped with a large acorn tip. Cones (pine, &tc.) may also be used for this—making excellent tools of growth magic. In divination for "love," a couple may each drop an acorn in still water and watch to see how they respond to each other. In a spell to encourage a friend to initiate a romantic interest, seven acorns are placed on a small square of white cloth and tied up with a red cord or ribbon to form an "amulet bag." After sleeping with it under their pillow for three consecutive nights, it is buried beneath a rose bush and then the person calls out for the other to come. The acorn is also a nut-food or it may be crushed into "oak flour."

Apple-seeds are natural items of love-drawing magic—though also poisonous in large quantities. The common apple tree is actually a hybrid effort—the result of years of crossbreeding to bring us the familiar fruit we know today. The original apple species—the crab apple (*malus hupehensis*) produces much smaller fruits, resembling cherries. The *Rosaceae* family of apples is shared by over 3,000 different species, including the ash, bay/laurel, cherry, hawthorn, peach and plum trees. In Druid folklore, apple is associated with *Queris* or the *Quert Ogham* and is the traditional wood of love magick.

Most Celtic scholars associate apples with the Isle of Avalon, called "*Emain Ablach*," which some also interpret as "Isle of Glass." In fact "*Affalon*" may be a mutation of "Appleland,"—perhaps an ancient orchard or grove. One famous magical tool in lore—referred to previously—a Celtic shaman's wand called the "*craebh ciuil*" or "Silver Branch," was fashioned from apple-wood. The fruit is also sacred to Mystics because it bares the image of a pentagram when cut at its midsection, and is particularly significant to the harvest—the festivals of Lughnassadh and the autumn equinox. In ancient times, the harvest traditionally began with a toast of cider. At Yule, the apple-wine "*wassail*" was used ceremonially for tree blessing. Apples are found in natural healing remedies for anemia. They are good sources of Vitamins A and E, which may assist purifying the body of toxins and lowering blood pressure.

According to faerie lore, bay leaves ward away the enchantments, spells and glamour of others when placed under the tongue. Pine-cones—when found by moonlight—are symbols of good fortune, health and well-being. Perhaps the most famous herbal 'Elf-Amulet' is the "*trefoil*," "*trifolium*," "*shamrock*" or "clover" that is so commonly identified as a symbol of luck—or to ward away warfare. All the herbs mentioned require cutting or removal from the land, so it is customary to "ask the plant's permission" in order to officiate an understanding that a spiritual intelligence exists within all life. A common incantation of the "magical herbalist" is:

"With this strike may you grow stronger."

"Magical herbalists" have also designated specific herbs that are held particularly sacred in Elven-Ffayrie Magickal Tradition. These include: dandelion root; chamomile; mistletoe; elder flow'r: hops; Irish moss; rosemary; rose-hips; raspberry leaf; mint; mullien; skullcap; and slippery elm bark. These may be used by themselves or in conjunction with each other for attracting the attention of "Otherworldly folk" in ritual as well as mixed with black tea and drank as an infusion. They calming herbs—and they may aid one in attuning to the energies of the "Green World" and "Faerielands."

To protect a home, an Elvish shaman might use sage and fern to clear out negative energy. Sigils of protection could be traced on the four outer walls to conjure a "magick shield." One might use the "Elf-Sign" (star) or another protective "rune," "Ogham"—even the "Dragon's Eye"—will generally suffice for banishing and warding against "typical" types of unfriendly (or malignant) energy. A traditional Gaelic-Welsh incantation for this purpose is:

> *Cosaint agus beanachtai yn n'Deith do talamh seo. Dibir na ole agus dona.*

Ask the aid of "helpful" Elementals. Decide and fix on a target or energy current (or ray) that you wish to block. Envision a representation of the unwanted energy or current and feel that it is the embodiment of that what are you are warding away. See the auric energy projected from as being blocked or shielded—as if encased in a bubble—which dissolves into the astral aether as you say:

> *I command you, by the names and letters of the Most High, to depart in peace!*

Keys to effective spellcraft are: clarity of intention; the ability to raise internal energy and merge it with assisting external ones; visualization of desired goals clearly; and the willpower to properly release energy so summoned from within and without. The keys—in this order—form the fundamental steps taken in all practices of "spellcraft." The following are some additional tips to aid your faerie spell-weaving:

—Incorporate only tools and items of a "like energy" to that which you wish to connect with. All others are distractions.

—Visualization skills make-or-break your mystical prowess of directing energy with the Mind, according to Cosmic Law.

—Only call forth or summon spirits and energies specific to your purpose; and only those that accelerate your cause.

—Ask the "Universe" (and "spirit guides") for assistance in carrying ("channeling") or directing the release of energies via the appropriate channels.

—Do not dwell on a ritual working already performed, or on what the nature of the results will be, for at least three days afterward. This keeps any energy used for that ritual-spell "out there" "working for you" and not contained or restricted to the vicinity of your thoughts.

—Most importantly, it is essential that you believe in your abilities. Remember the ancient proverb that: *all intentional acts are magical.*

—Elven Wizardry—
Rites of Healing & Protection

Consecrate a "Circle of Power" in a place receiving blessing, protection and/or healing. Set out your ceremonial tools—or representations of the "Gifts of Faeire"—in their correlating directions. Enter the circle from the northeast by procession if there are multiple practitioners. Go to the center of your workspace unless you are working in a group that allows for using "Elemental Stations." Light a white candle and say:

"May there be peace within my being."

Each participant should do the same. You can then proceed to address each of the directions from the center (altar)—or if performed in a group, other participants may be stationed at each Elemental "quarter."

NORTH: *May peace ring out and extend across northern expansions.*

EAST: *May peace ring out in the east and extend across the furthest plains.*

SOUTH: *May peace ring out in the south and extend to the peaks of the tallest mountains.*

WEST: *May peace ring out in the west and extend to the depths of the deepest sea.*

Light more white candles—as well as a blue and a red one if using this rite for "healing." You may even state affirmations as you light them, before continuing with the rite.

NORTH: *May peace, love and harmony extend to every living being and space in the Universe, especially [name of what/ who is to be blessed/protected/healed]. Great Bear of the North, I call now on your strength and the wisdom of the Earth Element. Offer your blessing towards me and extend your protective/healing power on [n].*

EAST: *May the purity of the Air Element enrich all work performed here. May the Winds aid me in purifying the energies of [n]. Hawk of the Eastern Dawn, I call now on your agility and the wisdom of the Sky Element. Offer your blessing toward me and extend your protective/healing power towards [n].*

SOUTH: *May the purifying flame purge and annihilate that which is unclean, especially in this place/for [n]. Great Stag of Southern Flame, I call on your virility and the wisdom of the Fire Element. Offer your blessing toward me and extend your protective/healing power towards [n].*

WEST: *May the blessing of the purifying and healing powers of the transforming waters be upon me in the work that I do towards [n]. Wise Salmon of the Western Sea, I call upon thy True Knowledge and the wisdom of the Water Element. Offer your blessing toward me and extend your protective/ healing power towards [n].*

Return to the center of your workspace and recite the "Elvish Wizard's Benediction"—or the "Gorsedd Prayer" of Druidism. You may use a version from some other ceremonial source or the more commonly known one, provided here:

Dyro, Dduw, dy naw erth, deall Ae yn heal gybod; Ae yng n gwybod, gwybod y cyfiawn; Ae yng ngwybod y cyfiawn; Eigarn Ac a garu, caru pobhanfod; Ac ym mhob hanfod caru Duw. Duw a phob dai oni.

Grant us O God, thy protection; and in protection, strength; and in strength understanding; and in understanding, per-

iception; and in perception, the perception of righteousness; and in the perception of righteousness, the love of it; and in the love of it, the love of all life; and in the love of all life, the love of God and all goodness.

May the Source of All Being and Creation extend currents/ rays to protect/heal this place/person.

Bless the "target" with "saltwater" and "burning incense." A "smudge-stick" of sage, reed or fern might also be used. Bless the "bowl of water" and sprinkle it on the person and around the person, or in each room of the house and around the outside of the property. With the "salt-water," say at each point:

By the Elemental Powers of Earth and Water do I so cleanse and consecrate [n].

With the incense, at each point:

By the Elemental Powers of Flame and Wind do I so purify and bless [n].

Returning to the center of the circle, complete this portion of the rite by saying:

May there be peace [in this home/at this place/with this person]. May it/they absorb the protection/healing channeled to this space "now made sacred" [or if at the Grove, "most sacred"].

If there is a faerie-shaman or Druid present, they may wish to seek the nature of an ailment of a person—or the energetic disturbance of an area—by communicating with Otherworld "shadows," "spirit guides" or other kind of energy work that allows for "astral" communication. Supplemental healing and protection spells may be performed here. Once the ceremonial goals are satisfied, thank the powers and extinguish the energies of the "Magick Sphere."

—The Elven Ways—
A Self-Dedication Ceremony

Regardless of whether or not you formally decide to join (or develop) a "coven," "circle" or "grove" of the Elven Tradition —whatever name you use to call such a close-knit magical group—you will first need to perform a personal "Self-Dedication" rite to the Elven Way. Dedication rites are traditionally different from "initiations," because a dedication rite is performed in solitary—alone in the woods or wilderness. This ceremony is not necessarily a "magickal spell" in the traditional sense—it is a personal "Rite of Passage" observed much like the "seasonal celebrations" of the "Wheel of the Year."

The Self-Dedication Ceremony is a form of psychological magic—it effectively changes an internal set or mode of thinking that determines our perspective in life. One such premise for a true Self-Dedication Ceremony: the Elven Wizard—or Elvish Wizard-*to-be*—has just discovered some strange arcane tome, such as the one you currently hold, and realizes —or awakens to a realization—that either they personally share the Elven-Faerie-Dragon legacy themselves, or for some "unknown" reason, they feel a peculiar inclination to these mysteries, innately drawn to the path via self-initiation.

Although this rite did not appear at the beginning of the original "Elven-Faerie Grimoire"—which the current author has made every effort to relay here in proper tribute—it would be logical that this is among the first, if not *the first*, ceremonial observation made by a practicing *Seeker*. It provides a decent introduction to the psyche to this world of ritual symbols and abstract energies. It may be performed without "tools," or as a solidified sentiment after these are made and consecrated.

Focused meditation and self-dedication rites performed in Nature may aid in bridging the relationship with the natural, spiritual—or otherwise "metaphysical"—side of Reality. All skill and ability is accumulated over time as a result of consistent growth of this relationship, which breaks down the artificial barriers of fragmented separation between the *Self* and the *Cosmos*—what is considered "Magical Authority" or "Power," but which is really derived from the ability to operate the *Self* in perfect clarity—or what we call "*Self-Honesty.*"

Conjure the "Magick Sphere"—or *Nemeton*—in a manner that you have practiced—even if you have only envisioned doing so in your mind, as you read this "grimoire," which is a form of magic in itself when energy is properly directed. This time, as you move about to trace the boundary of the circle, by hand (or wand), you will set out an "Elemental Candle" at each cardinal direction—a common practice in all forms of Elemental Magick and Wizardry. Choose one of an appropriate Elemental color for each direction. Wait until you are addressing each element during the Self-Dedication Rite to light the candles—and do not use the incantations from the "Casting the Circle of Power" section until you are already a "self-dedicated practitioner."

Once the area has is deemed "Sacred Space," go to the center of the circle—you do not need an "altar" for this rite—and stand or kneel, facing north, saying:

> *In my mortal form I am known as* [name all know you by] *but today/tonight I come to you in my Elven-Ffayrie form with the name* [a chosen magickal name or "true name"]. *I come to you now, Spirits of the Universe as an "Elf-Child"* ["*Ffayrie-Child*" for females; "*Elf-Friend*" for mortal practitioners who are not certain that they are personally a representative of the Elven-Faerie legacy.]

Take a "bowl of salt" and remove a pinch, placing it on your tongue. Feel the salt of the Earth entering your bloodstream and becoming a part of your entire body as you say:

> *I am a child of Earth. I am a child of the stars. I have studied on my own in preparation, but now I seek the Spirits of Nature to be my teacher, to instructor me in the true sciences of the Cosmos. Hidden in your folds lies the answers of Creation and Life. We are one. I am one with the entire Universe. I seek to share a relationship with thee.*

Stand and move to the north, light a "green candle," saying:

> *Spirits of the Enchanted Forest, of plants and rocks and trees, awaken and know me [your magickal name]. I come with peace within, seeking your aid in learning thy mysteries. I vow to ever uphold thy secrets, walking the path of wisdom and enlightenment. I am a follower of the Elven Ways.*

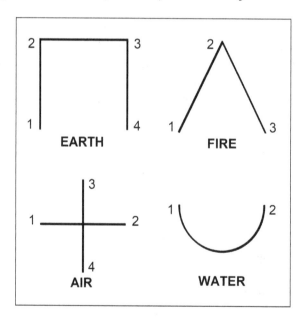

Trace a seal or symbol of the Earth Element that you will use regularly in your rites to incite energetic activity of the Elements. Examples shown here are based on the traditional Druidic interpretation of Elemental Magick.

Envision the "Sign of Earth" as green in color, as you intone:

By this Sign shall we know each other.

Go to the east; while lighting the "yellow candle," say:

Spirits of the Enchanted Breeze, of winds and sky and Air, awaken and know me [magickal name]. *I come with peace within, seeking your aid in learning thy mysteries. I vow to ever uphold thy secrets, walking the path of wisdom and enlightenment. I am a follower of the Elven Ways.*

Trace your "Sigil of Air," envisioning it yellow, saying:

By this Sign shall we know each other.

Move to the south and speak the following as you light the "red candle" there:

Spirits of the Enchanted Mountain, of sun and star and flame, awaken and know me [magickal name]. *I come with peace within, seeking your aid in learning thy mysteries. I vow to ever uphold thy secrets, walking the path of wisdom and enlightenment. I am a follower of the Elven Ways.*

Trace your "Fire Sign" and see it red, saying:

By this Sign shall we know each other.

Move to address the west, light the "blue candle" and say:

Spirits of the Enchanted Sea, of waves and lakes and rain, awaken and know me [magickal name]. *I come with peace within, seeking your aid in learning thy mysteries. I vow to ever uphold thy secrets, walking the path of wisdom and enlightenment. I am a follower of the Elven Ways.*

Trace your "Seal of Water" in blue as you intone:

By this Sign shall we know each other.

Return to the center and take some anointing oil—a type of your personal choosing. Spiritual traditions teach to "anoint" with oil from the feet to the head (upward)—and bless or wash from head to foot (downward). Anoint your feet and say:

> *Blessed be the feet that bring me here this day/night and enable me to touch the ground, to walk the path of the Ancients, treading the 'Right Way' always, never deviating from the path of enlightenment and wisdom.*

Anoint your knees, saying:

> *Blessed be the knees that bend to give reverence to the Higher Power of the Universe, to the Source of All Being in the Cosmos that gives me the strength to move forth on the path of light and the ability to make or break my stride.*

Anoint the palms of your hands and say:

> *Blessed be the hands that lift in praise of the Universe and all Life. They are my commanding hands I raise in power and I acknowledge their ability to direct my will, as they are extensions of my active mind.*

Anoint the heart—left breast—saying:

> *Blessed be the flame that burns within my heart, that I may know the True Love of the Universe and in so doing, that I may recognize the Right Way by what I feel deeply burning in my very spirit.*

Anoint the lips and say:

> *Blessed be the lips that speak the sacred words of incantation. May the words they speak only advance my evolution further and never idle or in vain. From my mouth, I utter the words of*

*power and share in the breath of the All, yet remaining silent
to non-believers.*

Finally, speak the following as you anoint your forehead:

*Blessed be the mind that seeks to understand its own nature
and connection to the true Self, that allows me the ability to
seek true knowledge and guidance from my true Self into this
body, which is at one with my mind. Let my thoughts be pure
and only of a nature that will contribute positively to my
Ascension.*

Elven Wizards and Mystics often consecrate a personal item,
emblem or artifact—like a pendant or necklace—which is
later worn as a symbol of dedication to the Elven Way. Hold
up your talisman saying:

*May the Spirits of Nature and the Universe beyond, see and
bless this symbol of my dedication—recognizing it and me in
our future exchanges.*

Thank the energies and extinguish the circle, completing the
ceremony.

—The Elven Ways—
Circle-Initiation Ceremony

"Sylvan Magick" is mainly related to trees and so groups of practitioners coming together to learn and practice the Elven Way will often call themselves a "grove" instead of a "coven." Magick may be performed as a solitary, but "circle magic"— or "group magick"—generally requires a minimum of three people, one to represent each of the most basic Elemental Stations: Land, Sky and Sea. You know from previous study that relevant Elemental schema run as high as nine different "*duile*" or Elemental aspects that participants may occupy without having to divide the system further. Larger groups may designate tree or "Ogham" names for an outer circle of practitioners requiring congregational/ceremonial stations.

A "coven" or "grove" logically begins with members initiating each other. But this doesn't always make much sense at the initial inception of a group. In the past, the leader of a coven was so by her status; a leader of a grove or Arch Druid might be elected by a council. These High Priests and Priestesses were not "initiated" into their social positions—they were "installed." Today, most are ceremonially installed into the group by other initiated members.

It is difficult in modern times to actually find a group using an authentic Elven-Faerie Tradition that is not diluted by the general pop-culture interpretations of the Western Magickal Tradition. This is not surprising due to a lack of true mainstream Elven-Faerie lore to draw such practices, especially those not restricted to a specific lineage or family tradition. This particular rite was adopted in 1998 by the "*Elven Fellowship Circle of Magick.*"

The area of initiation should be an outdoor *Nemeton*. Choose a place where the group can meet repeatedly and form a connection with this terrain over time. This place must allow for an absence of worldly distraction and the ability to practice rituals without the unnerving discovery from disruptive onlookers. Construct your *Nemeton* of stones, being sure that the diameter is large enough for all participants. A group of three can easily use a circle nine feet in diameter. Do not overlook the significance of the "Megalithic Yard" when constructing these henges. A single unit (1-MY) is equivalent to 2.72 feet, making appropriate ceremonial sites approximately 8.16 or 10.88 feet in diameter by this rule. Be creative.

A "Magician/Sponsor" leads the blindfolded "Initiate" to the northeast corner of the *Nemeton*, where the Leader—a group founder or other "ceremonial magician" hereafter referred to as the "Guardian of the Grove"—greets them. The "Guardian" stands in wait at the northeast threshold, holding a sword.

GUARDIAN OF THE GROVE: *Who is it there that you bring here to the very Gates of this sphere most sacred and secret?*

MAGICIAN/SPONSOR: *A child of Earth and Star seeking entrance—to be set on the path of our mysteries.*

GUARDIAN: *Do you then present this person to the Grove, vouching before us for their conduct and their dedication to our circle and the Elven Ways?*

SPONSOR: *I do. I sponsor this child of Earth and Star, and must take responsibility for them now. They remain in a state of darkness—blinded to the mysteries of our Nemeton.*

GUARDIAN: *Then, as Guardian of this Gateway, I open the Portal to our Sphere—but it is never broken. You may enter this time by the Unspeakable Password.*

The "Magician/Sponsor" guides the "Initiate" to the center of the circle, where they are set before the existing membership of the Grove.

> GUARDIAN: *Answer, Initiate. Do you seek entrance into the mysteries of the "Elven Fellowship Circle of Magick"* [or another name for your personal group]?
>
> INITIATE: *I do.*
>
> GUARDIAN: *Answer, Initiate. Do you come here of your own free will, free from the pressures of peers or others and free of ulterior motives?*
>
> INITIATE: *I do.*
>
> GUARDIAN: *And finally, answer, again: Are you willing to swear an oath to the secrecy by the ancient covenant of the Mystic Wizards of the Earth now raised before you, and this Council, and the spirits we have called to our nemeton?*
>
> INITIATE: *I do.*
>
> GUARDIAN: *Kneel and submit yourself to this Elven Council.*

The "Initiate" kneels and the "Guardian of the Grove" begins to encircle them in *deosil* rotation—drawing up the primal energies of the Earth planet.

> GUARDIAN: *You are entering deep woods, the Enchanted World of the Elven-Faerie unsolicited. You step foot on the ground held most sacred to the Keepers of the Earth that maintain and celebrate the ancient Ways. Under penalty of death, no mortal shall step foot on our court unbidden, and thus you now render yourself to the mercy of the Court. You enter a place that is not a place in a time apart from time and still you are here.*

Fear has no place in our world—here in the Otherworld—and it is our will that you should perish from the spear-blades and arrowheads aimed at you by our Elven military as a sentence for such blasphemy. If you bring mortal fear in your heart to our world, you will undoubtedly summon your demise. How do you enter our world, Initiate?

INITIATE: *With perfect love and perfect trust.*

GUARDIAN: *I ask the Sponsor: has this Initiate been properly prepared? Has s/he completed their Self-Dedication to the Elven Way? Is the Initiate recognized by the Elemental Portal Guardians of the Watchtowers?*

SPONSOR: *They are prepared. They are dedicated. They are recognized by the Elemental Realms.*

GUARDIAN: *We shall find out. May the Source of All Being and Creation grant us protection; and in protection, strength; and in strength, peace; and in peace, understanding; and in understanding, knowledge; and in knowledge, wisdom; and in wisdom, love; and in love, the love of all things; and in the love of all things, the love of the Universe.*

The "Sponsor" summons the "Initiate" up from their knees, guiding them on a cross-quarter Elemental journey before returning the center again. In ancient times, this would have been conducted in a cave or underground labyrinth. This text is read as the "Sponsor" guides them first to the south, as the "Guardian" reads from the center of the circle:

In the beginning was the infinite void of Nothing, a canvas with no form, a screen without picture. But then came Light, the Dragon, the Cosmic Law, that which gave all existence its form, waves of potentiality sprawling across the matrix-fabric of the Universe.

The "Initiate" is brought to the east:

When the fires of life burned down to glowing embers, they breathed into existence the Air, the element of knowledge, and the Elven-Ffayrie spirits of the trees and breeze.

Across to the west:

More and more tangible did the formless Spirit of Light become, when the Waters emerged, ripples sent out to every corner of all encompassing sea. But the currents of energy chased one another and became even more solid.

And, around to the north:

The Formless Fire gave birth to Air; the gaseous Air gave way to water. The sea would yield finally to the land, to the Element of Earth, a powerfully strong and stable foundation to hold up the less tangible manifestations. This Earth is the planetary spirit of G'ea and She has had 'Keepers' and 'Guardians' at all times and places to maintain the balance of the Elemental World and thwart all that would cause disharmony on Earth.

Returning to the center:

As you have come to us in the darkness of ignorance, know that we are the 'Keepers of the Earth,' the 'Guardians of the Green World' and 'Scions of the Secret Knowledge' from the ancients. As you emerge, reborn into a realm of Light and enchantment, your existing name is no longer appropriate and is retired at the boundary of the Sacred Grove. We shall know you as [circle name for Initiate]. *Welcome Elf/Ffayrie Child, Lord/Lady* [n].

The blindfold is removed. Existing members come forth and greet the Initiate, followed by a celebration in their honor.

—The Nemetona—
Eisteddfodd Liturgy

The *Nemeton* may be conjured by means already suggested, an astral version thereof, a mixture of "Casting" and "Group Liturgies," or simply by using this rite alone. Some incantations used in solitary Ritual Magic are not necessary to observe "seasonal celebrations" and "rites of passage." The liturgy presented here closely resembles the structure for a gathering of Welsh Druids and Bards, called an "Eisteddfodd," which is a public festival event.

This rite may be amended for any type of group energy work, gatherings and "circle magic" for any number of participants. The ceremonial observation is most effective within a circle of trees and/or stones. Once the participants are prepared, procession to the northeast corner of the *Nemeton*, bringing all tools and necessary items with you and begin.

—OPENING BENEDICTION—

<u>King of the Elves</u>: *May the Source of All Being and Creation grant us favor and protection; and in protection, strength; and in strength, peace; and in peace, understanding; and in understanding comes the True Knowledge of the 'Right Way'; and in the grace of this knowledge may we be granted the will to use it; and in that will, the wisdom to temper the use of knowledge; and in temperance comes mercy; and thru mercy, love; and in love we find the Source of All Being and Creation.*

<u>Faerie Queen</u>: *The recursive spiral path passes through Annwn ('ah-noon') and returns to the love and favor of the Source. Blessed be the All.*

<u>All</u>: Blessed be the Universe.

—GRAND INVOCATION—

<u>King of the Elves</u>: *To bathe in the aethyr of new light and life that swirls about the galaxy. To cleanse away iniquity and mortality so we may join in the harmony of all living beings. Here we stand, beneath the Oaks, beneath the Stones, coming to the place we watched our ancestors go to commune with the Spirit of the Universe.*

<u>Faerie Queen</u>: *The stars shine brightly upon this meeting of our people. The Divine Star shines brightly on us now at the hour of our meeting.*

—ELEMENTAL BENEDICTION—

<u>Faerie Queen</u>: *Let peace ring out through the four quadrants of the Universe. Within our being may we find peace at the center. In the Secret Grove we meet to share peace. Then, as we go about the lives we lead on the 'Surface World,' we radiate the currents of love and peace and attract the same.*

<u>King of the Elves</u>: *Here we stand strong, coming together in answer to the call of our inner vow as Guardians and Keepers of the Earth. Here we stand, side-by-side, heart-to-heart and* [the circle joins hands] *hand-in-hand.* [Release hands.]

<u>Northern Guard</u>: *Guardian of the North, realm and spirits of the Earth Element, 'nature spirits,' Gnomes, Kobold and Drwyds of Falias, hail and welcome to this Nemeton. Extend the currents of peace and stability.*

<u>Eastern Guard</u>: *Guardian of the East, realm and spirits of the Air Element, Ancient and Shinning Ones, Elves and Drwyds of Gorias, hail and welcome to this Nemeton. Extend the currents that enable enlightenment.*

<u>Southern Guard</u>: *Guardian of the South, realm and spirits of Fire, Dragon Priests, fiery sprytes, pict-sidhe and Drwyds of Finias,*

hail and welcome to this Nemeton. Extend the necessary energy for strengthening the will.

<u>Western Guard</u>: *Guardian of the West, realm and spirits of the Water Element, ancestral spirits, merfolk, Drwyds of the past and the Otherworld city of Murias, hail and welcome to this Nemeton. Extend the currents of personal well-being and those that enable the insight of wisdom.*

—BARDIC VERSE & STORY—

Traditionally, a gathering of Elven-Faerie, Wizards, Druids and Bards includes recitation of lore and legend to preserve their legacy. It is this very practice that earns the liturgy the name "Eisteddfodd."

—FESTIVAL OBSERVATIONS—

Perform magical operations or ceremonial celebrations that the group has come together to accomplish. You will need to "Cast the Circle" if performing "ritual magic."

—THANKING & DISMISSING ELEMENTAL SPIRITS—

<u>King of the Elves</u>: *May the Source of All Being and Creation grant us favor and protection; and in protection, strength; and in strength, peace; and in peace, understanding; and in understanding comes the True Knowledge of the 'Right Way'; and in the grace of this knowledge may we be granted the will to use it; and in that will, the wisdom to temper the use of knowledge; and in temperance comes mercy; and thru mercy, love; and in love we find the Source of All Being and Creation.*

<u>Faerie Queen</u>: *Let peace ring out through the four quadrants of the Universe. Within our being may we find peace at the center. In the Secret Grove we meet to share peace. Then, as we go about the lives we lead on the 'Surface World,' we radiate the currents of love and peace and attract the same.*

<u>Western Druid Guard</u>: *Guardian of the West, spirit of the Wave and realm of Sea, we thank thee for thy attendance this day/eve as you witness and remember the ceremony we practice in memory of the rites of our ancestors. May you return again when hence we call. Hail and Farewell. Go in peace.*

<u>Southern Druid Guard</u>: *Guardian of the South, spirit of the Flame and realm of Fire, we thank thee for thy attendance this day/eve as you witness and remember the ceremony we practice in memory of the rites of our ancestors. May you return again when hence we call. Hail and Farewell. Go in peace.*

<u>Eastern Druid Guard</u>: *Guardian of the East, spirit of the Wind and realm of Air, we thank thee for thy attendance this day/eve as you witness and remember the ceremony we practice in memory of the rites of our ancestors. May you return again when hence we call. Hail and Farewell. Go in peace.*

<u>Northern Druid Guard</u>: *Guardian of the North, spirits of Stone and Wood and realm of Earth, we thank thee for thy attendance this day/eve as you witness and remember the ceremony we practice in memory of the rites of our ancestors. May you return again when hence we call. Hail and Farewell. Go in peace.*

—CLOSING BENEDICTION—

<u>Druid King/Arch Druid</u>: *Before departing from this place, we release the field surrounding this sacred nemeton, grounding the energy of Earth, releasing to the Sky the energies of Air, pushing down the currents of Fire deep into the 'Core of Gaea' and pouring the Waters back into the Sea. So mote it be.*

<u>Druid Queen/High Priestess</u>: *As we have come in peace, so do we leave in peace. We are the 'Children of the Stars,' beings of light, life and love. In departing, we project and radiate peaceful energy and positive power throughout the Universe, dispersing the energies of light and truth gathered here this day/night. Blessed Be.*

<u>All</u>: *Blessed Be.*

—The Alardana—
Seasonal Ceremonies

Many modern "neopagan" traditions observe some form of annual "revival calendar" or "Wheel of the Year." Most are inspired by actual "pagan" holidays and festivals based on an ancient observation of "natural cycles" or "seasons," especially those related to agriculture. During the early 1900's, a modern standard of eight "*sabbats*" or "grove festivals" was developed by Gerald Gardner (for *Wicca*) and his friend Ross Nichols (for *Druidism*). It still remains in popular use today, evenly spacing festival observations six-to-eight weeks apart. However, there is some redundancy inherent in the symbolism. For example—the Celtic festival of *Beltane* (May's Eve) correlates with the summer solstice, and both are landmarks for summer, the season of maturation. The festival of Beltane is a "flower festival" marked by an observation of short-lived "may-blossoms" visibly in Nature. This begins the "agricultural summer." Another "astronomical summer" is observed as the "summer solstice"—which is a celestial or astrophysical event marking a "turning point" in the year.

To observe an eightfold "Wheel of the Year," the four "*Fire festivals*"—Beltane, Lughnassadh, Samhain, and Imbolc—are drawn from Celtic lore to supplement two equinoxes and two solstices. It is metaphorically referred to as a "wheel" that is constantly "turning" the seasons through an annual cycle. Different types of "regional-cultural revival" will also carry distinct language-vocabulary, or names, for these same kinds of celebrations—such as in the Druidic Tradition practiced by many Elven-Faerie folk, the solstices and equinoxes are called the "*Four Albans*"—or "Four Lights"—coinciding with a traditional "Wheel of the Year" used by the ancient Welsh Celts.

Research suggests the Roman Church and "Celtic Church" set their holidays to coincide with dates and relative symbolism of pre-Christian "pagan" customs and holidays. Not only did this aid in smoothing over a conversion of rural agricultural pagan folk—but the Christians were still actively developing a "religion," and incorporated many aspects that do not appear in the Hebrew-Kabbalistic tradition that Jesus actually practiced. Keep in mind—Jesus was a Jew, but he was also shown in scripture as a descendent of the throne of David, and thus a part of an arm of the Dragon Legacy once preserved by the Essene and Gnostic sects. John the Baptist was also an Essene, evident by his use of Essene baptismal rites, borrowed from the pagans, and only used at that time and place by that particular mystic sect. The Church later took ownership of this type of ceremony as well.

The following are standardized dates of the traditional pagan festivals along with the more commonly known observances corresponding to the same times and/or energies.

"ALARDAN"—SEASONAL FESTIVAL CEREMONIES

April 30-May 1: Beltane, May's Eve, Calen Mai ("First of May"), Tana's Day, Walpurgisnacht and May Day.

June 21 (20-22): Litha, summer solstice, Alban Heruin, mid-summer and St. John's Day.

July 31-August 1: Lughnassadh ("Marriage of Lugh"), Cornucopia, Calen Awst ("First of August"), Lammas and Lammas Eve.

September 21 (20-23): Mabon, autumn equinox, Alban Elved, harvest-equinox, Rosh Hashanah and Thanksgiving Day.

October 31-November 1: Samhain ("Summer's End"), Shadowfest, Calen Gaeof, Feast of the Dead, All Saint's Day, All Soul's Day and Halloween.

December 21 (20-23): Yule, winter solstice, midwinter, Alban Arthuan, Jul, Saturnalia and Christmas.

January 31-February 1: Imbolc, Brighid's Day, Calen Geaef, Oimelc, St. Blaise's Day, Candlemas, Valentine's Day and Groundhog's Day.

March 21 (20-22): Ostara, Eostre, spring equinox, Alban Eiler, Akiti, Sheelah's Day, St. Patrick's Day and Easter.

SAMHAIN – ALARDAN FESTIVAL

Some controversy still exists concerning a proper 'New Year' observance—but Celtic traditions usually begin their calendar on Samhain, November's Eve, or October 31. This time period, much like Beltane, is an energetic threshold when the "veil" between the "physical world" and the ALL is thinnest—in this instance, from the *outside*. Pagans traditionally observed the "Feast of Ancestors" during "Samhain" (pronounced *sow-en*) meaning "Summer's End," and today we know the remnants of these ancient customs as "Halloween." This includes events like "bobbing for apples" or "pumpkin-carving" (reminiscent of the ancient gourd-carved heads). "Faerie lights" or painted glass orbs with candles inside are suspended from the trees around the *Nemeton*—emitting cool UV or cobalt blue light.[*] Seasonal rites may be performed within a *Nemeton* using the "Eisteddfodd" or "Group Liturgy." They may also be practiced as a solitary, addressing each of the directions in turn.

NORTH: I call thee Northern Spirits of *Lasse, Cloch, Arbor* and *Elessar*. Join me powers of Leaf, Earth, Tree and Stone, in this celebration of my ancestors. I come to the Sacred Grove this *estevar* ["evening"] to be reunited and guided by their *asha* ["spirit"].

EAST: I call thee Eastern Spirits of *Gaeth, Gwai, Nel* and *Fin*.

---

[*]   Similar to the *Pelen Tan* described in *"The 21 Lessons of Merlyn"* by Douglas Monroe.

Join me, powers of Wand, Sky and Cloud, in this celebration of my ancestors. I come to the Sacred Grove this *estevar* ["evening"] to be reunited and guided by their *asha* ["spirit"].

SOUTH: I call thee Southern Spirits of *Re'Aitai, Anar, Arva* and *Teine*. Join me, powers of Skyfire, Sun, Flame and Fire, in this celebration of my ancestors. I come to the Sacred Grove this *estevar* ["evening"] to be reunited and guided by their *asha* ["spirit"].

WEST: I call thee Western Spirits of *Kh'dek, Muir, Kyela* and *Pehlora*. Join me, powers of Ice, Sea, Water and Love, in this celebration of my ancestors. I come to the Sacred Grove this *estevar* ["evening"] to be reunited and guided by their *asha* ["spirit"].

NORTH: *Glora Duath*. The Sun is overcome by darkness. On this *estevar*, a night that is not a night, the invisible *evala* ["cloak"] between this world and our ancestor's realm in the Other-world is thinnest—from their side.

EAST: I call upon the ancestral power of Elvenkind within me. Give me clear knowledge of *Kaloren* [the "Right Path"].

SOUTH: I stand on a threshold between time to witness the death of one year reborn to another. As Keepers of the Earth, Guardians of the Elven *Cor Anar* ["Wheel of the Sun/Year"], I charge the *Duath* ["darkness"] to give way to *alb* ["light"] at Midwinter—the turning point of the Sacred Earth Year.

WEST: In the name of the covenant sworn by Ancient Elvish Wizards that first enticed and communed with spirits of the Otherworld with food offerings, I call out to my ancestors from *Arth Asha* ["the spirit world"] to share in this feast with me. Take from this offering the essences you so require.

You may then celebrate your feast. Be sure to leave a portion of it in the northern quadrant as an offering.

NORTH: Behold, I see before me, the Sidhe. They have graced my vision with their presence. They manifest to me, crossed over, transitioned from the Realm of the King. From ancestral mounds they have come this night to celebrate the *Samhain Alardon* ["Festival"] with me.

EAST: Here I stand at *Saeth Duir*, Guardian of the Threshold. I am a portal messenger. Before me the winds rise up to offer their hail and I thank thee spirits of the eastern direction for celebrating with me.

SOUTH: As the ancestral *asha* ["spirit"] depart, I wish peace and love for them on their return to the ancestral plane. I ask only that you leave me with your hereditary guidance that it may be a light to illuminate *Kaloren* ["the Right Way"].

WEST: From the ninth wave I emerge and from nine elements was I created. In nine states of being I channel my power and radiate peace multiplied times nine. By the power of nine may I hope to enjoy the fruits and bounty of another year.

NORTH: And finally—Here, I stand in the north on Earth as Guardian of the Threshold. I here seal the Otherworld portal. The ancestral energy and spirits of the dead have passed by this gateway and I bid them peace on their departure. New life comes from death and Nature once more unfolds her mysteries to her initiates. As Keeper of the Earth I shall await the New Light when we shall again meet this winter.

ALBAN ARTHUANN – ALARDAN FESTIVAL

Long before modern observations of Christmas, ancient cultures celebrated the (re)birth of the Sun King at Midwinter on the evening of December 21st—the longest night of the year. Pine trees; evergreen wreaths; symbolism of Oak, Holly and Mistletoe—all originate with "pagan" Druids. We have retained customs of "Santa Claus"—that *"jolly ol' elf"*—where we encourage a visit by leaving a "fairy offering" of milk and sweetbreads (cookies). Consider using red, green and white candles to illuminate your night work—all traditional colors of Druidism and the winter solstice. You might even affix the candles to a "Yule Log." The *"Alban Arthuann"* festival—meaning the "Light of Arthur" or "Light of the Bear"—is observed in the evening. After this night, the daytime grows longer and so the Sun is deemed "reborn."

NORTH: I call upon the Spirit of the Forest this eve. Come forth *Aldaron, Herne, Dagda, Kernunnos*—the Green Man and the Antlered One. You do I call upon, the strength of Earth, the elemental forest spirits, on this the darkest of nights.

EAST: *La'Aer, Gaeth, Suk'anar Estevar.* I call upon the power and energy of the Winds and spirits of the Air Element, on this darkest of nights, and a time of new beginnings.

SOUTH: From the south I bind energies of *Re'-Aitai*, Skyfire, *Leollyn*, Great *Anar*, Sun—whose power grows steadily.

WEST: *Muir. Muir. Suk'anar Estevar.* I call upon the power and energy of the tides, activity of splashing water, spirits of the wave and sea, on the darkest night of the year, as Midwinter turns and the Sun's course follows.

NORTH: The turning point is a new birth, one marked by the growing power of the Sun Father, *Leollyn*. As Keeper of the Earth I stand witness to new life coming from death. I stand guard to a gateway of the Cosmic Law that all things changes.

EAST: The *Cor Anar* ["Wheel of the Solar Year"] turns. I stand waiting encased in a season of hibernation. I am the Morning Star *"el tuile"* ["Spring"] and offer a season of new beginnings and new hope.

SOUTH: *Gaea. Vasta. Gaea. Vasta.* I awaken and arouse the Earth Mother to bare witness to the rebirth of the Sun King.

Send forth your energies of creativity and inspiration. Lend us your fiery strength.

WEST: In the *Suk'anar* ["darkest"] *Estevar* ["night"] I call the energy of *Leollyn* ["Sun King"] who is born and reborn here at *Alban Arthuann* [the Winter Solstice] as the "Child" Sun King. From *Numen* ["the west"] I ask to receive the intelligence and wisdom to better use my abilities. Through self-knowledge, I increase my understanding of the Universe.

Light the solstice candles on the Yule Log in the north. If you use evergreen wreaths, light candles in these too.

NORTH: On this *Suk'anar* ["darkest"] *Estevar* ["night"] I call forth the Lord of the Forest by the names: *Aldaron*, *Ninastre* and *Saelr'ir*, to celebrate and observe the great mysteries of seasonal change and cosmic cycles.

EAST: The time draws near. The Sun King is to be reborn as a child. May all spirits and animals of Nature awaken and know his birth.

Wait in your circle until midnight, continuing your festivities until you wish to close by celebrating the Sun-birth itself. You can continue at midnight, have an all-night vigil until dawn, or you may return just before dawn the following morning.

EAST: *Vasta. Vasta.* Come forth and awaken, power and spirits of *Gaeth* ["wind"], energies of *La'Aer* ["the Air Element"]. Hear me; hear the call of the *Ekahal* ["Elven Wizard"] as I rouse you from hibernation. Rejoice! Rejoice! The Sun King is reborn!

SOUTH: *Vasta. Vasta.* Awaken ye powers and spirits of *Arva* ["flame"], energy of *Teine* ["the Fire Element"]. Hear me; hear the call of the *Ekahal* ["Elven Wizard"] as I rouse you from hibernation. Rejoice! Rejoice! The Sun King is reborn!

WEST: *Vasta. Vasta.* Awaken, powers and spirits of *Muir* ["the sea"], energy of *Ear Pehlora* ["the Water Element"]. Hear me; hear the call of the *Ekahal* ["Elvish Wizard"] as I rouse you from hibernation. Rejoice! Rejoice! The Sun King is reborn!

NORTH: *Vasta. Vasta.* Come forth an awaken, ye powers and spirits of *Aldaron* ["the forest"], energy of *Lasse* and *Gael* ["leaf and stone"]. Hear me; hear the call of the *Ekahal* ["Elvish Wizard"] as I rouse you from hibernation. Rejoice! Rejoice! The Sun King is reborn!

IMBOLC – ALARDAN FESTIVAL

Imbolc is a Celtic "Candle Festival"—observed with a candle light vigil from the evening of January 31st into the following dawn of February 1st. Even if a vigil is not observed, a candle may be left to burn all night for the protection of the home and family. Meditation on the candle flame has an ability to put you into a trance-hypnotic state. Fire gazing, in general, is known to produce similar calming states. Such activities allow the "inner mind" to be more receptive to visions and prophetic skills may be heightened. Divination may be performed, but most of the subtle energies of this time of year are received at night during subconscious dreaming.

NORTH: I call thee Northern Spirits of *Lasse, Cloch, Arbor* and *Elessar.* Join me powers of Leaf, Earth, Tree and Stone, in this celebration: a turning of the *Cor Anar* ["Wheel of the Solar Year"] and the strengthening of *Glora Anar* ["the Sun"]. Bless now this *Tuile Alta* ["Springtime Light"] and lend your powers to this candle. [Blessing a candle to be used for the vigil.]

EAST: I call thee Eastern Spirits of *Gaeth, Gwai, Nel* and *Fin.* Come join me, powers of Wand, Sky, Cloud and Rain, in this celebration of the turning of the *Cor Anar* ["Wheel of the Solar Year"] and the strengthening of *Glora Anar* ["the Sun"]. Bless now this *Tuile Alta* ["Springtime Light"] and lend your powers to this candle.

SOUTH: I call thee Southern Spirits of *Re'Aitai, Anar, Arva* and *Teine*. Join me powers of Skyfire, Sun, Flame and Fire, in this celebration of the turning of the *Cor Anar* ["Wheel of the Solar Year"] and the strengthening of *Glora Anar* ["the Sun"]. Bless now this *Tuile Alta* ["Springtime Light"] and lend your powers to this candle.

WEST: I call thee Western Spirits of *Kh'dek, Muir, Kyela* and *Pehlora*. Join me powers of Ice, Sea, Love and Water, in this celebration of the turning of the *Cor Anar* ["Wheel of the Solar Year"] and the strengthening of *Glora Anar* ["the Sun"]. Bless now this *Tuile Alta* ["Springtime Light"] and lend your powers to this candle.

NORTH: May all of the Nature spirits and beings, woodland creatures and bipeds, find security, warmth and protection in the *Alta Nwyrve* ["light of the sacred fire"], which I extend as an expression of peace, radiating perfect love throughout the Cosmos.

EAST: From the Radiance within and the new *A'lahn* ["light"] that shines in the *Aiet* ["east"], may all the beings of *G'ea* ["the earth planet"] no longer be subjected to impenetrable *Duath* ["darkness"].

SOUTH: *Tuile F'yonn*, the "Light Season" is soon upon us. As some sprigs of *Tuile* ["the spring season"] and new hope od life appear, the Elven-Faerie Wizards come to commune with the "Elements of Nature," gathered here in this *Kirc* ["sacred circle"] in springtime anticipation.

WEST: *Gaea* breathes the breath of renewal, weaving a web of enchantment that spreads across the land. May the spirits of *Tuile F'yonn* ["the season of light"] bless this land with love and abundance. Energies of *Ear Pehlora* ["the Water Element"] send forth thy spring rains to nurture all life as it strives to grow and mature.

NORTH: Great Lord of the Forest ["*Aldaran*"], come forth and use your ancient magicks to bless the land, making it fertile and green. Bring renewal to all life—every living *Asha* [spirit/soul] of *Arda G'ea* [the earth-planet plane of existence] above and below the Surface World.

EAST: Voice that beckons in the winds of dawn, grant me thy guidance and inspiration.

SOUTH: Voice that echoes strangely through the stillness of the noon's midday heat, speak quietly your secrets.

WEST: Vision that emerges to give form to the voice heard at sunset and in the moonrise, bless me with thy gifts.

Whereas most Alardan liturgy may be amended for use by any number of participants, you will retain the "I" (singular tense) as you imagine or visualize this following imagery.

EAST: I am the wind across the plains and sea. I am a hawk high above the cliffs. I am a raven on a Druid's shoulder.

SOUTH: I am the fire inspiring the minds of sentient spirits. I am the flame that burns in the passion of lovers. I am the beacon of light that permeates throughout the Universe.

WEST: I am a wave crest of the sea. I am the variegated sound coming from the rushing waters. I am a valley lake nestled between two plains.

NORTH: I am a hill of poetry. I am finest of flowers and trees. I am a stone standing watch since the beginning of creation.

Thank and dismiss the energies—wishing them peace as they depart—as with all ceremonies. Then return to your place of dwelling; taking your blessed candle with you. You may consecrate an area of prosperity and protection in the home with it—and if possible, allow it to burn down, extinguishing itself.

ALBAN EILER – ALARDAN FESTIVAL

The Spring Equinox goes by many names, including Ostara, Eostre, Ostera, Eastre and finally Easter. *Alban Eiler* is often observed on the dawn of March 21st. These kinds of festivals once ran three or more days in duration—observed perhaps from the 20th to the 23rd. In ancient Babylon, the New Year festival of Akiti and first month of Nissanu began on this day —observed by the entire population for ten days. If ground conditions allow, you might make this a seed-planting ceremony. You may use "pots" if outdoors is not an appropriate choice. Both the spring and autumn equinox mark points of equality between daytime and nighttime.

NORTH: I call upon the Spirit of the Forest at the dawn of the *Tuile F'yonn* ["Spring Season of Light"]. Come forth *Aldaron, Herne, Kernunnos*—you who come when I call on the strength and power of the Earth Element and forest energy. Merge your stream with this Grove, this Sacred *Nemeton*. Come and celebrate the Springtime Equinox.

EAST: *La'Aer, Gaeth, Tuile F'yonn.* I call upon the power of the winds and energies of the Air Element on the dawn of the Spring Season of Light, this time of new beginnings. Be here now to witness and remember my ceremony.

SOUTH: From the south, I bind the power of *re'-aitai*, skyfire, and *Glora Anar*, the strength of the Sun that has returned. The air of the east blows to the south and it is warmed. Come now and celebrate *Alban Eiler* ["the spring equinox"].

WEST: *Muir. Ear Pehlora.* Energy and power of the waters and sea, I call thee here now to share in an ancient observation of the equinox, the festival of balance between day and night.

NORTH: As all beings yield to the new *A'Lahn Tuile* ["light of the spring season"], I plant new seed and call upon powers of the "Elements of Nature" to bless and encourage its growth.

As part of a seed-planting ceremony, you might choose an appropriate flower/herb for each direction, or use "pots." If necessary, you may even visualize the seed-planting process.

EAST: At the eastern ward I plant new seeds of psychological well-being.

SOUTH: At the southern ward I plant new seeds of spiritual well-being.

WEST: At the western ward I plant new seeds of emotional well-being.

NORTH: At the northern ward I plant new seeds of physical well-being.

EAST: Spiritual powers of *La'Aer* ["the Air Element"], care-takers of all flowers and trees—take and scatter my seeds among fertile soil. Bless and keep safe all new life that begins in *Tuile* ["the spring"].

SOUTH: *Sier Arva* ["sacred fire"], searing flame, spirits of the same, ensure that the Radiance of *E'Graine Glora Anar*, bright sphere of the Sun above, shines down to nourish these seeds with life-giving warmth and light.

WEST: Spirits of *Ear Pehlora* ["the Water Element"], the gentle rains and *Muir*, Element of Sea, come forth and bless this new life with your lustral waters, moisture and nourishing rains.

NORTH: I place the life of all new seed in the hands of *Gaea* and the invisible caretakers of the Green World of Nature. O Spirits of *Talamh* ["the Earth Element"] accept the seeds of new life into your folds.

EAST: Spirits of the *Duile* ["fey elements"], you have been called to this *Kirc* ["sacred stone circle"] *Nemeton* to observe, recognize and remember the ancient tradition observed.

SOUTH: Today, I call upon and receive the strength of the heavens, warming light from the Sun, to invoke the splendor of the Element of Fire...

WEST: Depth of the Sea and radiance of the Moon...

NORTH: Stability of Earth and firmness of stone...

EAST: Speed of lightning and swiftness of Wind.

NORTH: The cyclic phases of *Gaea* and the laws of the Green World of Nature are marked and observed with the rotation of the *Cor Anar*. The Great Wheel turns again.

BELTEINE – ALARDAN FESTIVAL

The *Belteine* or Beltane festival is named such after the "Fires of Bel" or "Belinos"—most likely a remnant of Bel Marduk or "Lord Marduk," patron god of Babylon, known elsewhere in the mutation of "Baal." It was actual on the dawn of an ancient Belteine when the *Tuatha d'Anu* arrived in Ireland and set fire to their own ships. The most commonly known tradition of May Day is the "May Pole"—a symbol of the "World Tree" that is usually danced around while weaving ribbons. "May Day" is, of course, May 1st, though the festival begins the night before—on May's Eve—with the construction of two large bonfires built side-by-side, which are then consecrated to Bel before set aflame. Ancient Celts marched their cattle in procession between these two flames as they led them out to pasture for the year. Some evening observances may be held, however this following rite is typically observed at noon.

NORTH: I greet you *Alardon*, Spirit of the Grove, Spirit of the Green World. I call forth northern energies of *Lasse*, *Cloch*, *Talamh* and *Arbor*. Join me, powers of Leaf, Stone, Earth and Tree as we celebrate the mysteries of creation at the height of *F'yonn Thuile* [the "season of light"].

EAST: I greet you *Gwai,* Spirit of the Sky. I call thee forth from the east to celebrate the forthcoming *Laer Reudh* ["summer season"] marked by the Fires of Bel. Energies of *Gaeth, Fin* and *Nel*—spirits and powers of the Wind, Air and Cloud—grant me thy inspiration and guidance.

SOUTH: Spirits of *Laer Reudh Arva* ["summertime flame"], now is the time to emerge, come forth and shine brightly. Power of the southern spirits, open your *Evala Duir* ["hidden door"] of mysteries. Join me in celebration of summer's anticipation.

WEST: I hail from the *Kirc,* this sacred *Nemeton.* Hear me, *Kh'dek, Muir* and *Ear Pehlora.* Spirits and powers of the last receding Ice, the warming Sea and the Element of Water, join me now, this *Beltaine Alardon* ["Beltane festival"].

All ritual candles should be lit from a central flame or bonfire consecrated to "*Bel.*" In the event that candles are not appropriate, you may substitute lanterns or torches. Color themes for Beltane are red, yellow -gold and green.

NORTH: Lady of the Earth, Lord of the Greenwood, Spirits of the Grove, nature spirits and woodland creatures, come now to this *Nemeton* and share in the spiritual fire of *Bel.*

EAST: May this sacred time of *Belteine* rekindle the heart and inflame the spirit of all living things in creation.

SOUTH: As a Keeper of the Earth, Guardian of the Elemental Mysteries, I stand to observe a turning of the *Cor Anar* ["Solar Wheel of the Year"]. *Glora Llew Anar* ["spirit of the Sun"] I await the day of your solstice apex and keep watch as you grow in strength each day.

WEST: *F'yonn Thuile,* the Light of Spring is coming to a close, making way for *Laer Reudh* ["the summer season"]. Today begins *Twythron Thrimidge* ["the month of May"] sacred to the *Dwyr* ["great Oak Tree"].

NORTH: Elements of Nature, Forces of the Green World, heed my call this day. Open up your oaken door and reveal thy mysteries to me, a servant of the Earth Planet and follower of the Elven Ways. I seek the wisdom of creation and abilities to channel all energy currents of the cosmos. And to the same, I am a keeper and guardian for all my days.

At this juncture, you may consider a recitation of the *"Cad Goddeu,"* or "Battle of the Trees." In any case, retain the "I" in these following statements as they are visualized.

NORTH: I am a *Cloch* ["stone"] hidden in the *Saeth* ["unseen folds"] of *Talamh* ["the Earth"] and in *Milana Abrahor Terrest* ["an ancient emerald forest"].

EAST: I am a yellow *Alta* ["ray of light"] of *Glora Anar* ["blessed Sun"].

SOUTH: I am a *Dwyr Arva* ["flaming door"] concealing the secret laws of creation.

WEST: I am a blue-crested wave under *Isil El'orel* ["the Moon"] concealing mysteries of the purple depths of *Muir* ["the sea"].

You may observe the tradition of the Maypole and feast. After the feast and any activities, the convocation concludes.

NORTH: *Laer Reudh* ["the summer season"] comes upon us quickly. It graces now by every bud, blossom and leaf.

EAST: On the dawn of the morrow, the Earth shall be set upon her "Golden Path" toward the season of maturity.

SOUTH: The great *Cor Anar* ["Solar Wheel of the Year"] continues to turn once more, now bringing us every nearer to the "Red Season," but ever turning.

WEST: And may peace radiate throughout the universe.

ALBAN HERUIN – ALARDAN FESTIVAL

The "Summer Solstice" marks a time of mystical significance throughout ancient Æurope. For as long as we can remember, Elves, Druids, Mystics and Wizards performed Midsummer Rites. In Western Europe, these were frequently vigils held at sacred stone "*Kircs*," like Stonehenge on the Salisbury Plains in England. [There are thousands of "*Kirc*" remains scattered throughout the mainlands.] While the festival may begin the day before, this rite begins approximately ten minutes before the dawn of the solstice itself—usually June 22nd. It is the longest day of the year.

NORTH: I call upon the Spirit of the Forest in the twilight of the great Elven-Ffayrie Rade between the worlds, before the dawn of *Laer Reudh*, the "Red Season" of summer maturity. Come forth *Alardon*, *Herne*, *Kernunnos*, the Green Man—those entities that arrive when I call on the strength and energy of the Earth Element and the Enchanted Forest. Share your energies with this Sacred Grove.

EAST: The threshold is drawing near. The forthcoming power of *Glora Anar* ["the Sun King"] peaks to bless the lands of *G'ea* in celestial marriage. May the spirits of *La'Aer* come forth to share in this great observation of the season.

SOUTH: Hark! On the horizon awaits the Sun on the longest day of *Cor Anar*. *Arva*, *Teine*. I summon the spirits of flame and the power of high noon's heat to come forth on the occasion of this *Alban Heruin* ["summer solstice"].

WEST: The dawn of *Glora Anar* ["the Sun"] is upon us/me, only moments away. I call ye spirits and energies of *Muir* ["the sea"] and *Duile Ear Pehlora* ["Element of Water"] to come forth and share celebration of this Summer Solstice with me.

NORTH: *Glora-Anar*. Mighty Sun Father, share your power with me now in your time of greatness. I am a Keeper of the northern ward, and Guardian of the Earth while you sleep.

EAST: *Glora-Anar*. Mighty Sun Father, share your power with me now in your time of greatness. I am the Keeper of the eastern ward, guarding the direction of your birth.

SOUTH: *Glora-Anar*. Mighty Sun Father, share your power with me now in your time of greatness. I am a Keeper of the southern ward, Guardian of the mid-day peak during your travels through the sky.

WEST: *Glora-Anar*. Mighty Sun Father, share your power with me now in your time of greatness. I am the Keeper of the western ward, guarding the station of your daily retirement.

Moments before dawn, the leader says: "*Mighty Sun, be here now.*" Then the rite continues after dawn has peaked.

EAST: As Guardian of the East, I hail that the Sun is upon us.

SOUTH: Hail to the Great Sun King Llewollyn rising in the sky.

WEST: Hail to the Great Sun King that warms the oceans and the sea.

NORTH: Hail to the Great Sun King, the supreme light bearer parading through Enchanted Forests.

EAST: I smell the fragrance of the summer flowers.

SOUTH: I am warmed by the spirit burning within all life.

WEST: I am blessed by the love in all life flowing throughout the Green World of Nature on Earth and in the Universe.

NORTH: May the love and energies called here for the *Alban Heruin Alardon* ["festival of the Summer Solstice"] be radiated as perfect peace by all spirits present for this occasion.

LUGHNASSADH – ALARDAN FESTIVAL

The ancient Celtic festival of *Lughnassadh*—pronounced *"loo-nass-ah"*—is observed on August 1st (or the eve of the same) and means literally: "The Wedding of Lugh"—a solar deity in the Celtic pantheon derived from the *Tuatha d'Anu*. This marriage of the "sun and sky" with the "land" marked the start of the harvest cycle—which runs through the autumn season until the eve of *Samhain*. The *Lughnassadh* festival is a time for blessing an forthcoming harvest and offering the first grains cut as a sacrifice back to the Earth and its spirits. For this ceremony, bring a sufficient supply of fresh bread and wine to the *Nemeton*. Traditional lore also suggests the custom of *"Lammas Towers"*—a competition to see who can build a larger bonfire that stands upright for the longest period of time. The rite is aligned to the sunset/dusk (autumn) threshold.

NORTH: I call thee Northern Spirits of *Lasse, Cloch, Arbor* and *Elessar*. Join me, powers of Leaf, Earth, Tree and Stone, in this observation of another turning of the *Cor Anar* ["Wheel of the Solar Year"]. Bless now this harvest time. Darkness appears distantly in the north as the Wheel continues to spin.

EAST: I call thee Eastern Spirits of *Gaeth, Gwai, Nel* and *Fin*. Come and join me, powers of Wand, Sky, Cloud and Rain, in this observation of another turning of the *Cor Anar* ["Wheel of the Solar Year"]. Bless now this harvest time as we must prepare for an inevitable winter.

SOUTH: I call thee Southern Spirits of *Re'Aitai, Anar, Arva* and *Teine*. Join me, powers of Skyfire, Sun, Flame and Fire, in this observation of another turning of the *Cor Anar* ["Wheel of the Solar Year"]. Bless now this harvest time, spirits of *Dan Harad* ["the southern direction"].

WEST: I call thee Western Spirits of *Kh'dek, Muir, Kyela* and *Pehlora*. Join me, powers of Ice, Sea, Water and Love, in this observation of another turning of the *Cor Anar* ["Wheel of the

Solar Year"]. Bless and observe this harvest, and the wedding feast of Lugh here observed by the ["name of the Grove"].

NORTH: This *Calen* ["day"]/*Estevar* ["night"] I gather in the sacred *Nemeton* of the Grove to observe the Ancient Elven-Ffayrie festival of *Lughnassadh*. Here we mark the beginning of the harvest season. Here we celebrate the wedding feast of *Lugh*, hence all friendly spirits are invited.

KING OF THE ELVES: In order to eat, whether plant to us, or meat to other-kin, something must die. This is the law of Nature: that no energy shall be created or destroyed, only finite in number, changed and altered through processes. The energy may be exhausted if not renewed, so it must be maintained responsibly.

FAERIE QUEEN: When we eat of the sacred harvest, or the hunt, honor must be given to the sources of that energy that we take into ourselves. By this we honor the being that is the source of the food and its life, and the Source of All Being and Creation who is the source of the essence of life that is within the being and food, and life must be maintained responsibly.

Go to the central workspace and take up the bread, holding it outward and asking for benediction from the spirits present.

NORTH: Elemental powers of the ancient and sacred *Terrestai* ["the everlasting or eternal forest of the Universe"], spirits of Nature, Earth and Stone, you that arrives when I call on the power of *Tuath* ["the north"], spirits of the fields and harvest, spirit of the grain, I thank thee for your precious wheat, fruits and roots. All who share in the feast of this bread will also share in your eternal blessings of bounty and prosperity.

Return to the central workplace and replace the bread with the wine, taking it up and extending it ourward as you ask the spirits for benediction.

WEST: *Duile Muir Ear Pehlora*, Elemental powers of Water and Sea, powers of of *Muin* ["the vine"], I thank thee spirits for your precious drink, as we might drain blood, so do we drain the wine from the grape in our harvest. Spirit of the wine, bless this drink and all who share it.

NORTH: All ye friendly spirits gathered at this Sacred Grove, this most holy *mandala* ["magic circle"], may you share in this feast in honor of the first harvest, the covenant of agricultural tradition, shared in offering for the wedding celebration of *Lugh* to the land.

Here you may celebrate the feast, sharing the "bread and wine." Remember to bring a portion of this feast in offering, placed at the northwest, saying: *"May the spirits of Nature accept this sacrifice, sowed and reaped using the knowledge granted by the covenant between the Earth Children and the Ancient and Shinning Ones."* Each participant may wish to offer a portion of their feast in a similar fashion before completing the rite.

NORTH: Nature is the greatest of all teachers. The Keepers of the Earth share these mysteries of creation as Guardians of the *Cor Anar* ["solar year"]. We come each turn in seasonal celebration eight times annually. Here in the sacred place of ancients I gather Elemental energies to weave a place worthy of such celebration.

EAST: Split wide the fruit of the seeds that have been sown and open the door to the ancient mysteries. As we share in the harvest, we share the wisdom of the cosmic law and the universal energy that makes all growth and life possible.

SOUTH: Source of All Being and Creation, kindle the formless and sacred *Nwyvre* ["divine fire"] of *gnosis*, inspiration and true knowledge in my head. Share in the eternal *Alta* ["light"] that is inextinguishable and an ageless source of true wisdom.

WEST: Great Spirit of the Western Winds that blow over the

sea, energies and beings radiating from the sunset's beauty and evening twilight, come and share these blessings from the "elixir of wisdom" before departing this *Nemeton* in peace and perfect love.

NORTH: Deep within the secret folds of the forest lies the source of Elven knowledge—the Sylvan Library. Open your "Books of Light" and grant us true knowledge. Share with me your ineffable wisdom as I share with you the ancient covenant woven into this mystic elemental temple, consecrated here and now to observe *Lughnassadh*. Partake in our harvest and accept the sacrifice of ["name of the group or Grove"].

EAST: Change is ever upon us as the great seasons cycle. We must prepare for this each year, the changes. So, the harvest must be brought in to sustain life in a season of death. Spirits of *La'Aer* ["the Air Element"], *Giet Romen Gaeth*, powers of the Eastern Wind, come and share in the energy of this "Magick Sphere," bless and receive this combined sacrifice—a labor of love between the Earth and its children. Depart in peace to spread the winds of fortune on all harvests in the world.

SOUTH: Behold the passion of *Laer Reudh Anar*, the "Summer Sun" that dims as the *Duath* ["dark"] half of the year turns. Its lifeforce received in the growing things which we receive in our nourishment. But change is always present in Nature, and we must observe and live in harmony with these changes, as the cycle of life, death and renewal turn once more. Mark well and remember this observation of the ancient covenant, departing in perfect peace and perfect love, and returning to this place again when we celebrate the turning of the Wheel.

ALBAN ELVED – ALARDAN FESTIVAL

An ancient name for this festival may be translated literally as *"Light of Elves."* This ceremony is traditionally practiced as a part of a "Thanksgiving Feast" in honor of the harvest, and as an observation of the "Autumn Equinox," the rite is a part of a festival peaking on September 21st. As with *Alban Eiler* (the Spring Equinox), forces of light and dark—or day and night—are in balance with one another. With light giving way to darkness, the season of death is soon setting in. Harvest festivals are often observed at dusk. [This ceremonial liturgy incorporates a "consecrated feast" and creation of a "*satchet*" or "pouch" containing "Mistletoe."]

NORTH: This *Kus'anar* ["evening/twilight"] I do call upon *Aldaron* ["spirit of the forest"], *Herne, Dagdha, Kernunnos*, and the Green Man spirit. You are summoned to gather here for this *Alban Elved* ["Autumn Equinox"] observance. I call to you that answer when I summon the solidity of Stone and powers of Earth. Come forth now and be present to celebrate these ancient mysteries.

EAST: This *Kus'anar* ["evening/twilight"] I do call upon *La'Aer* ["Element of Air"]. You are summoned to gather here for this *Alban Elved* ["Autumn Equinox"] observance. I call to you that answer when I summon the intensity of Wind and powers of the Sky. Come forth and be present to celebrate these ancient mysteries.

SOUTH: This *Kus'anar* ["evening/twilight"] I do call upon the Southern Ward, radiant energies of *Re'Aitai*, Skyfire and the final rays of strength extended from *Glora Anar* ["the Great Sun King"] now fading. You are summoned to gather here to observe this *Alban Elved* ["Autumn Equinox"]. I call to you that answer when I summon up the strength of Flame and powers of Fire. Come forth and be present to celebrate these ancient mysteries.

WEST: This *Kus'anar* ["evening/twilight"] I do call upon *Muir*, *Ear Pehlora*, and the spirits of the place where the Sun sets. Hear the summons to gather here and observe this *Alban Elved* ["Autumn Equinox"] ceremony. I call to the spirits that answer when I summon forth the fluidity of Sea and powers of Wave and Water. Come forth and be present to celebrate these ancient mysteries.

NORTH: At this time of year, those who live by the ways of nature—magical folk and woodland creatures—all make haste to ready their harvest before the frost. Now we take rest and offer thanksgiving to the spirits of the harvest and of Earth.

EAST: I come to acknowledge and observe the ancient ways; ancient ways that I maintain and uphold whenever I remember and keep the Elven Tradition. I adhere to the secret and sacred covenant between *G'ea* ["spirit of the Earth planet"] and the Keepers of the Earth, her mysteries and traditions.

SOUTH: I stand in recognition to observe the ever turning *Cor Anar* ["wheel of the Solar Year"] at the time of equinox, the balance of light and dark. The harvest season is midway and all preparations must be made to survive the winter. The last scythe shall fall at *Samhain*. So, we come to extend our thanks for the food that will sustain all life through the dark months.

WEST: From the *Gwaith* ["shadows"] of *D'yonn Reudh* ["the autumn season"] comes the cycle of *Hrive D'yonn* ["winter"] and death. *Gaea* ["the Earth Mother"] shall never perish so long as her faithful Elven-Ffayrie Guardians are there to serve and protect her. This is our responsibility.

NORTH: As the harvest is taken in, winter plans are made. I guard a season of inner exploration as the Earth ["*Gaea*"] and Sun ["*Glora Anar*"] hibernate in winter ["*Hrive D'yonn*"].

EAST: The secrets of the *Cor Anar* ["Wheel of the Sun"] are symbolic and well-hidden, but they offer to us the keys of self-realization. I will stand guard and wait for the season of new growth and beginnings as *Gaea* ["the Earth Mother"] and the Sun ["*Glora Anar*"] awaken in *Tuile F'yonn* ["the spring season"].

SOUTH: The ancient power of the Elves, Faerie, Druids and Wizards shall never perish if the traditions do not cease to be observed. This is our responsibility. At this time of year, the Keepers of the Earth gather in the secret forest to reaffirm their Oath to Nature and remember the ancient covenant as it recedes in slumber. Let the Earth rest easy in her season of hibernation, knowing that her Guardians are ever-present in stewardship while she sleeps. I stand guard a wait for the season of fullness and maturity as *Glora Anar* ["the Sun"] warms in *Laer Reudh* ["the summer"].

WEST: It is the equinox. At this time *Isil El'orel* ["the Moon"] sits in balance with *Glora Anar*. I stand guard and mark the ebb and flow of Autumn [*D'yonn Reudh*] and ask all the forces of nature to bless our food, our spirits and our path.

At this juncture, members prepare an amulet-bag containing the herb, mistletoe. It is consecrated in ceremony (using the consecration rites), then later hidden away for future use. At the northern quarter, each participant takes their amulet-bag to be blessed.

NORTH: May this sacred herb of the ancient—the Mistletoe— be consecrated for the future use of *Sylvan Druidecht* ["Elven Forest Magick"]. May its contents activate all herbal remedies and potions that I prepare during the forthcoming year with goodness and love. May the amulet bag itself be charged as a symbol to guard away misfortune in my life and home.

Invite friendly spirits gathered at your *Nemeton* to join in the essence of the feast you have prepared, making certain to leave a formal offering in the north—inviting the energies or entities present to partake in the bounty before thanking and dismissing them.

GREENWOOD GRIMOIRE

—The Greenwood Grimoire—
Magick of the Enchanted Forest

Green is the universal color of Life and Nature—a color most sacred in Elven-Faerie Tradition, from which the *"Green World"* is named: the "place of enchantment" where "Forest Magick" permeates the air. True "Elven Magick" is performed in the "Green World" and pertains to its elements more strongly than any other magical system. The place of operation is in Nature— no dank chambers or elaborate wizard vaults will do.

The *"Green World"* is described in lore as that space in the physical world that resonates an affinity with all natural energies of the Elemental Kingdoms—and therefore raw forces of Cosmic energy may be tapped, unhindered by the tampering of Man. Practice of "Forest Magick," by definition, is primarily concerned with Earth and Air Elements. It is in these forms and manifestations that an Elven Wizard, Mystic or Druid is able to use to capture the essence of "Earth Magic" as related to trees.

A *"silva"* (or *"sylva"*) is a treatise or discourse cataloging the nature and function of the forests—with psychological, spiritual and emotion properties all designated to coincide with the physical lore. Most current forms of "tree magic" linked to the Druid *"Ogham"* (or *"Ogam"*) are derived from the *"Book of Ballymote"*—or *"Sylva d'Ogam."* This current "Greenwood Grimoire" included in the *Elvenomicon* is based on a manual titled *"Sylva Druieachd,"* meaning "Treatise of the Elven Forest Wizard" or "Treatise on Elven Forest Magick," from the same source tradition that provided the current author with materials to prepare our previous "Elven-Faerie Grimoire." For those with a deep inclination toward "Tree Magic," this will serve as an incredibly faithful guide to the Enchanted Forest.

It is important, from the start, to address an idea put forth by anthropologists called "tree worship." Ancient Druids, Elves, Mystics and Wizards *did not* "worship" trees any more than a person might worship some other sacred symbol used to represent the "Divine" in a religion. Elves *revere* trees as an icon of the ALL, the Source-of-all-Being and the Cosmic Law that guides and defines all existence. By understanding the trees and the way in which they grow, Elves also understood the expansiveness of fractal existence of Reality long before and far clearer than Fibonacci and other modern mathematicians.

All life, matter and energy across space and time is a progression of Cosmic Law that moves or grows in the same manner, code or program as trees. This is an important key to the system of Elven Magick. It is often thought that trees are simply inanimate and unintelligent beings, and yet this could not be more untrue. Although they may not share the same degree of "movement freedom" as many other creatures in the wild, their "Earth memory" is far older, clearer and more accessible than what is encoded in shorter-lived beings. Trees also have the ability to be charged (absorb energy) from their natural surroundings, and like other lifeforms, prefer to live in "groups" and "communities."

"Awakened" trees—those interacting with Elven magick—will more easily communicate with one another, and if there is a shortage of trees to talk to, they will produce them, through "*layrs.*" The branches or roots will actually re-root to form a new tree, while still connected to the mother. The more we interact with them and learn, the more we realize that trees are actually quite sentient beings and they have the ability to communicate with us when their spirit is "Awakened" or "remembered" intentionally with Elven magick.

Traditional lore describes the "spirit of a tree" as a "*Dryad*"— borrowing the Greek term used to define a female Druidess, or "Lady of the Woods." The *Dryad* "spirit" is an intelligence or spiritual growth program inhabiting and driving the living system manifestationi that we call "tree." The same patterns and tree-like consciousness are seen in neural formations of the brain called "*dendrytes*"—the word "*Dryte*" is a masculine equivalent to "*Dryad.*"

The "spirits" within trees—which have many names in the Elven Tradition—are a part of any wood taken from it for magical purposes, just as a fractal or genetic print retains the entire code within each part. In fact, nearly all of the objects and tools used in Elven Forest Magick are crafted from trees. It is the manner in which the wood is taken and how it is used that distinguishes the Elven Way from the ways of Humans. This begins with a high reverence for the Green World and all life in Nature, including asking permission from the spirits of a tree before taking any part of its lifeforce. We see a similar practice among archaic shamans and modern herbalists. By "permission seeking," the practitioner is further developing a communicable relationship with the Green World—and this is reinforced in consciousness with each "communion."

With the exception of the title of this "grimoire," the term "*wood*" is hereafter applied to parts of a tree no longer attached to a living tree—either from intentional removal, or some other natural means. There are essentially three types of "*wood*" indexed by loremasters of the Elven Tradition:—

> *Deadwood / Dredgewood*
> *Wickwood / Wetwood*
> *Livewood / Wizardwood*

Wood that you find littered all throughout the forest floor is "deadwood." For whatever reason, it has been broken away from the trees—and it always does—mixing with fallen leaves and decaying foliage to form the soil after its decomposition. It is the fine for kindling fire, but be sure not to clear it completely away from the forest floor, as it is a necessary part of the ecosystem.

While deadwood may be used for amulets, talismans and various magical crafts, is not generally preferred for permanent or serious ritual tools. An initiate might first discover a staff or wand in this manner—though the intentional creation of ritual-magic tools and ceremonial objects often requires live sources with wood collected by a true dedicate of Elven Ways.

"Wickwood" is *any* wood taken from the forest that is not properly removed by a magical practitioner. This means any wood harvested as lumber or broken by carelessness without following the Elven Code of permissions. When wood is taken in this manner, the spirits of the tree actually retract from it, making it quite unsuitable for magical work, particularly of the Elven-Druid variety. Humans have a tendency to remove plants and trees with hostility and ignorance—for whatever the reasons—and this energy is also present in wood that is harvested by that same sentiment.

"Livewood"—or "Wizardwood"—is *any* wood taken from a living tree by an Elven Wizard, Druid or Mystic Herbalist after first following the Elven Code of permissions. This also includes thanking the tree (or plant) for its sacrifice. The article removed from the tree respectfully preserves the spiritual essence of the living spirit of the tree—as a result the wood is blessed by the "Nature spirits" and is positively charged with perfect love, peace and cosmic unity. If you feel inclined to leave an offering to the "Nature spirits" in exchange for their sacrifice, then by all means do so. *Always follow your intuition when walking the path through the enchanted forest!*

—Elven High Magick—
The Light Body & Astral Grove

Many techniques of Elven High Magick are categorized as "energy work," "light work," or "astral work" using New Age vocabulary. An ability to use currents of natural or cosmic energy in "magick" is dependent on the true understanding and realization of a "higher omni-dimensional web-matrix" or "field" in which all energy exists and acts beyond the surface images and forms we might believe we are interacting with. It is really this underlying energy that is exchanging and moving, and only bands of light within a specific spectrum give rise to visible manifestations in the "world we see."

It is essential that an Elven Wizard is fluent in their knowledge and use of the "subtle" underlying currents of universal cosmic energy found throughout all Nature and within and as all Life. These frequencies or vibrations—often interpreted as "auric energy"—emanate from all systems: people; animals; trees; rocks; minerals ...*everything*. Certain individuals may even increase their sensitivity to regularly perceive these energetic interactions at the most basic underlying degrees of awareness. A kaleidoscope of energetic currents or "rays" are abundantly processing around you—and through you—even now. Energies transmitted through all environments, actions and thoughts are all constantly interacting with one another, even when we are not "aware" or do not see a visible change.

Try this exercise:—Go outside on a clear day when the sky is light blue and lay down in the grass, perhaps on a hill. Allow your attention to drift as you quiet your mind. Focus on the clouds, if any, otherwise, the blueness of the sky. Bring your awareness away from the things of a mortal world and life.

Raise your arm and hold your hand about a foot in front of your face so that your vision of the blue sky is backing it. Place your index finger and thumb together as if you are pinching something and rub the slowly in a circular swirling motion. Bring them apart about an inch and soften your gaze to look between them. *What do you see? What is that?* Energy streams and strings are indeed all around us. They project from all living things and may be altered with emotion and intention. Even physical placement of non-living objects—as made famous in recent revivals of *"feng shui"*—has the the ability to affect the motion of energy currents around us, and in turn, our own vibrational states in their presence.

"Dowsing-With-Your-Feet" is one technique taught to Elven/ Sylvan (Forest) Wizards that assists sensitivity development. They learn to free their minds and allow inner intuition to guide their "actions" when selecting a particular tree, rock, stick, *&tc.*, which we might relay as having a particular aspect "speak to us," or that a particular tree (*&tc.*) has "chosen" us. The relationship between a Wizard and the Green World is unique for each instance—and nearly impossible to "grade" as many have attempted in their formation of certain 'Orders' and 'Lodges'—which is why the "Inner Teachings" are always revealed by Nature *herself.* The core material in the *Elvenomicon* is meant to provide intrepid seekers the keys to unlock the "Great Mysteries" by sheer dedication and sincere desire. Potential "Forest Wizards" will have to enter the Green World for an extended period of time to work with these energies directly—yet, once we shared communion with these forces, the "Astral Grove" always exists within us to work from.

According to Elven Tradition, *all* trees have healing qualities. Almost any species of tree is capable of channeling pain and negative energies down into the magma core of the Earth for transformation. It may seem odd to send such energies down into the Earth to be incinerated, but they are more destructive when left unchecked on the surface. Since we are all one organism, Wizards must cure their own pain to properly ease the pain of anyone else—including the Earth itself. Equally so, it is actually in our best interests to help in relieving the suffering of the surface world—ourselves and our environment—so that it does not restrict the future global process of Ascension that we are all participating in. Everything is connected together in the Universe—meaning all of *us*—and what one or two people may feel in one place, is not at all restricted to affecting only them alone. Every course we take sets out causal ripples or tides of manifestation across seas of infinity—and we must take the responsibility for every single one of them if we are to assume any "control" over their "power."

You might practice "Dowsing-With-Your-Feet" for intuitively selecting a "Healing Tree" to perform the following exercise. Ask the tree's permission to heal your pain—emotional, physical, *&tc.*—then soften your gaze and attempt to perceive a visible auric glow emanating from the tree, similar to the bands you may have seen between your fingers in a previous exercise. Sit up straight with your back to the tree—using its trunk to support your spine, keeping sure you are in a comfortable position. Feel and see your "auric body" merge with that of the tree. Focus on your connection to the tree until you no longer easily distinguish boundaries between your body and the tree. Bring your pains to the surface and send them down the trunk into the ground with each breath. Feel and see that you and the tree are pushing it deep down into the fiery core below for incineration and recycling. You may wish to visualize any remaining energetic cords or ties to the energy as equally dissolved. Always thank the Nature-spirits when you have completed energy work in the "Green World." It is also customary to "tend to"—or "groom," in the Animal Kingdom—the fellow life in Nature that we are stewards of or share kinship with, furthering our ecological responsibility.

Whenever activating your consciousness within your "astral form"—just as you would to partake in "Astral Projection"—you are entering your "Light Body" or "Body of Light." If you do this in wakened states without, the intention of Astral Projection, you may be able to use this shift in consciousness as a catalyst for better recognizing the "subtle energies," streams and strings that seem otherwise invisible to the uninitiated. This technique for "astral preparation" is the same method used for "energy work," "light work" and Tree Magick.

Entering the "Light Body" is an application of Visualization and Will to direct intention. This is the same for all "energy work" and "light work." Such methods differ greatly from the vocal dramas and ceremonial forms of ritual magic popular in other systems, including "Elementalism." Energy currents of the forest are strong, but are slow in their build-up of "eventual power." As a result, "Forest Magick" does not carry the same "flare of immediate accessibility" that many practitioners search for—such as we see in the more active Elements of Nature and its corresponding "spirit world." In the forests, progressive learning and communication efforts tend to be slower—matching speeds of frequency in the Green World. To participate in "woodland magic," a Sylvan Wizard must slow their vibrations to the "heartbeat of the forest" and envision their own "light-shield" as the same brilliant emerald green.

Try this exercise:—Sit comfortably with your back erect or lie down. I do not suggest sitting cross-legged, with any parts of the body crossing, or without back support, when first attempting. Begin by focusing all your awareness as a light in your feet, initially drawing this energy up from the ground, and concentrate all of your focus and awareness on this area until it is completely filled with light. Slowly bring this light awareness throughout your entire body, moving it from your toes, feet, ankles, legs and knees upward into your thighs, pelvic region, solar plexus, stomach, chest and shoulders, then finally into your arms, neck, head and reaching its destination in forming a halo-crown about the top of your head. By this method, the Wizard becomes a "Pillar of Light." Feel this light extending from your body and strengthening your auric shield. [The "Western magical tradition" even observes a similar version of this rite, called the "Middle Pillar."]

Accessing the "Astral World" begins first with the ability to project one's consciousness into their "Light Body." Secondly, the Wizard must consciously detach their "Light Body" from its fixed awareness to the physical simulacrum that it localizes as a "home" or "genetic vehicle" (for the physical degree of material existence within the Human range of normative sensory perception). In Forest Magick, the Wizard does not detach into the astral, but maintains this heightened sense of awareness as a magical prerequisite to performing any light-work or energy-work—in Nature or otherwise. The Shaman that visits the "Otherworld" to perform their "magic" does this too. Rather than performing a ritual or ceremony within the physical *Nemeton*, the magic is conducted directly on the "Astral Plane" within the "Astral Grove" or some other locale.

"Astral Travel" taps an imaginative part of our consciousness that is most active in children before civic systemology takes a greater hold on neural activity. But we are all "Children of Light" and "Children of the Stars"—and it is that "star-light" for which the "*astral*" is named. By raising our consciousness and awareness to connect with that ancient source of our *Self*, we are reaching closest to the light to become the free spirits again that we once knew as children, to partake in the amazing spiritual bliss that results from communion with the ALL. To visit your "Astral Grove" it is critical that you first become proficient in entering your "Light Body."

Once you are able to enter the "Light Body," the practice of "Astral Travel" may be achieved by envisioning a catalyst for teleportation—meaning a "threshold," "gateway" or "portal," to launch your astral form through. The Element of Water is a powerful common "portal" element—representing the most fluid-like yet physical substance to bridge between "worlds." Females will find a sense of familiarity using dark pools and mirrors as a doorway. The "Earth portal" or stone megalithic "Trilithon" gateway is another stereotypical "portal" icon, used popularly in Druidism. Other Personal symbols or glyphs may be used to direct awareness as you pass into "Faerie."

Whatever method you choose, you must be able to project your conscious awareness into your Light Body and then project that body through an envisioned portal or representation of a door. This helps trigger the subconscious into releasing the mind into the "Astral Field" and appropriates our attention awareness in the process. Simply envision the portal firmly, seeing it standing before you in your mind's eye. Some practitioners have also found success by visualizing a "Flaming Door." Spend time practicing and refining your skills in assuming this state. Note all of its details of the visualization until it seems as real as any other experience. Using Will, you may direct your astral form through the portal, and maintain a belief that you occupy *this* physical body in the "Astral."

Once you have successfully launched yourself through the imagined portal, anything might occur. You may emerge in darkness—the Underworld Initiation—in which you will be forced to move your mind through a complex labyrinth, often the result of blocks or barriers of the uninitiated mind. You may find yourself in the "astral stellar void"—where all kinds and natures of energy and light moves this way and that, existing as "waves of possibility" and never really taking on a concrete form in one shape or another sometimes known as the "White Place." Or, perhaps you will cross to the Abyss and find the shell of the void—before the First Cause—where all is the Infinity of Nothingness. If you fix in your mind to reach the "Astral Grove" upon entering this state of consciousness, then you may arrive in a greenwood forest setting.

The "Astral Grove" is within the *"Infinite Enchanted Forest,"* and if you do not directly arrive there from your portal, you must "will" yourself there. Your "Astral Grove" is composed of infinite streams of light and energy, formed and constructed by your intentions. Nothing on the astral plane has form except as a finite perspective of an individual observer experiences it and interacts with it. Thus, there is a lot of room for games, magical practice and other experience in the Otherworld, especially if your access to a physical grove is limited.

—Elven High Magick—
Enchanted Trees, Forests & Groves

Elemental Magick explored in the "Elven Faerie Grimoire" is performed within a ritually consecrated "circle." Forest Magick of Sylvan Elven-Ffayrie tradition uses a circle or natural clearing for its rites, one that is in the midst of a "grove" of trees. This "grove" becomes the *Nemeton* for an Elven Wizard.

"Ogham Groves" were once intentionally planted and tended by Elvish Drwyds or Druids. A ring of specific species of tree and plantlife would be maintained as an observatory-temple. The concept of a "tree calendar" most likely emerged from such practices, where wise Wizards were capable of literally "reading the signs of Nature" and interpreting natural conditions from the appearance of these trees—including the time of season. Many have assumed that Ogham lore is primarily a means of "fortune-telling" or mundane divination, yet these natural observations could also predict weather, animal behaviors and other natural effects of the environment. Certain times of year, or other natural conditions, were reflected by the different species of the grove in specific ways—and this lore was carefully observed and cryptically recorded.

Elven Forest Magick lore describes no requirements concerning the boundary of a "ritual circle" or its marking. Large stones are not always appropriate, and they may disrupt natural energies of groves, circles and clearings that may already visibly appear as distinct "circles." Forest Magick is less formal, and more intentionally deliberate, than "ritual magic"—even when it is performed in a woodland setting. You might carry a small bag or pouch of smaller gems/stones used to temporarily designate points of the circle or as a focal aid.

Circle stations are not clearly indicated in the rites of Forest Magick as they are in Elementalism and traditional ritual magic. This is in part because magical work performed by the Sylvan Wizard is primarily internal and often practiced alone. An urban citizen may find difficulties in planting and tending a physical grove. The ability to do this not only distinguishes the type of "magick" involved, but also the type of individual that is able to advance through the Elven Forest Magick system. The natural area guarded is revisited frequently for both mystical operations and meditative exercises which contribute a "charge" or quality of "Enchantment" to the terrain.

The following groupings of tree species repeatedly appear in Elven-Faerie and Celtic-Druid lore:—

· The Elven-Ffayrie Triad Trees are *Oak, Ash and Thorn.*

· The Seven Chieftain Trees of the Cad Goddeu are *Apple, Ash, Hazel, Holly, Oak, Pine and Yew.*

· The Seven Noble Trees of the Grove are *Apple, Alder, Birch, Hazel, Holly, Oak and Willow.*

· The Nine Sacred Woods of Needfire include *Ash, Apple, Cedar, Hazel, Holly, Mistletoe, Oak, Pine and Poplar.*

· The Traditional Tree Calendar Grove consists of *Birch, Rowan, Alder, Willow, Ash, Hawthorn, Oak, Holly, Hazel, Apple (or Vine), Ivy, Reed (or Pine) and Elder.*

The "Greenwood Grimoire" includes several rites that may be used individually or in succession as the application requires.

<u>THE BLESSING OF THE SAPLINGS</u>

Before planting the grove or breaking ground, take all of the trees you intend to plant to the location. All members of the "fellowship" may also be present. Any participants involved should perform all tree-work from the "Body of Light."

The leader (or land steward) stands in the center and says:

Here I [we] have [are] gathered in this place of light. Here I [we] find a place to weave a Sacred Space that I wish to honor with the planting and stewardship of a Sacred Grove of trees. May this Holy Nemeton be a place of peace and power.

Conjure the circle, using stakes to mark its boundary—where the trees are to be planted. Use the most appropriate liturgy. Nature-spirits of the foresy will not be as concerned about your "ritual formalities" as they wll be with your planting.

NORTH: *I [we] come forth to this sacred place and call the spirits of the land to join us here. At this Nemeton do I [we] ask permissions to raise and tend a Sacred Grove of trees, following the tradition of my ancestors.*

EAST: *Here at this sacred place do I [we] acknowledge my [our] vow[s] as Keeper[s] of the Earth. Here I [we] pledge to be Guardian of the Grove, a consecrated Nemeton ever sacred. Here may the sylphs, sylves and Nature-spirits of the woodlands, come and bless, making holy and enchanted.*

SOUTH: *May these future trees of this Grove, these saplings presented here, be blessed by the good Creatures of Faerie, the Four Elements and the Sun above. May the light, love and strength of the cosmos nourish these trees and offer all life sanctuary when visiting here in peace and love.*

WEST—holding hands over buckets of water: *May the spirits and powers residing in the Elements of Water, Sea and Rain come forth and bless these vessels of water. I use them to now share you blessing with these saplings, that they may receive your grace. I ask that you be generous in nurturing this Sacred Grove with your gentle life-giving rains.*

Burn incense and carry it thrice around the circle boundary, working clockwise. Feel the energy in the area equalizing to the land changes about to occur. Conjure a clear image of the completed project and project it as you inform the spirits of Nature—and the trees to be planted—of your intentions. Say:

> By the grace and permission of the Forces of Nature and the Spirits of the Universe; in accordance with the covenant sworn between my ancestors and the Ancient and Shinning Ones; I now break ground in perfect peace, perfect love and compassion and understanding. I open this circle now to perform the work, but the circle is never broken.

CONSECRATION OF A NEWLY PLANTED GROVE

After planting the grove trees, bring some remaining soil to the center of the grove circle and say:

> May all good Spirits of the Earth and Land bless this soil, the land where it is used and the life in nourishes. Bless those who use it as an expression of perfect love to nurture this newly planted life.

Bring this consecrated soil to each of the trees, sprinkling it over the topsoil around each one. Depending on species and climate, wood chips may be used if more appropriate. Feel the love and compassion for Nature and life flowing through you as you complete the planting stage for each of the trees.

Return to the center to consecrate more water, saying:

> May the Spirits of Water and Sea bless this water, the land where it is used and the life it nourishes. Bless those who use it in their expression of perfect love to nurture this newly planted life.

Take the water around to each (as previously with soil). Then clean and clear the area before performing a "Dedication."

THE RITE FOR PLANTING A SINGLE GUARDIAN TREE

This rite may be used to plant a specific "Guardian Tree" or it may be used for each tree planted in the "grove." Go to the space and ask the spirits of the land for permission before you break ground. Follow the basic steps outlined in previous rites—making certain to perform all work from your "Light Body." As you dig and plant the single tree, say:

I plant this tree in perfect peace, love, compassion and under-standing. May it be to others and myself a symbol of the same.

When are ready to complete the work with topsoil and/or woodchips, consecrate the materials, saying:

May this earth feed and nourish this sacred life, a symbol of perfect peace, love and compassion and understanding.

Complete the planting, then consecrate vessels of water, saying:

May this consecrated water bless and nourish the life of this sacred tree, and may all good Elemental Spirits of Sea and Water ensure the rains to ever maintain it.

Water the tree liberally with your consecrated water and then connect with the auric/light field of the tree—something that becomes easier as your proficiency in Tree Magick grows—saying:

By the Elements of Nature were you sown. By perfect peace and love are you grown. I am a Keeper of the Earth and have overseen your birth. I am a Guardian [Scion] of Elven Ways and your steward for all my days.

Close the rite (if planting a single tree)—or continue with each tree of the grove before performing a *"Grove Dedication."*

ADDENDUM—DEDICATION OF THE GROVE and STEWARDSHIP

A grove is consecrated and dedicated prior to its use as a *Nemeton*. The rite may also be used repeatedly over time. You may even use this rite to dedicate existing groves growing in the wild.

> NORTH: *May the Sacred Grove awaken to the mysteries of the Everlasting Forest. May it grant Elven Wizards, and those who come in peace, the same strength and protection the Sacred Grove offered the Ancients. May the sacred ground on which it stands, be purified and blessed.*

> EAST: *Here now before the Sacred Grove and the Nature-spirits awakened and drawn to my work, do I vow stewardship to the Sacred Grove and the mysteries of the Everlasting Forest. I am a Guardian of the Earth Mother, keeper and protector of her ancient ways.*

> SOUTH: *I summon forth the energy and power of the Sky and Sun. Come forth spirit that grants light and life to all creatures on the Earth. Send forth thy Rays of Radiance and instill strength and well-being throughout the Sacred Grove.*

> WEST: *May the spirits of the Water and Rain Elements look upon and bless this Holy Nemeton, consecrated and dedicated to the mysteries of the Universe. Nurture and give life while protecting from deluge and fierce storms.*

You may wish to supplement this rite with individual "Tree Awakenings" and "Rites of Elven-Ffayrie Calling" to more intensely "awaken" and "enchant" the land. With repeated use, this Grove portion of the forest will eventually stand apart, noticeable to folk with even the slightest sensitivity, and may even appear more "alive."

Such is the nature of true *Elvish Magick!*

—Elven High Magick—
Rays of Light & Energy Play

According to traditional lore from Bards and Druids, "Three Rays" compose all energetic manifestations, passing through the "Three Spheres"—or great divisions—of Existence.

 The smallest inner circle is "*Abred*," which is the physical world, a plane of condensed energy, including the "Green World of Nature." The next sphere is "*Gwynedd*," the Otherworld—or Astral—which exists as a "higher" spatial dimension that envelopes the physical world. Finally, there is "*Ceugent*," which is to say "*Nirvana*," or the "Kingdom of Heaven," where resides the Source-of-All-Being-and-Creation and, in some traditions, those spirits that have achieved "Supreme Ascension"—those who have successfully climbed the "Ladder of Lights" back to the Source.

True "Elven Magick"—energy work and light-work—requires calling on and using "Divine Radiance," which manifests as colored "Rays" of the "Forces of Nature." These auric streams of energy and consciousness are summoned by will, intention and emotion collectively. Once a Wizard has projected awareness into the Light Body, the color of the auric "Light Shield" may be altered to meet a desired energy vibration. Call the energy down as a beam of light from the stars and then allow yourself to assimilate its essence.

The properties of the "Three Rays of Awen" are forthcoming. The "Three Rays" of Divine "silver," "crystalline" and "gold" are further divided—fragmented or condensed—into the *seven* bands of light. The primary Rays are called upon in Elvish

High Magick. Modern practitioners find that identifying the *Rays* by color is a most convenient and accurate way of differentiating their relative degrees on a continuous "spectrum." The color—and thereby, nature—of one's own "Light Shield" is transformed by the work to match and attract the desired energetic currents. Remember, as you experiment with the *Rays* and light-work, that these various colored degrees are all derived from three primary rays, which in turn are the manifestations of a singularity of *All-ness*. Using visualization and Will, you may call down the radiance of the "*Rays*" and allow yourself to absorb it through all of your pores and then radiate it from your aura and each breath. Classifications of the *Rays* are as follows:[*]

THE SILVER (LEFT) RAY

Sound/Letter: I ("*ee*")
Polarity: Female, dark, passive, lunar.
Quartile Element: Water (some Earth)
Elvish Element: The Sea
Physical Manifestation: The Mineral Kingdom
Threshold Time Period: Dusk, sunset, autumn.
Elessar (Elf-Stone): Silver (hematite)
Light Bands (Rays): Indigo, violet and blue.

The Silver Properties of the Light Rays

VIOLET (Saturn): Astral vision, darkness,
    Otherworld work, wisdom, wards.
      Domain: Element of Vapor/Cloud
INDIGO (Jupiter): Beauty, enchantment,
    emotions, love, music, play.
      Domain: Element of Rain
BLUE (Luna): Compassion, dreams, healing,
    peace and understanding.
      Domain: Element of Sea

---

[*] Classifications excerpted from *"Draconomicon: The Book of Ancient Dragon Magick"* by Joshua Free.

THE GOLD (RIGHT) RAY

Sound/Letter: O ("*oh*")
Polarity: Masculine, light, active, solar.
Quartile Element: Fire and Air
Elvish Element: The Sky
Phys. Manifestation: Animal & Human Kingdoms
Threshold Time: Dawn, sunrise, spring/summer.
Elessar (Elf-Stone): Gold (tiger's eye)
Light Bands (Rays): Yellow, orange and red.

The Golden Properties of the Light Rays
YELLOW (the Sun): Knowledge, intellect,
    confidence, and inspiration.
    Domain: Element of Skyfire
ORANGE (Mercury): Communication, courage,
    being aware, wishes.
    Domain: Element of Star
RED (Mars): Transformation, healing, strength,
    willpower, and leadership.
    Domain: Element of Flame

THE CRYSTALLINE (MIDDLE) RAY

Sound/Letter: A ("*ah*")
Polarity: Neutral, crystalline, reflective
Quartile Element: Earth ('Quintessence.')
Elvish Element: The Land
Physical Manifestation: Plant & Tree Kingdom
Threshold Time: Twilight, midnight, winter.
Elessar (Elf-Stone): Black (obsidian) or Green
Light Band (Ray): Green

The Crystalline Properties of the Light Ray
GREEN (Venus): Life-force, balance, healing,
    growth, true love.
    Domain: Element of Earth

The traditional "Elven-Faerie Star" is a seven-pointed septo-gram. Elemental symbolism differs from the more commonly known Earth Wizard "pentagram"—which obviously repres-ents Earth, Air, Fire, Water and *Akasha*. The Elvish Wizard sees such elements as more than simply "rock" and "wind," but as the very manifestation of the Seven Rays of Creation, powers descended from the Source-of-All-Being that make up the myriad of lights that we call manifestation. The "Seven Rays" also correlate to the traditional "seven energetic cen-ters" of the body—called "calen" and "astyr" or "chakras" in various traditions—all related back to the primary Three Rays and the holistic singularity.

THE VIOLET RAY—INTERCONNECTEDNESS

Spiritual Element: Fire-of-Spirit (*Nwyvre-of-Akasha*)
Light-Centre: The Crown or Flower of Life (*7th Chakra*)
Gemstone: Amethyst specifically.

One of the core beliefs and teachings of the Elven Tradition concerns the unity of all life. Everything shares energetic ties to everything else—and everything is connected together at the "highest" spatial plane of existence. Quantum metaphysi-cists is already beginning to demonstrate how this works at a subatomic level. The mainstream consciousness of Humans is slowly migrating back into this paradigm. Sylvan light-work, such as that which allows a seed to grow faster, is dependent on a belief or premise that "thoughtforms" and emotion have the ability to charge or affect the energy around us. This en-ergy may be focused as a colored *Ray*—filtered with intention and emotion, as if placing a piece of colored film over a white light projection. The energy of the "Violet Ray" is the highest frequency—and shortest wave-length—of all the vibrations treated in this system. As such it should be only used for the highest caliber of mystical work, Ascension work and Tran-scendental magic—matters involving activation of the "true Self," inner development, "star-walking" and reconnecting with the ALL.

> ### THE PURPLE RAY—THE SEA
> Spiritual Element: Water-of-Spirit and Water-of-Earth
> Light-Centre: Heart or Merkaba (*4th Chakra*)
> Gemstones: Quartz, quicksilver, silver, sapphire, and
> turquoise.

The Sea is powerful. It is the perfect "liquid" manifestation of the "inter-connectedness" envisioned at the first point. The tides of the Cosmic Sea are the waves of potentiality—they represent the Will and Ability of Cosmic Law in motion. The Sea and Water Elements also possess a long-standing association with the Moon and the "emotional condition" of our make-up—that which bridges the "Mind" with the "physical body," a vast network of energetic communication and exchange. The ebb and flow of these waves of energy manifest as both gentle tides and fierce rushing currents. This "Purple Ray" is called upon to aid in centering and purifying our emotions and, in effect, the proper use of Will and intention. It is the second "highest" "magick" on the "Ladder of Lights," by which one can reach a *Self-Honest* experience of life from the Violet rung.

> ### THE BLUE RAY—THE MOON
> Spiritual Element: Earth-of-Water and Water-of-Air
> Light-Centre: Sex Organs (womb) and Spleen (*2nd Chakra*)
> Gemstones: Hematite, Pearl, Topaz and Lapis Lazuli.

Indeed, the Sun is a necessary condition for life derived from light, but the Moon *influences* the beings of light. The ancients believed that the Moon was a luminary body, but of course, we know now that it actually reflects the Sun's light—much like the reflective surface of the Sea. Tidal cycles of water are influenced by a magnetic pull on the earth from the Moon. There are thirteen lunar cycles in a 365-day solar year—and just as many menstrual cycles for a woman. The Moon might affect cyclic psychological, hormonal and otherwise behavioral biorhythms on Earth. For example—different people generally maintain "higher" or "lower" energy levels cycling with different times of day, week, month and year. These patterns are unique to each individual and may be discovered only though self-reflection and self-analysis. The "Blue Ray" is called for perfect peace and protection—which is why it is used for casting a Circle of Power. Disruption of the Blue Ray (*2nd Chakra*) causes depression and anxiety—the polar opposites of the peace and security spectrum—and so use of this *Ray* may aid in restoring a personal balance as needed.

THE GREEN RAY—THE WOODLANDS

Spiritual Element: Earth-of-Earth and Earth-of-Air
Light-Centre: Ground (feet) or base of spine (*1st Chakra*)
Gemstones: Amazonite, Aventurine, Emerald, Moss Agate
    and Serpentine.

An inclination toward the "Green World," and its currents, is the epitome of "Elven Magick." Woodlands and forests are for the Elven-Ffayrie what water is to fish. The "Green Ray" life-force energy is used in all "tree communication rites" and "growth magick." A subversion of the "Green Ray" in its pale (greenish-yellow) form may produce jealousy, envy and discord. When used properly, a Wizard will change their "Light Shield" to match color hues of the forest they are communing with. Trees are the most sacred icon of the "Green Ray"—growing their branches out like the dendritic snowflake, the "Sign of Awen" or the "Elf-rune." Additionally, the "Green Ray" may be used in rites/meditation for personal grounding (centering) and to assist healing.

THE YELLOW RAY—THE SUN

Spiritual Element: Earth-of-Fire, Starfyre and Air-of-Fire
Light-Centre: Mind (Third Eye) or Brow (*6th Chakra*)
Gemstones: Citrine Diamond, Gold, Tiger's Eye and Topaz.

As the Moon is the celestial sphere most sacred to the "Silver Ray," so the Sun brilliantly illuminates the "Golden Ray." All Three Rays of Illumination were once thought to originate with the Sun—which like all other Stars, must originate in the "White Place," a plane of *Infinite Light*. White Light is indicative of the Middle or "Crystalline Ray," and the use of a prism reveals that all Seven Rays are actually contained within one. Crystals may be charged with any *Ray*-color (frequency) or intention through Will and Emotion. The "Yellow Ray" is called forth in connection to the intellect, mental faculties and the accumulation of wisdom—by whatever class (and color) that may fall under. It is interesting that the "Blue Ray" and "Yellow Ray" on either side of the "Green Ray" also share some of the reflective properties of the Green Ray—and as we know in our experiences with artistic colors: mixing yellow and blue results in green. The Elven-Faerie Star paradigm is quite fluid in this way, demonstrating interconnectivity, *not* separation.

THE ORANGE RAY—THE WINDS

Spiritual Element: Air-of-Air, Air-of-Earth and Fire-of-Air
Light-Centre: Throat (Respiratory) or Breath (*5th Chakra*)
Gemstones: Amber, Carnelian, Jacinth and Opal.

Winds are particularly sacred to the Sylph-Ffayrie types. It is the power of the Air Element, with warm currents driven by the Sun, that blows seeds containing the spark of life ensuring the continuation of Nature. Powers of the breeze or wind element are often overlooked because they are represented by the most intangible and unseen symbols—but reflect some of the strongest manifestations of energy in motion. When the wind is "at your back," in may help carry you further. If blowing in the proper direction, in may aid in delivering clear communication at a distance. Otherwise, the "Orange Ray" is only used to relay information that you *really* want to stand out and draw attention to. Next to red, it carries the longest-wavelength, and demands attention, which is why so many in positions of leadership radiate orange in their "Light Shield."

THE RED RAY—THE MAGICK

Spiritual Element: Fire-of-Fire and Spirit-of-Fire
Light-Centre: Solar Plexus (stomach) (*3rd Chakra*)
Gemstones: Red Jasper, Red Agate, Ruby and Rose Quartz.

Practical Magick—such as the "Elementalism" introduced in the "Elven-Faerie Grimoire"—is often a *seeker's* first step on the path to clearing and defragmenting the programs of the "Mind-system" and the Reality experience of the Human condition. Ritual-magic and similar forms of ceremonial practice may aid the novice in understanding and developing their own abilities—but we must make sure that we do not falsely attribute power to these "rituals" themselves, and that we do not fall into the trap of over-identifying dependence on such "external" forms as our only means of thinking "magically." All intentional actions—or movements of energy—performed deliberately are considered "magical," and only when a true conscious understanding of these principles and dynamics becomes automatic second-nature to us, do we begin to say that we are practicing or operating "magick." It is a process and a progressive journey toward active participation as *Self* in *Self-Honesty* with Cosmic Law of the ALL—and these are not the statements of someone who lives life only in response or as a victim, no indeed, we are actively creating with the "Red Ray" and it manipulates the emotional states of passion, consummate love and anger—currents with the longest wave and most immediate tangible results.

—ℰlven High Magick—
Communing With Nature

Prior to working with the entire spectrum, an initiate should begin their journey into "Light Work" or "Energy Work" with the "Three Rays of Radiance." The following "Triad Rite" will assist in this. Once a familiarity with the system is reached, Rites of the Rays may be performed anywhere—in a physical setting or purely while working on the astral plane—and always from the perspective of *Self* within the activated "Light Body."

THREE RAYS OF RADIANCE—"TRIAD RITE"

- Face the northern direction.
- Call down the Radiance of the "Silver Ray."
- See and feel the "Silver Ray" descend upon you, and to the left of you, as you intone the sound "I" (or "ee").
- Raise your arms as you inhale the tone; bringing them down to your sides as you exhale and intone the sound—using your arms to draw or pull down the "air" (*Ray*).
- Do this with the Middle or "Crystalline Ray."
- See and feel the "Crystalline Ray" descending upon you, and through you, with the sound "A" ("*ah*").
- Repeat the process, calling the "Golden Ray" down upon you, and to the right of you, with the intonation "O" ("*oh*").
- With practice, the rite may conclude by drawing down all "Three Rays" using the three processes simultaneously: "I-A-O."
- You might also try experimenting with other Elven sequences, such as "A-O-I."

Elven lore includes many references to an "Astral Grove" and "astral plane"—suggesting this environment as most suitable for meditation and ritual work. But, this is only available to those with proficiency in accessing such state of consciousness. To assist in this development, there is one safe effective exercise—called "A Day at the Pool"—that teachers offer their students to practice directing (projecting) mental energy in the astral. Try this:—Enter the Body of Light and begin first at your Astral Grove, asking for the grace of the Cosmic Source to protect your True Spirit as you work. Now travel through the "Everlasting Astral Forest" until you find a still pool or lake—making certain you are experiencing all of the sensory details of your surroundings as you move through this fluid-like degree of existence: the colors; smells; the feeling of the ground beneath your feet... Then begin to practice your intentional interaction with the environment—draw in energy (inhaling through your astral form) to make deliberate movements and actions with the Astral Body. For, example, extend the energy with an exhale as you bend down to pick up a rock from the waters edge. Hold it a while, feeling it completely in your hands, making certain the imagery is concrete as you build your Will and to focus. Continue to perform simple actions, tossing the rock from one hand to the other, inhaling energy and exhaling action. Then use your will (and exhale) as you cast the stone across the still waters of the pond—releasing and projecting the energy. Pause a moment to witness the results. Did you see ripples across the pond as consequence of the energy you directed? [This type of exercise may be repeated as desired for cumulative experience.]

To summon the Radiance of peace and protection about yourself—or to a specific locale—conjure a "ball" of compressed blue-white energy rays between your hands. Feel its radiance warming and cooling your hands simultaneously. It may help if you perform a "Triad Rite" first and call on the "Blue Ray" directly as you construct the "ball." Use the "Three Rays" to give the ball substance, then incorporate the "Blue Ray" to provide its "shield" or energetic filter. If this does not work

for you at first, try rubbing your hands back and forth together repeatedly while initially drawing down the Radiance, and
then bring them apart several inches and focus your energy
and attention on the space between your hands. When the
ball is adequately visualized and experienced, feel the "*Radix*"
or "*Rad*" of the ball emanating out, affecting the surrounding
environment with its radiation, driving all out-of-phase frequencies and negative conditions away. Then direct the
"positive" Radiance of the ball toward a target, or absorb it
internally. This practice is otherwise known as a "*Blessing.*"

We have mentioned Light Shields of living beings in passing—
but these same "auric covers" exist in all things. They are the
energetic frequency signature of that "thing"—now fragmented in exclusion to "other things"—a filtering determinant of
the energy projected and received by that existence and in
relation to *All* other existence, as One. Colored bands associated with living beings are consequences of energetic activity
moving through the body on all degrees/levels of existence.
These colors may typically distinguish what energy type—be
it *Ray, Chakra, &tc.*—is most actively projecting into the field.
Each color carries frequencies associated with basic attributes (as relayed in the previous lesson-chapter) that may be
either under-stimulated or over-active, generating "positive"
constructive frequencies in our life and work or "negative"
wave-interference patterns. Understand that we are not here
speaking in absolutes—"good" and "evil"—but, what we *have*
discovered is that there are modes of operation that contribute either *toward* or *away from* progression on our "Path of
Ascension," and that these also tend to solidify or manifest in
our daily lives and directly related to our spiritual evolution,
emotional well-being and even yes, even our physical health
—all of which is interconnected and nothing is in exclusion.
There is nothing wrong with treating physical ailment symptoms with physical medicine as a tool that better enables the
"Mind" and "Spirit" to focus on its own degrees of health. But
when we focus on the physical ailments and remedies in exclusion, the underlying "problems" continue to resurface.

Esoteric lore from the "Ancient Mystery School" also evokes the existence of the colors and Rays in its description of the degrees/levels of existence that make up the identity of *Self*. It states that: at the innermost core of your being there is a "violet egg" or oval-like elliptical sphere containing the essence of your True Spirit. All of the rest—all the other bands and layers—are further and further shells that resonate with more and more condensed degrees of existence. And this includes our "biochemical" genetic vehicle that the Spirit calls "home" for its earthly condition of experience.

Elven lore describes the "violet egg" as "amethyst" (or violet quartz)—and that it is a "fragmented shard" of a now "Dark Crystal," something that even seems to resonate with a certain brand of modern-day fantasy. The "amethyst crystal" of our True Spirit is protected in an encasement of spiritual skin —a pink shell that radiates the true love and absolute purity of the ALL. This violet-pink hued spiritual existence is the truest part of our identity, which came from and may return to the Source—the destination of Ascension called *"Ceugent"* in Welsh literature. This state of our True Spirit is the connection link back to the Source—a column that is also aligned with the "Middle Ray" or "Crystalline Ray" (from which both the "Silver Ray" and "Golden Ray" divert from) that activates our personal energetic propulsion system as an "Identity"— the light centers within us that align to variously perceived degrees/levels projecting our very existence—and ability to simultaneously exist—at all degrees/levels of the ALL at once. Without such a function, we would have no consciousness, no ability to relate to our created environment and no memory to retain either.

When the white crystalline energy of the Light Body has stabilized (equalized) or is "clear," it is then able to manifest all colors of the spectrum perfectly. These Rays use the body's *Chakra-system*—or "*Calen*" system—as an energetic "step-down transformer" connected to "Divine" Radiance of the Cosmos. The fourth level of your spiritual existence consists of both a silver and a gold shell that wraps around the crystalline one, sealing the primary auric energy in as part of the Identity. The fifth level is the "Light Body" itself—the "outer aura" and "Light Shield." It is the part of us that people may see when they say they can "see auras." Your energetic and emotional state influences the type, nature and strength of your auric "Light Shield"—and vice versa, because all energetic activity is an "exchange" in some way. It is possible to neutralize negative or destructive aspects of an emotion (color) by changing the "Light Shield"—and therefore our conscious attention—to an opposing color. For example—a person might counter the "red" they see when angry with "blue" peaceful hues. When we meditate on the nature of this multiplicity of oneness that we perceive as levels of the "spiritual self," we may strengthen our abilities to consciously interact with these energies as a part of a daily holistic practice.

The same degrees of consciousness and energetic interaction that we apply to ourselves is also present in other forms of life—including animals and trees. Therefore, it is important that an initiate is first aware of how this energetic system operates on *themselves* before attempting to interact, commune, or otherwise exchange energies directly with Nature—and specifically the *trees* that we will be focusing the remainder of this "grimoire" toward.

"Tree Magick is a unique personal form of practice used by Elvish Wizards—and later Druids—to awaken the individual consciousness of trees on Earth, one by one. These awakened trees form groups or "chains," composing a complex network of communication—and energetic exchange—with the other awakened or "Enchanted" trees. Through the "high magical" processes of "Communion with Nature," an Elf is capable of learning otherwise undisclosed spiritual lessons from Nature and awakened tree-spirits, because they are all linked to the entire planetary pool of "Earth Memory," just as each of us is influenced by encoded genetic memory within our design that may even be billions of years old.

An advanced use of these abilities might include activating a ring of awakened trees to guard an area like your home. Linking with the Forces of Nature, a sensitive adept may notice when the surrounding area has a "visitor" or is disturbed, like the strings of a spider's web. Other more abstract practices could include accessing data from the Elven Libraries—what some refer to as the "Akashic Records." The Forest Magickal Tradition is so vast and colorful that entire lifetimes could be dedicated to its ways and unlimited applications. To "Commune with Nature," your skills developed from previous exercises in Visualization and Willpower will be tested.

The following are prerequisite steps of the traditional "Commune with Nature" spell-rite that must be met before other specific applications are performed.

- Go to the sacred woods where you practice your art of energy-play and light-weaving. This will most likely be the *Nemeton* or place where you most often spend time developing your aptitude in the "Elven Way."
- Spend some time meditating on the "Elven Tradition."
- Project your awareness into your "Light Body."
- Adjust your "Light Body" to match the green energy vibrations of the woodlands.
- Use muscular inclination ("Dowsing-With-Your-Feet") to guide you to a specific tree. At first you may want to work with only a few tree types—but eventually you will be able to awaken the entirety of the forest.
- When working with individual trees, approach slowly and from the north (when possible) and with a quieted "mind." Do not bring a head full of cluttered worldly matters to your Elven Green World energy-work.
- Sit close—within an arm's reach—and focus on both your "Light Shield" and the "auric radiation" of the *tree*.
- Spread your palms wide on the surface of the trunk.
- Match your frequency and vibration (color) with the tree and then merge the two energy fields.
- Retain contact with your left hand, completing the

circuit with your right hand by using some catalyst for the energy—such as sticks, stones or the ground, depending on your other intended practices.

Now that the preliminaries are performed, what follows will depend on what type of Green Magick you have intended. Not all Nature-communion sessions are for literal "communication," which can be quite a lengthy process. Basic communion is the first step regardless. Visualize—and maintain an awareness—of a clear circuit of energy. The pillared trunk of the tree represents the "Tower of the Green Ray," the Middle Ray of pure crystalline reflection. Take this energy into your circulatory and nervous system through your left (or receptive) hand spread on the trunk. Make it a part of you, and then send it forth to the ground after cycling it through your catalyst or tool—just as you would an electric circuit! The root structure of the tree takes this in, circulates it through its own internal nervous system—passing through trunk, branch and sprig—before it is passed back to you. When both aspects are sending and receiving simultaneously, there is no energy "drain." When life-force energies are cycled, they actually are filtered as a result of the process—which may be beneficial when it is clear *Self-Honest* filtering, much like removing corrosion from a wire connection or contact. Similar exchanges take place in sexual encounters—where energy is projected, permanently changes by the "energetic signature" of a partner, and then returns. When we engage in such activities without performing proper energy-work, there is a risk of damaging or depleting energy from our *"chakra-system"* and/or "Light Bodies."

Once you commune, you can communicate:—Close your eyes and see a whitish etheric cloud between you and the tree, slightly above your head. Both of you share this field and have the ability to project into it. Understand: trees will not verbally "talk" to you. They prefer—and are restricted—to communicate in a timeless language of symbols and imagery; hence in this instance, a "picture is worth a thousand words."

So long as there is true communion between you and Nature, the verbal use of communication—for example, in rites and rituals—are mainly for your benefit, and to assist focusing on actual communicable energy transmissions. Members of the animal and plant kingdom are more likely to hear and respond to tone and "emotional charge" (or your "Light Body") than the words themselves. Use the cloud previously described as a "thought-bubble" to facilitate communication. Then wait and be patient to see what happens. Tree communication is often slow work—even for an adept.

The Elven Forest Magick system is loosely aligned to the later Druidic classification of *Ogham* trees, a systemology derived from the former. There are three different traditional sets of *"Ogham Tools"* that are often all haphazardly referred to as *"Ogham Sticks."* Elven tradition gives each of the versions its own title and each are kept separately in their own magical pouch—called a "Crane Bag" in the *Ogham* (or *Ogam*) system.

Ogham Sticks
Ogham Rods
Ogham Wands

OGHAM STICKS—Twenty sticks/twigs of the same type/species, cut to the same size and polished. An alternate version uses wood-chips as "runic wood-stones." Each of the sticks or chips will have one of the Ogham glyphs burned (preferably) or painted thereon. The "Ogham Sticks" are used for high-divination and "cryptomancy."

OGHAM WANDS—Ranging from eight to sixteen inches long, each wand should be constructed from a correlating tree for each Ogham rune—or a tree of similar energy for ones not available in your area. The "handle" of the wand should be shaved flat on one side so there is a surface to burn or paint the Ogham mark. The other end should be shaved to a stake-like or spear-like point so it may be pushed several inches into the ground. During communion or communication, the

Elven Wizard holds the handle of the wand to complete the energetic circuit. The "Ogham Wands" are primarily used for communication and spiritual communion with Nature.

OGHAM RODS—Twenty-one pieces of dowel or thin wood that are cut to equal lengths and used specifically for divination. Some scholars suggest this ancient tool set is responsible for the children game "pick-up-sticks"—which is what an object-ive observer might see when the set is cast, interpreted and retrieved. They "Ogham rods" are held in one hand about a foot away from the ground, and then dropped. Using runic and Ogham signs as reference, the Wizard may interpret any omens found or "read."

When used in conjunction with tree communication and com-munion with Nature, even simple acts of "divination" may become very powerful workings of "Elven High Forest Ma-gick." The *Elf Stones* are a perfect example of this.

ELF-STONES (*Elessar*) are among the most sacred tools used in "Sylvan Magick." They may be used for any purpose: divina-tion, tree communication and/or energy/light-work. Elven lore suggests many different versions—including all-blue and all-green—but in the traditional *"Triscale Set,"* each of three equal-sized stones taps into the energetic heart of one of the "Three Rays of Radiance" or Elven *"Awen,"* as follows:

> "Golden Ray" – Tiger's Eye
> "Silver Ray" – Hematite
> "Crystalline Ray" – Obsidian[*]

The "Elf Stones" are a perfect catalyst for divination and tree communication, acting as a an energy-testor, similar to the function of a "pendulum" or "dowsing rods." The standard "Triscale Set" may be used to indicate a positive or negative response based on where the gold and silver stone fall in rela-

---

[*] Some sets substitute aventurine or bloodstone for the obsidian.

tion to the black/green crystalline indicator. To use the Elf-Stones in relation to introductory "Tree Magick," you might try the following:—Link up to a tree energy from your Light Body and ask it if it is in need of a Guardian and Caretaker or if it wishes to begin a mystical and spiritual relationship with you. Drop the stones at the base of the tree and see how they fall. If the gold one is closest to the indicator, the answer is "yes." The answer is "no" if the silver stone is closer.

Practices related to *Ogham Tools* and *Elf Stones* are all great for developing skills of "Elven High Forest Magick," but they are dependent on sensitivity and awareness of a practitioner for effectiveness. Any of these tools/techniques may also be used to "Awaken the Forest." The final rite offered in the original "Greenwood Forest Grimoire" is none other than a direct means to accomplish just that:—

ELVEN HIGH FOREST MAGICK—"TREE AWAKENING"

• Enter your "Light Body."
• Call down the "Radiance of the Three Rays."
• Make physical contact with the tree.
• Perform the "Tree Communion" spell.
• Speak the "Elven-Gaelic name" for the tree species three times, followed by the "English name," and finally the names "Aldaron," "Daghda" and the "Guardian-name" (associated with the type/species).
• Knock three times and break contact.
• The tree is *awakened!*

—Sylva Druieachd—
Sylvan Forest "Ogham" Catalogue

THE ALDER TREE

Elvish-Celtic Name/Letter: Fearn/"F"
Druid Guardian: Forann
Archetypes & Deities: Strength, Bran the Blessed and Macha.
Quadratic Element/Colour: Fire/Crimson (*'flann'*)
Polarity: Male (solar)
Month of Cor Anar: January
Sacred Animal/Bird: Fox, Ram/Gull (*'faelin'*) and Ravens
Gemstones: Beryl, Serpentine and the Gold Elf-Stone.
Ffayrie Herb(s): Fern
Traditional Uses: Charcoal, dye, and housing foundations.
Divinatory & Energy Expressions: Foundation, protection,
   guidance, resistance to water/enchantment.

Oghamic lore attributes the Alder Tree to the element of Fire; however, investigations into its mysteries would reveal that it also carries an affinity for water—because Alder wood holds up quite well against it. In fact, *Fearn* is capable of actually living in water. Parts of many "water-towns" such as Venice are built on piles of Alder wood. Since the element of Water and the magic of enchantment and glamour are so closely related, this Ogham may also ward away such when used as a talisman —protecting against enchantment from others. As a result of its unique aquatic growing ability, it represents a bridge or link between this world and the Otherworld—and "bridges" in general.

One clear indicator that this is a Faerie-tree is that when it is first cut, it appears as though it were bleeding. Such omens forced the ancients to consider that maybe this wood should not be often cut, and so there is a mystical taboo or *"geas"* concerning its use—though it often is used. It allegedly makes the good charcoal and the bark yields a blood-red dye. Fresh shoots produce a more cinnamon-hued dye.

The Fire Element and red attributes apply to its use in battle. According to the *"Cad Goddeu"*—"Battle of the Trees"—Alders are at the head of the battle—"first in the foray"—right there on the front line. Warriors often sought Alder wood for their shields. The blood-like sap of *Fearn* is equally reminiscent to wounds endured in battle—such as those of Bran the Blessed. Alder energy drives the warrior spirit, allowing one to stand fast in battle or conflict, or when confronted with an over-abundance of external pressures. Just as the head of Bran arrived in the midst of battle to reveal important prophecies, so must an Elven Wizard be open to the inner voice at all times.

Wards made from this wood—meaning wands used for protective talismans or "magical artifacts" to keep away certain energies—are highly effective. Of course, to obtain Wizard-wood you must touch the tree with a blade, which is taboo except by most adept of Elven Wizards. Ask spirits of the tree to enter the ward and to aid safeguarding against the will, magic and enchantment from others toward you, your family —or for the owner of the ward.

Alder is sometimes used for medicinal purposes. The inner bark may be boiled in vinegar and used to anoint the skin to remedy various skin conditions, it tightens gums when used as a mouthwash (or soothes a toothache) and has even been used to help kill head lice and assist the scalp recovery afterward. [As with any "folk medicine" discussed within these pages, the present author suggests the reader/seeker embark on extensive investigation into all homeopathic and holistic medicine—including a discussion with a health care professional—before self-treating with any natural suggestions.]

THE APPLE TREE

Elvish-Celtic Name/Letter: Quert, Queris/"Q"
Druid Guardian: Qualep
Archetypes & Deities: Empress, Avalon, Kerridwen (or
    Cerridwen) and Mannan Mac Lyr.
Quadratic Element/Colour: Water/Green ('*quair*')
Polarity: Female (lunar)
Sacred Animal/Bird: Unicorn/Hen ('*querc*')
Gemstones: Rose Quartz and the Silver Elf-Stone.
Ffayrie Herb(s): Wild Strawberry and Rosebush ('*quenda*')
Traditional Uses: Dietary (fruit) major food of the Elves,
    drinking (cider,) woodcarving, and the "Silver Branch" (or
    "bough") or "Apple Wand."
Divinatory & Energy Expressions: Love, beauty, the union of
    mind and spirit between lovers, eternal life (perpetual
    youth), abundance, fertility and healing.

Many Celtic scholars interpret the name of the *Isle of Affalon* (or "Avalon") as the "Isle of Apples"—also known as the "Isle of Glass." Both the Apple Tree and Avalon share a peculiar connection to the Elven-Ffayrie Otherworld. An examination of ancient lore and references to Avalon suggest it was called "Apple-land,"—and most likely home to an orchard or elaborate arrangement of Apple groves.

An Order of priestesses and Druidesses maintained a mystical tradition in Avalon sacred to the Silver Ray and using Apple Wand in their ceremonies. The *Craebh Ciuil* wand or "Silver Bough" is used for healing, beauty, peace and harmony, in addition to Otherworld Magick. The "Apple Branch" is also a central tool to several magick rites that summon or call the *Fey*. Lore suggests that it is a forked branch, unpainted, with three silver bells hanging on white, silver and/or blue ribbon.

Another reason Apple is sacred is that when the fruit is cut in half, you can see the image of the pentagram—the five-rayed star. *Quert* is sacred to the harvest, festivals of Lughnassadh and the Autumn Equinox. A toast of cider is always conducted in the honor of the Apple Tree Spirits at the beginning of the harvest to bless and consecrate the harvest season. All of the dietary hybrids of the Apple now common throughout the world first emerged from the original Crab Apple tree. The fruit also appears in folk remedies to soothe asthma or chronic pneumonia sufferers, possibly inspiring the old saying that: "*...an apple a day keeps the doctor away.*"

THE ASH TREE

Elvish-Celtic Name/Letter: Nuin, Nwyn, Nion/"N"
Druid Guardian: Nebgadon
Archetypes & Deities: The World/Universe, World Tree, Lugh, Ogma, and Odin/Woden.
Quadratic Element/Colour: Air/Green or Clear ('*necht*')
Polarity: Crystalline (reflective of any polarity)
Month of Cor Anar: March
Sacred Animal/Bird: Adder or Serpent/Snipe ('*naescu*')
Gemstones: Sapphire and the Green or Crystalline Elf-Stone.
Ffayrie Herb(s): Magic Mushroom ('*fly agaric*' in Europe or otherwise '*psilocybin*')
Traditional Uses: Spears, maypoles, pool cues, paddles, oars, hockey sticks, wands, dream pillow herbs, sea/water magick and healing.
Divinatory & Energy Expressions: Triumph, completion, overview, protection, overcoming mental strife, and the 'World Tree' that links the inner and outer worlds.

There are three main wands of the Sylvan Tradition – excluding the Apple Branch formerly mentioned. They are Oak, Ash and Thorn. While the Celtic *Drwyds* are best known for their Oak wands, the legendary Spear of Lugh was fashioned from Ash wood. The first Elven wands were then of the *Nuin* current, in imitation of this spear, and often carved into a spiral, like a Unicorn's horn—always representative of the Air Element. Ogham tools constructed from Ash wood are used for inspiration, enlightenment and most obviously, knowledge.

Nwyn is the most likely candidate for a "Tree of Knowledge" or "World Tree" (Yggdrasil) often referred to in Nordic-Elven lore—or even the Semitic Kabbalah, which is based on Meso-potamian lore of the *date-palm* as the "World Tree" or "Tree of Life." In all of its forms, the "World Tree" is a holistic mi-crocosmic-macrocosmic representation or Cosmic model—its branches each representing different degree/levels of exist-ence (or dimensions) yet still a part of the singular Tree. Elves sometimes refer to the "Middle World"—or "physical plane" experienced by the Human condition—as "Mid-Branch."

As one of the few truly crystalline tree currents, Ash trees possess the ability to be one sex and then switch based on re-productive needs. According to folk remedy lore, Ash bark may assist in reducing fevers; and the leaves may be used to remove bio-toxins as a laxative, or externally to treat snake-bites. When leaves are unavailable (out of season), the bark is often used with similar results and the sap is sometimes ad-ded to teas and infusions to aid relieving kidney stones and bladder infections.

THE ASPEN TREE

Elvish-Celtic Name/Letter: Eadha, Aethin, K'emmir/"E"
Druid Guardian: Essu
Archetypes & Deities: The Tower, Brighid, Rhiannon and
   Keyne.
Quadratic Element/Colour: Water/Silver or Red ('erc')
Polarity: Female (lunar)
Other Trees Sharing the Current: Poplar & Cottonwood
Sacred Animal/Bird: White Mare/Swan ('ela')
Gemstones: Grey Topaz, Opal and the Silver Elf-Stone.
Ffayrie Herb(s): Bracken
Traditional Uses: Shapeshifting magick, divination, shields
   and Rites of Passage.
Divinatory & Energy Expressions: Overcoming barriers and
   problems, facing fears, overcoming death, working through
   emotional distress and matters of ambition.

The Aspen Tree is aligned to the use of intuition and the un-covering or revelation of secret or esoteric knowledge. Long have Wizards sought Aspens as "Oracle Trees." From a meditative state—the Body of Light—they watch as winds blowing through the leaves produce a sound and flickering sight that is conducive to skrying and receiving visions and prophecies. Slightly more robust, the Poplar and Cottonwood Trees carry the same energy current. Cottonwood, particularly, is more highly aligned to masculine/solar polarities, also known as the "Giant Aspen."

The *Eadha* current represents mysterious lessons that are necessary to overcome in order for spiritual completion on the Earth Plane—and finally the "Grand Ascension." Aspen Trees have many associations with death, as both Jesus and Judas of the Judeo-Christian tradition hung from them. Aspen wands and Ward-talismans represent overcoming death and bad habits. They are also used in "karmic balancing" rites and for revenge. The measuring rod used to fit coffins for people was once made of Aspen wood. But Aspen is not the final Ogham Tree in the twenty-fold system—it is nineteenth—reminding us that the physical death transition state is *not* the end.

Elves, Wizards and Druids all maintain a "Doctrine of Transmigration of Souls" that indicates that the "spiritual egg"at the center or core of our True Self is not physically tangible at the normal human degree of perception and is not destroyed when the physical body or vehicle perishes. It instead extends its own light to maintain a spiritual existence or vehicle fit for higher degrees/frequencies of manifestation. If more lessons must be learned, the Light Body or spiritual self will travel to another catalyst or vehicle to access this knowledge—we sometimes call "reincarnation"—which continues until True Ascension takes place, and the being or spirit is so full of light that physical incarnations are no longer necessary, except in cases where a self-actualized Ascended Master returns by will to assist teaching others. The Aspen Tree does not have many medicinal uses, save one famous one: Nature's Aspirin. The bark is powdered and administered—perhaps in capsules or tea—to relieve fevers and mild tension or pain.

THE BEECH TREE

Elvish-Celtic Name/Letter: Phagos, Sultan, Atarya
   Dwyrion/"Ph"
Druid Guardian: Pharon or Oberash (Alba-Sun)
Archetypes & Deities: The Sun, Virgil, Grandmother of the
   Forest, Ogmha and Oenghus mac Og.
Quadratic Element/Colour: Skyfire (or Water)/Orange (or
   Sky Blue)
Polarity: Female (lunar) usually, otherwise reflective.
Sacred Animal/Bird: *'Draig-Teine'* or FireDrake/Crane or
   Bluebird
Gemstones: Fire Opal, Blue Topaz, Azurite and each Elf-Stone
   individually.
Ffayrie Herb(s): Morning Glory
Traditional Uses: Writing tablets, book covers, woodcraft, tree
   communication.
Divinatory & Energy Expressions: Archaic knowledge, writing,
   communication, the Summer Solstice (*Alban Heruin*), runes,
   victory, and letting go of old patterns.

Beech Trees are a secret Ogham character incorporated into a
later system—possibly by reconstructionists themselves. It is
an important tree, appearing in the first line of the "Cad Goddeu," yet it does not appear in any traditional twenty-fold
Ogham system. The Beech and Oak trees are the subject of the
first quatrain of the "Cad Goddeu" prose—and they share a
connection, representing ultimate "Godparents of the Forest"
(*Atarya Dwyrion*). Elvish lore often depicts the *Phagos* current
as a more "feminine" counterpart of the "masculine" Oak.

Phagos is a sacred tree to both Elves and Dragons. According
to lore, it is more closely aligned to humanoid energies than
other trees—and its "Dryad" spirit is often more receptive to
communication than many other species. In spite of this, the
Beech Tree is often slighted out of "New Age" texts regarding
"trees in magic" that are based exclusively on a modern Celtic Tree Oracle popularized by Liz and Colin Murray. But there
are other, and more antiquated, resources regarding Ogham
lore—much of which is found within the *Elvenomicon* and also

compiled within the current author's recension of *The Book of Pheryllt: A Complete Druid Source Book*. Communication is significant integral of the *Phagos* current. Beech wood was once the preferred material for writing tablets and even hardcover books. Resonating with the "preservation of knowledge," the *Phagos* current may also serve useful when working with ancestral spirits. The Beech Tree produces an edible nut called a *"mast,"* which is also traditionally used to make cooking oil.

THE BIRCH TREE

Elvish-Celtic Name/Letter: Beith, Beithe, Beth, Belwen/"B"
Druid Guardian: Boibel/Babel
Archetypes & Deities: The Stars, New Moon, Bel, and the
　　White Goddess.
Quadratic Element/Colour: Air/White (*'alban'* or *'ban'*)
Polarity: Female (lunar)
Month: November (New Year)
Sacred Animal/Bird: Cow/Pheasant (*'besan'*)
Gemstones: Flourite and the Silver Elf-Stone.
Ffayrie Herb(s): Fly Agaric Mushroom
Traditional Uses: Wands, broomsticks, protection for children
　　and wards.
Divinatory & Energy Expressions: New beginnings, renewal,
　　fertility, cleansing, purification and birth.

The Birch Tree marks the New Year on most interpretations of the Celtic Tree Calender and as such is sacred to *Samhain*. Its purifying energies are called to drive out old spirits and static energies of the old year. Such is also the primary ritual function of a "magical broom." Traditional folk magic rituals often began with sweeping out of the area to neutralizing the energy of a magical workspace or *Nemeton*. The "flying" aspect of the witchcraft tradition more likely emerged from the use of mushrooms that grew in the Birch shade and provoked "spirit flight" when ingested. Such methods of "astral travel" would lead seekers into the Otherworld via hallucinogens.*

---

* Although these practices of *"shadow magic"* are described in Elven-Ffayrie lore, legal restrictions regarding their possession in most of the

Beith is an energy of new beginnings, and the tree is notorious for producing new trees from fallen twigs. As the first tree of the Ogham system, it is commonly the first forest lesson encountered by an initiate. Only as a result of effective abilities to awaken, communicate and utilize currents of the Birch Tree, would a first degree student of "Elementalism" be permitted to enter the second degree of "Forest Magick." The New Year marks the annual transition into the "Dark Half of the Year"—from *Samhain* to *Beltane*. Although not observed even close *Samhain*, the Birch Tree is most closely aligned to energies of the Spring Equinox (*Alban Eiler*) forcing many scholars to question the validity of the accepted "Tree Calender" used by reconstructionists.

The Birch Tree is the "Lady of the Woods"—often replacing the Beech as the Silver Pillar (next to the Ash/Yew and Oak) in the Forest Magickal Tradition. Medicinally, the oil from the bark may be used to make a skin lotion, which may assist a variety of skin conditions. The buds of the Birch flowers are used to help stomach pains and ulcers. Chewing on twigs will helps keep teeth clean, and a tincture of the leaves and/or bark aids relieving mouth soars. Teas and tinctures have a purifying quality causing frequent urination when ingested. The oil in the bark may be used to repel insects. [Apparently, modern scientists discovered that a chemical in Birch known as "*methyl*," makes this all possible.]

THE BLACKTHORNE TREE

Elvish-Celtic Name/Letters: Straif, Straife/"St" and "Z"
Druid Guardian: Stru
Archetypes & Deities: Temperance (needed), The Falling Tower, The Arch Druid, Scathach and Skadi.
Quadratic Element/Colour: Earth/Purple or Bright ('*sorcha*')
Polarity: Female (lunar)
Other Trees Sharing the Current: Plum ('*emrys*')
Sacred Animal/Bird: Wolf and Black Cat/Thrush ('*stmolach*')

"western world" causes ethical issues in adovcating their use here.

Gemstones: All three Elf-Stones combined.
Ffayrie Herb(s): Stinging Nettle
Traditional Uses: 'Thunder and Lightning Staff' or 'Dark Staff'
(a.k.a. '*shillelagh*'), cudgel weapons and warding against evil
and illness.
Divinatory & Energy Expressions: Cleansing, control, operat
ing by force, confusion, restraint, resentment, sudden
change or renewal, strife and protection.

Blackthorne—also called the "Wishing-thorne" or the "Faerie
Tree"—actively reflects the "darker side" of Nature, and the
thorns may be carried (or used in ritual) as a symbol of this
part of the "Ffayrie Tradition." When allowed to grow wild, it
forms an impenetrable bramble—yet it is important to clarify
that when allowed to grow, Blackthorne is a tree, not a bush.
In the physical "Green World," a hedge of thorns may help to
hide a grove or other "secret portals" to the Otherworld. If
we apply the same symbolism to divination, the hedge may
represent barriers and distractions which promote confusion
and anger.

Dark Power is not restricted to "Dark Elves" and actually has
nothing to do with the *Unseelie Court*. Darkness and shadows
simply hide those parts of the world—and ourselves—that we
do not readily see or accept, like the "Shadow Self." When we
see observe the manner in which we handle frustration and
anger, we are often left to deal with aspects we do not like
and may seek to change. You can't change the fact that sometimes you get thwarted on your path and will come across
barriers and challenges. You can change your programmed
fight-or-flight response-reactions and your ability to cope, or
manage the "Game of Life."

A "*Shillelagh*" or "Sylvan Blasting Rod" is made from a Blackthorne branch with runes of power burned along its surface.
Lore suggests that a repetitive sequence of personal names
and words of power would be inscribed thereon. In spite of its
many titles, this is not a tool of malevolence. On the contrary,
it was used to protect against such malignant energy in an

active manner—perhaps as the original "ward-wand"—so as not to leave one defenseless against "Dark Arts." Strength, wisdom and self-actualization occur when you can face and control your own dark nature without being controlled by it. It cannot be healthily suppressed as "evil," because in doing so you are rejecting a part of yourself that will only surface later, unbidden and uncontrolled, and usually with unhealthy and/or destructive consequences.

Blackthorne tea—concocted from powdered bark—induces a calming effect, as is a common aspect of many Ffayrie trees when ingested, which may help to slow one's vibration down to "Green World" frequencies. *Straif* produces a purple berry called a "*sloe*," which is a necessary ingredient for "sloe-gin" alcohol. Ink and dye are also made from the sloe berry. Blackthorne is most sacred to *Samhain*, and second to *Beltane*.

THE CEDAR TREE

Elvish-Celtic Name/Letters: Chakris/"Ch"
Druid Guardian: Shavae
Archetypes & Deities: The Sacred Grove, Brighid and
  Arianrhod.
Quadratic Element/Colour: Air/Blue and Green or Pale
  Yellow.
Polarity: Masculine (solar)
Sacred Animal/Bird: Ewe/Goldfinch
Gemstones: Yellow Chrysopraise and the Gold Elf-Stone.
Ffayrie Herb(s): Juniper
Traditional Uses: Incense of purification, space and home
  blessings, calling and summoning spirits.
Divinatory & Energy Expressions: The height of psychic
  awareness and spiritual abilities and knowledge of all times
  and places.

Cedar is not a traditional Ogham tree. Along with the Beech, it was incorporated into the system more recently. The wood carries a long-standing tradition in the Ancient Near East for "binding" spiritual energies, and it is traditionally used in

210

construction of many sacred buildings, including Solomon's Temple. Some "New Age" Ogham revival systems classify the *Chakris* rune as the "the Grove" (*"Koad"*), most likely named after the Ceder Tree's ability to purify the area of the Grove (*Nemeton*). The runic glyph and energy current, however, is more appropriately attributed to the Cedar as an individual tree. In Elven Forest Magick, Cedar wood (and essence) is a purification incense, used in a similar manner as "sage." The smoke may be assist consecrating the Circle of Power, especially if ritual intentions include spirit summoning, ancestral work, or any form of Mesopotamian Neopaganism. It is called the "Tree of Light," sacred to the *Imbolc* and, as an evergreen, to the winter season (*Alban Arthuan*) and "Yule."

THE CHERRY TREE

Elvish-Celtic Name/Letters: Oadha/"Da," "Dh," and "Th"
Druid Guardian: Ambash
Archetypes & Deities: The Wild Hunt, Herne and Pan
Quadratic Element/Colour: Fire/Burnt Umber
Polarity: Masculine (solar)
Sacred Animal/Bird: Bear/Red-Tailed Hawk and the Phoenix.
Gemstones: Obsidian, Sard(onyx), and Crystalline Elf-Stone.
Ffayrie Herb(s): Cherry Fruit & Flowers
Traditional Uses: Communication with animals (brown magick,) kindling sacred fires, declaring and ending wars and woodcarving.
Divinatory & Energy Expressions: Sweetness, joy, delight, passion, love, conflict, competition and attraction.

Cherry is a popular wood for art and woodcraft because of its distinct coloration and ease of workability. Cherry wood is naturally charged to amplify Will, making a good wand for alchemy or transformation magick. The current can be used for intentions that further an existing war, or to end and prevent them. Cherries are symbolic of sexual passion—the power and intensity of the orgasm, and is sacred to *Beltane* and Midsummer (or *Alban Heruin*). *Oadha* is not an official Ogham Tree and yet, it seems incomplete not to consider it in our catalogue.

THE ELDER TREE

Elvish-Celtic Name/Letters: Ruis, Ysgawen/"R"
Druid Guardian: Ruben
Archetypes & Deities: The "Hanged Man," Vulcan, Boann and
   Nikneven.
Quadratic Element/Colour: Earth/Blood Red (*'ruadh'*)
Polarity: Crystalline or Female (lunar)
Month: The 13th Month (*Samhain*)
Other Trees Sharing the Current: Bourtree
Sacred Animal/Bird: Badger and Black Sow/Pheasant or
   Rook (*'rocknat'*).
Gemstones: Bloodstone, Red Jasper and the Crystalline
   Elf-Stone.
Ffayrie Herb(s): Nightshades
Traditional Uses: Exorcism, banishing, regeneration magick,
   elderberry wine and faerie-sight ointment.
Divinatory & Energy Expressions: Self-reflection (examina-
   tion) the end of a cycle, completion, change and crossroads.
NOT TO BE CUT FOR WOOD!
LEAVES MAY BE POISONOUS IF INGESTED!

Some superstitious folklore mistakenly attributes Elder as an "unlucky tree," but Elven-Faerie lore simply says that it is unlucky to cut one down, bring inside or even grow indoors. Those who cut them might fall to misfortune and death—and thus you have been warned now of this Forest Code. The Elder Knowledge is "Crone Knowledge," demanding protection and preservation—just as the elders of a spiritual society and their folk memory require the same. For *Oghamancers*, the *Ruis* current is one of the most difficult to awaken for "Tree Communication."

Elder is not a particularly large tree, reaching only 30 feet in height at maturity—but it is powerful and resilient. Its wood is strong, withstanding many harsh conditions. Elder bark—found as deadwood—may be used to develop a very dark dye and the leaves yield a rich "forest green" hue often used for riding/traveling cloaks. When mixed with alum and salt, the wood produces a deep violet dye.

The Elder Tree is very sacred in Elven-Ffayrie traditions, even apart from its Oghamic associations. According to lore, its sap may be used as to make a "Faerie-Sight" ointment—a head-dress or diadem fashioned from Elder deadwood twigs may grant the same ability to its wearer.

As previously stated, Elder is the "Crone of the Forest," the "Venerable Mother." She is so sacred to the forest people that her wood is protected in Celtic society by a "*geis*," a taboo against removing livewood—even by Wizards. Those who use the wood for furniture and miscellany may be haunted by the spirits of the wood, and fall upon misfortune. [After DeLorean cleared an ancient Elder and Thorn Faerie-forest to make room for a new car manufacturing plant in Ireland, the company disappeared altogether.] "Dark-natured" trees, called "unlucky" by some, actually tend to be the best species/types for ridding a space of negative energy or clearing away illness. Folklore suggests that a tincture Elder Flow'r will purify the bloodstream. Leaves may be infused into a solution that for externally dressing bruises and swellings—or as a pesticide. Elderberries are rich in Vitamin C and are used to make a delicious wine. They may also be boiled down to make a shampoo that will have a darkening effect on the hair.

THE FIR/PINE/ELM CURRENT

Elvish-Celtic Name/Letters: Ailim, Ailm, Elma, Ffynidwydden, Pinwydden/"A"
Druid Guardian: Achab
Archetypes & Deities: Green Man or Horned One, Merlyn, Abban, Am-Mesh (Gaea,) Arianrhod and Sezh
Quadratic Element/Colour: Earth (subordinate: Fire)/Jade Green, Light Blue or Speckled ('*alad*')
Polarity: Masculine (solar) but strongly aligned to the Earth Mother.
Other Trees Sharing the Current: Redwood
Sacred Animal/Bird: Cow, Stag or Deer/Lapwing ('*aidhirdeog*')
Gemstones: Moss Agate and all three Elf-Stones combined or by individual current.

Ffayrie Herb(s): Cowslip
Traditional Uses: Forest Magick, regeneration magick, Earth-
wands, torches and firewood for sacred fires.
Divinatory & Energy Expressions: The Elves, ancient knowledge, primal power, high views or objectivity, penetration,
strength and the eternal Earth-memory.

Trees of the Fir/Pine/Elm current represent the pure primal
Earth current and interconnectivity with all life in the Green
World of Nature—which is the epitome of the "Green Ray."
The Elm is especially distinguished as the "Tree of Elves," and
carries the same *geas* taboo against its use as the Elder. As a
result of the now frequent "Dutch-Elm Disease," the species is
not often planted/cultivated in modern society. Overcoming
this barrier of disease reflects the true strength inherent in
the *Elma* part of the current—and certainly the Elm shares
many spiritual attributes with the Fir/Pine (*Ailm*) part of this
energy, carrying affinities for "invisbility magick," agriculture and protective rites.

Fir and Pine Trees are tall and slender in comparison to the
Elm. They are also evergreens—the Elm is deciduous. The tall-
ness of the Fir, Pine and Redwood varieties of this current
demonstrate their "objectivity" and "high view"—their ability to see clearly and judge fairly. It is able to grow new trees
from old sprouts thought to be dead, making the Fir-Pine an
iconic symbol of endurance, eternal life, and of course, regeneration—which is why it is popularly featured in winter. We
can use modern science to divide this current into hundreds
of sub-species, but all of them represent the "Middle Pillar"
and carry the energy of the "Green Ray" in its clearest form.
Ease of communicating with this current and its frequent appearance in Sylvan Magick makes Fir-Pine a prime candidate
for early novice "tree work" before approaching other primer
trees in the forest catalogue, such as the Birch and Beech. The
Ailim current is useful for growth and fertility rites—for both
the "Green World" and personal needs, as well as rituals and
ceremonies pertaining to marriage and relationships. The Fir
Tree is also a natural source of charcoal, tar and turpentine.

THE FURZE/GORSE TREE

Elvish-Celtic Name/Letters: Ohn, Piswydden/"O"
Druid Guardian: Oise
Archetypes & Deities: The Sun, Lugh and Adraste.
Quadratic Element/Colour: Fire/Yellow and Gold ('odhar')
Polarity: Masculine (solar)
Other Trees Sharing the Current: Spindle ('gwyrthed'), the
    Linden Tree ('ohum') and Basswood or Lime tree.
Sacred Animal/Bird: Rabbits and Bees/Scrat ('odoroscrach')
Gemstones: Periodot and the Gold Elf-Stone.
Ffayrie Herb(s): Heather
Traditional Uses: Honey, food for animals, fertility magick
    and purification.
Divinatory & Energy Expressions: Wisdom, spiritual fulfill-
    ment, optimism, projection (like rays) and protection.

To call this Ogham a "tree" is bit of a stretch, but this hedge plant does grow a woody "bark" and it appears in the "*Cad Goddeu*" prose, describing a "Battle of the Trees." But, not all trees appearing in the verses are documented currents. Some scholars believe the "Battle of the Trees" was a metaphysical skirmish to determine rank and stature of the species composing the later Druidic Ogham Tradition. This low prickly shrub—not typically taller than a Human—is often present for purification rites and/or burned as incense.

To work with this current directly in your locale, you may need to find a suitable substitute tree that shares its energy—such as a *Linden* or *Lime* tree—especially if you intend to construct an *Ohn*-wand. The Gorse-Furze Ogham is also closely related to "Broom" and "*Ohun*," the Linden Tree or Basswood —but Americans without access to a Gorse bush are probably not going to find a species of Linden Tree naturally growing nearby either. "*Ohun*" is sacred to stars and astronomy, but also to magical rites or enchantments regarding love, beauty, glamour and personal attraction. Its metaphysical/ "*ray*" color is orange—as opposed to yellow for Gorse—but it retains a strong alignment with the element of Fire.

THE HAWTHORNE/WHITETHORNE TREE

Elvish-Celtic Name/Letters: Huatha, Huathe, Huath/"H"
Druid Guardian: Huiria
Archetypes & Deities: Judgment, Balance, Olwen and Hurle
Quadratic Element/Colour: Fire/Violet, Purple or "Terrible"
   ('*huath*')
Polarity: Crystalline
Month: April
Sacred Animal/Bird: Dragon or Goat/Night Raven ('*aadaig*')
Gemstones: Amethyst, Tanzanite and any related Elf-Stones.
Ffayrie Herb(s): Primrose Flow'r and May Blossoms.
Traditional Uses: Love and marriage rites, wands and wards
   acquired between April 21 or Beltane (May 1st) and the end
   of May. The wood is not usually taken otherwise or is grown
   locally for magickal protection.
Divinatory & Energy Expressions: Purity, restraint, chastity
   (but also love and marriage proper) and prosperity.

Huatha is another "Faerie tree" with a special "*geis*" (*taboo*) against wood removal—except in this instance there is a ten-day period preceding *Beltane* when wizardwood may be properly obtained. Hawthorn staves, wards and wands all have powerful protective properties, particularly against enchantment, spells or magic from others. This wood is used to make the famous "Whitewand," just as Blackthorne wood is used to make the "Darkstaff." A ceremonial rite should accompany all wizardwood removal as a sign of respect toward the spirits residing within that otherwise may bring misfortune.

Often cut back to form a "haw" or hedge, the hawthorn may enjoy a long time—even by tree standards—and reach dozens of feet in height. It makes a frequent appearance in fantasy or "fairy tales" as a magical barrier or wall around enchanted places or castles. Some Elven lore refers to it as the "Wishing Tree." Hawthorn berries, raw or in tea, may act as a blood thinner with calming properties to assist relieving heart issues. If the oak-resembling leaves are added to the tea, it may help a sore throat—and is sometimes added to grain alcohol for the same result.

THE HAZEL TREE

Elvish-Celtic Name/Letters: Coll, Koll/"C" & "K"
Druid Guardian: Kay (*'Cai'*)
Archetypes & Deities: The High Priestess, Star Mother
  (Goddess,) Llyr and Mannan mac Llyr.
Quadratic Element/Colour: Water/Midnight Blue or
  Brown (*'cron'*)
Polarity: Feminine (lunar)
Month: July
Sacred Animal/Bird: Salmon/Crane
Gemstones: Lapis Lazuli, Sapphire and the Silver Elf-Stone.
Ffayrie Herb(s): Bullrush
Traditional Uses: 'Dowsing Rods,' wands, divination sticks,
  baskets and thatch work. The nuts are used for love spells
  and to make drinks to induce 'Spirit Vision.'
Divinatory & Energy Expressions: Manifestation of creativity,
  divination, intuition, spirit vision and skrying.

The Hazel Tree appears to us as a current of great insight. Its nuts fall into lakes, which feed the "Salmon of Wisdom." The stream of Hazel-Salmon energy is the current or path of "inner knowledge," what is often sought from oracles and in divination: "perfect cosmic knowledge of all things." Hazel rods may be used to form an entire set of divination sticks—when tied together or carried in a "Crane bag" or pouch, actually represent a powerful ancient protective amulet. Forked branches are sometimes used to make "dowsing rods"—tools of energy-testing, for finding water, or tracking "ley lines."

Elven lore suggests the *Koll* current "Hazelnut Tree" is the "Tree of Sacred Knowledge"—a catalyst for learning the true nature of the *Self* and the Universe, and should not be confused with Eden's "Tree of Knowledge," which is metaphoric and related to genetics. The nuts of this tree are edible, and may be powdered to infuse a drink to induce "spirit vision," as well aid relieving colds and sore throat symptoms. The Water Element is strong in the *Koll* current, especially when it is frequently found around water. Its energy is most similar to that found with the Willow Tree and *Saille* current.

THE HEATHER & MISTLETOE CURRENT

Elvish-Celtic Name/Letters: Ur (Heather) & Uchelwydd
  (Mistletoe)/"U" & "W"
Druid Guardian: Uriath
Archetypes & Deities: The Hermit, All Heal, Freya and Grainne
Quadratic Element/Colour: Air/Purple or "Resinous"
  (*'usgdha'*)
Polarity: Crystalline
Sacred Animal/Bird: Bee and Lion/Lark (*'uiseog'*)
Gemstones: The Three Elf-Stones.
Ffayrie Herb(s): Heather and Honeysuckle.
Traditional Uses: Healing, attracting rain and perfume
  (Heather)
Divinatory & Energy Expressions: Healing, clarity, reviving,
  All-Heal and passion.

There are two types of *Ur*-Heather: red and white. The Red type attracts passion and is a symbol of sexual energy and lust. White Heather wards against passion and sex and symbolizes purity and chastity. While the Red Heather is sacred to, and picked, at Midsummer (or *Alban Huruin*), White Heather is aligned to the Spring Equinox (or *Alban Eiler*). As you may have guessed, Heather is one of those Ogham currents that not a tree in the proper sense. In some versions of the Oghamic system, this runic character and current is actually represented by "Mistletoe," which both Elven and Drwyd lore suggest is the most sacred of all herbs. Naturally, both Heather and the Mistletoe current share similar attributes.

Mistletoe lore is mainly the product of Celtic Druid Tradition. It was considered most powerful when found growing on Oak Trees—a rare but very real event (in spite of what modern skeptics have to say on it). It is aligned with the Air Element because it passes itself along tree top canopies and does not actually root in the ground. When cut with the Druid's Sickle, a white linen sheet would be placed below to catch it, being sure that its sacred essence never touched the ground. This herb was then consecrated and later added to all Druidic medicines—lending Mistletoe the folklore name "All Heal."

THE HOLLY TREE

Elvish-Celtic Name/Letters: Tinne, Celynen/"T"
Druid Guardian: Teilmon
Archetypes & Deities: The Golden Chariot, the Holly
    Man/King, Ares and Govannan.
Quadratic Element/Colour: Fire/Dark Gray ('temen')
Polarity: Solar (masculine)
Month: June
Sacred Animal/Bird: Warhorse and Warhound/Starling
    ('truith')
Gemstones: Ruby and the Gold Elf-Stone.
Ffayrie Herb(s): Monk's Hood (Aconite)
Traditional Uses: Spear making (combat and protection),
    Midwinter/Yule, chariot wheels, charcoal and grown to
    bring good fortune and ward off evil.
Divinatory & Energy Expressions: Movement, vigor, 'Best in
    Fight,' holiness and sacredness, the Wheel of the Year (Cor
    Anar), and Nature's cycles.

Many modern day Christmas customs emerged from preexisting Elven "Drwyddon," the ancient national religion of Celtic people once dominating the British Isles, Ireland as previously, the European mainland. Holly is a small evergreen and may have been the first "Yuletide Tree." All evergreens are actually sacred to winter and its seasonal festivals. Red Holly berries hang like ball-ornaments providing an iconic red and green theme. The three primary herbs of the Yule festival match three Oghams directly—Holly, Ivy and Mistletoe.

Lore suggests to grow a Holly Tree in your grove or garden to attract positive currents and ward against negative energy. Holly-wood burns well when still green (freshly cut) but it is taboo and against the Faerie Code to do so. Burning any pre-dried wood, particularly a species held so sacred to Elven-Ffayrie, is blasphemous. Holly wands may summon lightning, suggesting fire alignment as is the relationship with war and allegorical conflict of ongoing struggle for annual supremacy between the Oak King, ruler of the "light half of the year" and the Holly King who is keeper of the "dark half of the year."

The *Tinne* current shares many of the same energetic attributes as the Oak Tree—and with good reason. The only major frequency difference (aside from obvious size) is that Holly is an evergreen and Oak is not. At Midsummer (*Alban Heruin*) the Oak King loses the battle over the Sun's control to the Holly King, who yields it back to the Oak King on *Holly Day*, or approximately Yule. This is metaphorical, of course, and the lore is used to describe or explain the properties and polarity of natural forces that ebb and flow at varying times of year. [Holly leaves may also be used to brew detoxifying teas.]

THE IVY CURRENT

Elvish-Celtic Name/Letters: Gort, Uruin, Eiddew/"G"
Druid Guardian: Gahth
Archetypes & Deities: Justice, the Golden Spiral, Swan
  Maidens, Cuchulain, Cernunnos/Kerununnos and Orion.
Quadratic Element/Colour: Earth/Sky Blue (*'gorm'*)
Polarity: Feminine (lunar)
Month: September
Sacred Animal/Bird: Boar/Swan (*'geis'*)
Gemstones: Chryso(beryl) and any related Elf-Stones.
Ffayrie Herb(s): Lichen and Moss.
Traditional Uses: Exorcism rites and used to make the spiral
  that wraps around natural wands.
Divinatory & Energy Expressions: Cooperation, healing and
  the 'inner spiral.'

In the helix-style growth pattern of the Ivy, ancient Elves and Druids observed and recorded the "Golden Spiral"—else, the energetic serpent-entwining of DNA structures and life patterns. While not generally classified as a tree, Ivy possesses an ability to develop bark and grow strong when allowed to. *Gort* unifies the spiral with the wand—as a spiral (carved or metal) is sometimes wrapped around the length of a wand—or for a true herbalist, this might be the Ivy itself. Spirals represent "active creation," so incorporating it with any magical tool (or object) provides an additional "active" quality. It is sacred to the Autumn Equinox (or *Alban Elved*).

THE MAPLE TREE

Elvish-Celtic Name/Letters: Shorin/"Sh"
Druid Guardian: Mabon
Archetypes & Deities: Ymir the Giant (Norse) and Mabon
  (Celtic)
Quadratic Element/Colour: Fire/Fiery Red, Orange or Amber
Polarity: Masculine (solar)
Sacred Animal/Bird: Fox/Horned Owl
Gemstones: Gold Elf-Stone, particularly the Tiger's Eye.
Traditional Uses: Spells of binding, strength and unity of the
  family, maple syrup and red and orange-ray magick.
Divinatory & Energy Expressions: Energy (vibrancy), strength,
  good fortune, family life and transformation.

The Maple Tree is not a traditional Ogham character. In fact, it is not mentioned anywhere in "Celtic" Ogham lore. Maple is included here because North American and Canadian practitioners *do* share access to this current, and it is a powerful one. Ancient Druids of Britain and Ireland, where the Celtic Ogham was developed and refined, did not necessarily encounter the *Shorin* current, and little lore is ascribed to it. Its leaf structure is iconic—even gracing the Canadian national flag—visibly displaying the "Sign of Elves" and "Rays." The leaves also transition through all hues of green-to-red in the Autumn, near the "Equinox" (or *Alban Elved*). Maples may be used in magic to connect with other similar tree currents with types/species that are not accessible to the practitioner.

THE OAK TREE

Elvish-Celtic Name/Letters: Duir, Dwyr, Derwen, Dar/"D"
Druid Guardian: Daivaith or Dagda
Archetypes & Deities: The Emperor, the Oak King, the
  'Flaming Door,' Obraash, Lugh, Dagda, W'Odin, Thor and
  Helios (the Sun)
Quadratic Element/Colour: Fire/Gold and Black ('*dub*')
Polarity: Masculine (solar)
Month: May
Other Trees Sharing the Current: Hickory (and also Holly)

Sacred Animal/Bird: White Mare, Lion/Tiger, Salamander and Serpent or Adder/Peacock or Wren (*'druin'*)

Gemstones: Yellow Topaz, Amber (petrified tree sap), gold and the Gold Elf-Stone.

Ffayrie Herb(s): Acorn (*'uri'* or *'uru'*) and Mistletoe.

Traditional Uses: Protection for homes and doors, Elven-Druid magick, fertility magick and timber—especially for doors, bats, sticks and clubs. The 'gall' can be used as a powerful *"Naddred"* talisman called the "Adder's Egg," "Druid's Egg," or "Druid's Gem."

Divinatory & Energy Expressions: Strength, leadership, material gain, longevity (endurance), the doorway to mysteries, ineffable/absolute truth and solid protection.

The oak-acorn is a fiery seed of life—perhaps one of the most powerful elf-amulets found in Nature. Oak Groves—collectives of trees—have a tendency to grow because, as is said, the "acorn never falls far from the tree." Elven and Druid lore suggests that eating the acorns—or using oak flour—may aid in understanding "Divine" (Cosmic) and ineffable truth via inspiration (or *'gnosis'*), as similar to the *Hazelnut*. The Oak is a very "busy" tree with vast long-standing traditions of mystic lore—and it may very well be the most sacred tree on Earth.

Deep within the Greenwood forest stands a tall and gnarled Oak Tree branching out wide and drawing you nearer and nearer to the mysteries of the secret grove—the repository for all knowledge in Nature. There lies the "great door" leading to the inner mysteries of true initiation.

True magick is what brings us "Absolute Truth" and contributes to our evolution on the "Path of Ascension." It is often the Oak that is used to represent highest degrees or levels of study in Elvish Schools of Druidism, emphasizing the path to self-realization and absolute awareness. While it embodies the final most notable lesson for Oghamancers in their advancement to the *"Drywydd"* degree, it is listed seventh in the Oghamic alphabet, perhaps demonstrating a hidden awareness and appreciation of the original "sevenfold" system.

There is an old saying about how *Dwyr* is a long-lived tree: "300 years to grow, 300 years to mature, 300 years to die." In that time they will commonly acquire what are known as "galls." These spherical growths are sometimes the result of insect hives occupying beneath the trunk surface until their larvae are mature.

The "Grandfather of the Forest," guards the Oak door of May at *Beltane* and clearly aligned to the Fire Element. In fact, the *Duir* tree current carries such an affinity with fire that it has a tendency to manifest the element as lightning—which seems to strike Oaks more than any other species observed, almost as if they are "calling it down." Obviously the species defends its attributes of "strength and endurance" by withstanding such energy, resulting often in a much more gnarled, tangled and "interesting" looking tree.

A fiery energetic affinity between Duir and lightning makes the Golden Oakwand a highly sought after tool for Nature-oriented magic—adding to our arsenal of wand-lore:

TRADITIONAL ELVEN-FAERIE WANDS

Silverwand = Apple wizardwood
Wizardwand = Ash or Rowen wizardwood
Darkwand/staff = Blackthorne wizardwood
Whitewand = Hawthorn wizardwood
Goldwand = Oak wizardwood
Witchwand = Willow or Rowen wizardwood

Oak wood is a common material for ceremonial blade handles (corresponding with its fire alignment)—and another tree that closely shares the *Duir* energy current, though perhaps more passively, is the Hickory Tree or "*axara*." Its energetic attributes are similar to Oak, but applying to more worldly, mundane or tangible aspects—such as the acquisition of material gain, good fortune and abundance.

THE REED & BROOM CURRENT

Elvish-Celtic Name/Letters: Ngetal, Corsen, Erun/"Ng"
Druid Guardian: Noimahr
Archetypes & Deities: The Wheel of Fortune, Olbaal,
   Gwydion, Morgana and Morrighan.
Quadratic Element/Colour: Air (subordinate: Water) /
   Grass Green ('nglas')
Polarity: Feminine (lunar)
Month: October
Sacred Animal/Bird: Dog and Stag/Goose ('ngeigh')
Gemstones: Aquamarine and appropriate Elf-Stones.
Ffayrie Herb(s): Reed and Broom
Traditional Uses: Fertility and Love Magick, writing pens,
   brooms and pipes.
Divinatory & Energy Expressions: Effort, direct action,
   application and harmony.

Broom is a specific kind of tall wetland grass known as reed. It literally grows out of the water—and may even form an outer bark layer—making it the "Water Tree" of Elven Forest Tradition, though other systems often reserve this title for the Willow tree. But, while Reed is derived from the water, it is aligned with the Air element with a long-standing affinity for communication, writing and knowledge that originates in the *Ancient Near East*, specifically *Babylon*—where use of the "Reed stylus" was perfected for refined cuneiform script.

Reed represents a connection between the perceived "inner" and "outer" worlds and the harmonic balance of those energies. The Ngetal Ogham current is a subtle energy, slowly working its magic and enchantment from a point of stillness, with small ripples. Although aligned to air, the natural affinity between Reed/Broom and water makes it an appropriate addition to any rites aligned to an "aquatic" nature, or the consecration of water-elemental tools. The Broom type is actually named for its use in broom manufacture. In a previous lesson-chapter we discussed how brooms were used to sweep out and clear ritual space. Ironically, the Broom—both in its plant form or as an object—is sacred to *Samhain*.

THE ROWEN TREE

Elvish-Celtic Name/Letters: Luis, Ceridinen/"L"
Druid Guardian: Loth
Archetypes & Deities: The Star, Epona and Macha.
Quadratic Element/Colour: Air/Red or Gray ('liath')
Polarity: Feminine (lunar)
Month: November
Other Names for this Current: Mountain Ash
Sacred Animal/Bird: Bear and Unicorn/Duck ('lachu')
Gemstones: Smokey Quartz, Diamond, Silver and appropriate Elf-Stones.
Ffayrie Herb(s): Yarrow
Traditional Uses: Personal empowerment, protection against enchantment, Astral (Spirit World) and Otherworld work.
Divinatory & Energy Expressions: Awareness, insight, empowerment, self-control, evanescence, protection, nurturing and motherhood.

The Rowen Tree produces berries, which, much like the fruit from the Apple Tree, contain the five-pointed pentagram—the traditional sign of Nature's Elemental forces or the "Gaea system." The Ogham (talisman) offers protection while traveling and from the enchantments of others. For this reason, it is commonly used for walking sticks or staves and its protective properties make it beneficial to plant a Rowen Tree at the entrance of your home, property and/or Sacred Grove. *Luis* is called the "Quickening Tree" because of its active magickal power—combining active Air Elemental qualities with the feminine current. This Air of Moon correspondence makes its wizardwood a prime choice for a traditional "witches wand."

The leaves and berries, once dried, may be used as incense. Don't forget to add a pinch of Mistletoe. Burning this may call forth energies of the ancestral realm and Otherworld—as well as the "Nature Spirits." The Rowen Tree is represented by the Unicorn, the epitome of all that is beautiful and enchanting, also representing a link between worlds. The Unicorn current tempers that of the Dragon. These energies should always be used in balance of one another. It is easy to fall into the trap of over-analyzing and over-thinking and essentially all of the untempered qualities of the unbalanced "Dragonmind." It is most sacred to the annual beginning of winter (*Samhain*).

THE VINE CURRENT

Elvish-Celtic Name/Letters: Muin, Gwynwydden/"M"
Druid Guardian: Muriath
Archetypes & Deities: "The Lovers."
Quadratic Element/Colour: Water/Variegated (*'mbracht'*)
Polarity: Feminine (lunar)
Month: August
Sacred Animal/Bird: Scorpion and Lizard/Titmouse (*'mintan'*)
Gemstones: Aquamarine and appropriate Elf-Stones.
Ffayrie Herb(s): Neckweede and Blackberry/Raspberry.
Traditional Uses: Grapes, wine, meditation and revealing
   truths.
Divinatory & Energy Expressions: Inner-development, self-
   realization and comprehension.

The Vine, though not necessarily a tree, is ranked among the Ogham currents because it may develop a hardened outer bark. Its sacred annual threshold time is the harvest, specific-ally the Autumn Equinox (or *Alban Elved*). It has been used to make grape-wine for thousands of years. A tradition of wine used to "reveal truths" is derived from its ability to gain information gathered via loss of inhibitions. *Muin* represents hidden, just-below-the-surface realizations—sometimes only brought to the surface when dis-inhibited—that cannot be healthily suppressed if we are to break through to the next steps of our progression. With an ability to scale walls, the Vine truly knows no boundaries.

THE WILLOW TREE

Elvish-Celtic Name/Letters: Saille. Awn, Helyg, Helygen/"S"
Druid Guardian: Saliath
Archetypes & Deities: The Moon, The Silver Huntress, Diana of
   the Forest and Arianrhod.

Quadratic Element/Colour: Water/Bright, Opalescent or
   "Fine" (*'sodath'*)
Polarity: Feminine (lunar)
Month: February
Sacred Animal/Bird: Hare and Cat/Owl and Hawk (*'seg'*)
Gemstones: Opal, Pearl and the Silver Elf-Stone.
Ffayrie Herb(s): Moonwort
Traditional Uses: Lunar magick, feminine magick, fertility
   magick, banishing depression, baskets and wicker-work.
Divinatory & Energy Expressions: Beauty, enchantment,
   rhythms, cycles, secrets and an indication that emotional
   healing is necessary.

Willow Trees possess a high affinity for water: it drinks a lot
of it, soaking up as much as possible to develop a fast growing
trunk structure. A combination of water and the moon "Rays"
contribute energetic qualities of intuition, emotion, beauty
and enchantment. *Saille* represents the archetypal lunar-wa-
ter current resonating with the "Moon Goddess" or "Triple
Moon Goddess," aligned to feminine rhythms and cycles, and
not only in relation to monthly rhythms, but the greater life-
cycle of "maiden-mother-crone." The Willow Tree is metaphorically the "Grandmother of the Forest"—the one you can
tell anything to because she has already been there herself.

A Willow-wand may be used for lunar rites and/or water-ori-
ented magick relating to feminine needs, as well as dreams
and the old priestess tradition of "drawing down the moon."
Saille is a healing Ogham, mostly on an emotional level. By
linking/communing personally with Willows, you may open
channels necessary to sort, retain and release past emotional
pains and carried energy.

THE YEW TREE

Elvish-Celtic Name/Letters: Ioho, Ywen/"I," "J" & "Y"
Druid Guardian: Iachim
Archetypes & Deities: "Death," Arawn, Arianrhod, Dagda Mor
   and Hermes.

Quadratic Element/Colour: Earth/Dark Green or Very White ('*irfind*')
Polarity: Crystalline
Sacred Animal/Bird: Spider/Eagle or Eaglet ('*illait*')
Gemstones: Emerald and the Three Elf-Stones.
Ffayrie Herb(s): Bryony
Traditional Uses: Bows, poison and poisoned weapons.
Divinatory & Energy Expressions: Completion, changes, renewal, transformation forthcoming rebirth, the next step, the life and death cycle and communication.

Yew Trees typically stand at the end of the Ogham journey—regardless of which "alphabet" is used to catalogue it. *Ioho* is the sign of completion, in a manner much deeper than that felt with the *Ruis*-Elder Tree current. It is not so much an "ending," as much as it represents the gateway to the Other-world—or that is to say the absolute promise that there is life after death. *Ioho*-Yew shares an energetic frequency with a select few other Ogham Trees in the ability to (re)generate new trees from its "*layrs*."

At the end of the magical forest journey, the Yew Tree reminds us that it cannot be an ending—because nothing ends. By riding this energetic current toward Ascension, we are reborn and transformed into a new life. After completing the "Initiation of the Forest," the Initiate or "Oghamancer" may rightfully call themselves a "Sylvan Wizard" with the ability to awaken the woods and be known to all "Nature-spirits" as a forest-friend or "elf-friend."

The journey most certainly does not stop here. Mastery requires more than a few hours book-reading and a handful of visits into the forest. A perfection of the arts presented within the text of the *Elvenomicon* will require many years of true and faithful dedication, observation, personal reflection, extensive practice and holistic immersion...

...into Secret Traditions of the Elves and Faerie!

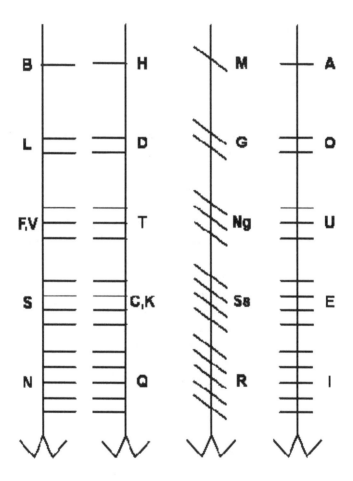

TRADITIONAL OGHAM SCALES

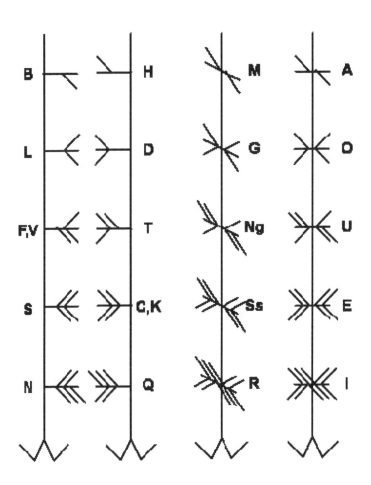

PROGRESSIVE-BRANCH OGHAM VARIATION

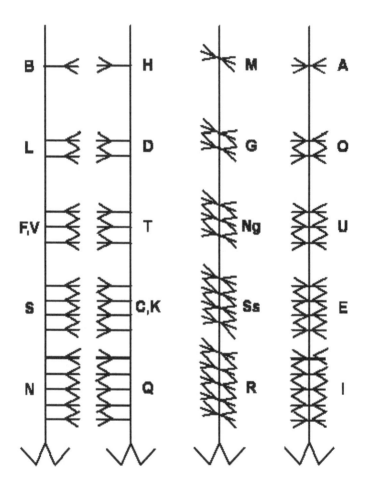

ELF-SIGN OGHAM VARIATION

APPENDIX

—Appendix I—
De'ea Canayen Istari Qlandra
| Cor Anar |

<u>DYONN—"The Dark Season"</u>

Narbeleth: Winterfilthe (October)
    2nd – Alardenna: Festival of Elven-Ffayrie
        Spirit Guides
    31st – Samhain: Night of Ancestors

Yestare: Newmoth (November)
    1st – New Year's Day
    11th – Lunatasidhe: Eve of Faerie

Rithon: Foreyule (December)
    21st – Alban Arthuann: Winter Solstice
    24th – Holly Day
    25th – Oak Day

Narvinye: Afteryule (January)
    18th – Danuhal: Festival of D'Anu

<u>FYONN—"The Light Season"</u>

Ninui: Solmath (February)
    1st – Imbolc: Festival of Brighid
    15th – Hal Pan: Festival of Pan

Sulime: Rethe (March)
    21st – Alban Eiler: Spring Equinox

Virith: Astron (April)
    7th – Yn Offeryn: Day of Offering to the Sidhe
    23rd – Hal Kernunnos: Festival of the Green Man

Lothron: Thrimidge (May)
    1st – Beltane: The Fires of Bel

REUDH—"The Red Season"

Norui: Forlithe (June)
>   21st – Lithe or Alban Heruin: Summer Solstice
>   23rd – Elnassadh: Wedding Festival of the King
>   and Queen of Faerie

Cerveth: Afterlithe (July)

Uruime: Wedmath (August)
>   1st – Lughnassadh: Wedding Festival of Lugh

Iavaneth: Holymath (September)
>   21st – Alban Elved: Autumn Equinox

[*Note*: Though the above calendar is partitioned to correspond with months that the modern reader is most familiar with, a consensus of ancient lore suggests that when plotted on a fixed calendar, transition from one month to another occurs on the 21st and not the 30th or 31st. Some versions are aligned specifically with lunar phases, beginning a month with the "new moon" or even the "sixth day of the moon."]

—Appendix II—
Elven-Faerie Dictionary
| Words of Light |

ABRAHOR: (A) The woodland realm of the Forest; the Wood Elves.

ABROREN: (A) Elves of Abrahor, the Forest and woodlands.

AETHYR: The substance of the Astral World; a sub-atomic field, which light exists on.

AFTERLITHE: July

AFTERYULE: January

AICME: (G) A set of five Ogham letters. There are four such sets in the original Oghamic system.

AINE: (G) The Queen of Faerie

AIRE: (Q) Holy or divine.

AIRBE DRUAD: (G) A mystical force field, esp. an impassable barrier or natural-appearing hedge.

AISILING: (G) A mystic vision or dream.

AIYA: (Q) Holy One, but not in reference to God.

AKASHA: The Fifth Element, spiritual fire that is embodied by the union of all Elements; quintessence at the core of all existence.

ALARDAN: (M) A festival or gathering of Elven-Ffayrie.

ALB: A prefix or root often referring to Elves; literally "Light."

ALBAN ARTHUAN: (G) Yule or Winter Solstice.

ALBAN EILER: (G) The Spring Equinox

ALBAN ELVED: (G) The Autumn Equinox

ALBANIA: "Land of Elves"

ALBAN HERUIN: (G) The Summer Solstice

ALBANY: "Land of Elves"

ALBION: "Land of Elves"

ALBREDA: (G) Wisdom of the Elves

ALDARON: (Q) Lord or spirit of the trees and forest.

ALDEA: (Q) Treeday, Trewsday or Tuesday.

ALFERIC: (SY) That which is Elvish Magick or Druidic Forest Magick.

ALFI: (G) Elf Power

ALFRED: (G) also *alfredo*; Elf-wise, both Elvish counsel and council.

ALGER: (G) Spear
ALTA: (Q) A brightness, bright light or light.
ALURED: (G) Elven council or court.
ALVA: Lugh's sister-in-law in Celtic Mythology.
ALVAR: (G) An army of Elves.
AMA: (SH) Blood
ANAIL: (G) Breath
ANAR: (Q) Sun
ANDUNE: (Q) West
ANG: (SY) The element and metal of Iron.
ANGA: (Q) The element and metal of Iron.
ANNUN: (SY) West
AOIFE: (G) The Queen of Faerie
ARDA: (Q) A plane or region.
ARTH: (S) A plane or region.
ARVA: (A) Flames, esp. the energy current of the Fire Element.
ASHA: (SH) Spirit or soul.
AUBREY: (G) Elf King
AURE: (Q) Daylight or sunlight.
AVERY: (G) Elf King
BA'ISTEACH: (G) Rain, esp. the energy current of the Water Element.
BAK'YAH: (A) A magick word used for counter-spells.
BARDD GWEWLL: (G) A particular shade of azure sky blue; dye used
    for Bardic cloaks.
BEAN-SIDHE: (G) A mourning spirit often appearing around the time
    of one's death.
BLEEDING: A part of *foison*; the inside of foodstuff is removed while it
    looks the same.
BRICHT: (G) Spellcraft or magick requiring a vocal incantation.
BROWNIES: Earth Elementals; the Elven-Ffayrie chefs.
BWCA: (G) also *bwbachod*, meaning Brownies.
CAERLLEN: (G) Ffayrie-mounds; literally "Ghost Hills."
CALAN: (S) Daytime or sunlight.
CERMIE: (Q) July
CERTA: (Q) A glyph, character or rune; pl. *Certar*.
CERVETH: (SY) July
CHOR'N: (A) A dark or black auric energy, esp. putrescence.
CIR: (SY) Circle or ring, esp. a stone circle.
CLOCH: (G) Stone
COIMIMEADH: (G) A Co-walker or Elemental being who appears to be
    Human.
COIRC: (G) A sacred vessel, esp. the ceremonial cauldron.

COOMLEAN: (G) An Elvensteed or horse.

COOSHIE: (G) An Elven Hound or familiar.

COR: (SY) Circle or ring, esp. a stone circle.

COR ANAR: (Q) The Solar Wheel of the Year

COROLLAIRE: (Q) Ffayrie-hill or "*howe,*" literally "green-mound."

CRANNCHUR: (G) The divinatory art of casting sticks, esp. Ogham.

DAETENIN: (A) Dark or unseelie, esp. dragons.

DAEVAUN: (A) Woodlands or forest.

DAN: (SH) South

DEEA CANAYEN: (F) Calendar

DELPHINE: (T) Elven

DESH-IRIAL: (T) Sister [proper]

DESH-KETAI: (T) Father [proper]

DESH-MIEVE: (T) Mother [proper]

DESH-MIRIAI: (T) Guardian of the Home

DESH-NERAIN: (T) Brother [proper]

DESHTAI: (A) To be honorable in following one's destiny.

DES'TAI: (TU) To be honorable in following one's destiny.

DEVIR: (A) To divert from the right path or follow the wrong destiny.

DICETIA: (G) A charm or spell.

-DOR: (Q) Suffix indicating a world or plane.

DORAI: (TU) Loyalty and duty felt towards loved-ones.

DRAKYR: (A) Dragon

DRAVIDIANS: The Tuatha D'Anu and later Sidhe.

DRYS: (GR) An Oak Tree, spirit of the tree or wren (bird).

DUATH: (S) Darkness

DUILE: (G) The Faerie Elements or Spirit of the Elements.

EA: (Q) also I'ria, the Source of All Being and Creation.

EAR: (Q) Sea

EASA'AHAE: (L) Peace

EDAPHIC: (SY) A stewardship lifestyle of tending the soil/Earth, esp. Elven/Sylvanus Tradition.

EKAHAL: (SH) Elf Wizard

EKAHUA: (SH) A female spiritual advisor or Ffayrie Enchantress.

EKAHUEI: (SH) A male spirtual advisor or Elf Wizard.

EL: (A) Prefix or root indicating Elf or star.

ELA: (SH) Stars

ELAITH: (A) The spirit of a being or Star-Essence.

ELAITH TOR: (A) "Tower of Spirit" or the auric-chakra personal energetic system of a being.

ELAN: (A) An Elf, literally Child of the Stars.

ELANDRA: (A) Elven

ELAYNOR: (A) also *elynor* and *elinor*, literally Star Dragon.
ELEN: (TU) Elf-Star or Elf-Friend.
ELENARI: (TU) Elf-Friend or Saturday.
ELENYA: (Q) Saturn-day or Saturday.
ELESSAR: (Q) Elf Stone
ELF-DAY: Tuesday
ELF LEAF: Rosemary
ELFRIDA: (G) Elf Power
ELFSHOT: In reference to when a mortal is struck by an Elf Arrow.
ELGAR: (G) Noble Elf, High Elf, or Danubian Sidhe.
ELIA: (A) The spirit or soul of a being.
ELM: Tree of Elves
ELOR'EL: (A) Moon
ELOYA: (A) Star-Heart
ELPHAME: Elfland, literally Protected-by-Elves.
ELVEN HISTORIANS: see remembrancers.
ELVEN HOLOCAUST: The Dark Ages, a period from 751 AD-1736 AD.
ELVIN: (G) Elf-born or Elf-Friend.
ELVIRA: (G) Elf-Friend
ELWIN: (G) Elf-Friend
ENDOR: (Q) The Middle Earth world of Humans or Physical Plane.
ENNOR: (SY) Derived from endor, meaning world of Humans.
-ENYA: (Q) Suffix meaning day or light.
ERA: (T) The Earth, land or Middleworld.
ERLINA: (G) An Elf, Sylph or Ffayrie.
ERU: (Q) The Source of All Being and Creation.
ERUSEN: (Q) Children of the Stars or Tuatha D'Anu.
ESHE: (SH) Elf-Friend
ESTEVAR: (A) Tonight, this night, evening or nighttime.
EVALA: (SH) Cloak
FAERIELIGHT: A folklore name for the Jack-O'-Lantern.
FAERIE RING: A naturally occurring circle or ring of high grass or
    mushrooms.
FANA: (IT) Goddess of the Woodlands
FANA: (Q) An invisible veil, esp. veil between worlds and dimensions.
FAUNI: (IT) Female equivalent of *silvani*.
FAUNUS: (IT) God of the Woodlands
FAY: (FR) Ffayrie
FEAS: (SE) Love towards a material object, e.g. "I love books."
FELONIA: (A) Sacred
FELN: (SE) Love towards magick and the Elven Way.
FER-DAN: (G) Bardic Druid scouts, messengers and news collectors.

FER-LAOI: (G) Bardic Druid metaphysical poets and musicians.

FEW: (G) An Ogham runic character

FEWS: (G) Ogham runic characters, plural.

FFERYLLT: (G) *Pheryllt.*

FIDTH: (G) An Ogham runic character.

FIN: (SH) Air Element

FIRIMAR: (Q) Mortal humans

FOISON: (SY) A game where Otherworld beings steal Human food.

FOLLETTI: (IT) Female woodland spirits, a lineage from the Etruscan Kingdom (Northern Italy).

FORELITHE: June

FUTHARK: (SC) The Norse Elven Runic alphabet.

F'YONN: (SY) Rebirth season, spring, literally the "Light Season."

GAEL: (A) Stone or gem.

GAETH: (G) Wind, esp. the energy current of the Wind Element.

GALADHAD: (Q) Trees, plural.

GALDROSTAFFYR: (SC) Using the Norse Runes in manners indicative of Ogham Magick.

GE'A: (A) also Gaea and Gaia, Spirit of the Earth.

GEIRT COIMITHETH: (G) see just-halver.

GEIS: (G) A mystical restriction or prohibition with costly physical and/or spiritual consequences if ignored.

GILLACHT: (G) Puberty

GLAM DIAN: (G) The most severe Druidic curse: excommunication.

GLAMOUR: A mystical enchantment where the physical nature/ reality is altered.

GLAMOURY: An Irish-Celtic revival of Elvish Otherworld Tradition.

GLORA: (SH) Sun

GNOMA: (GR) The genetic family of the Gnomes, Kobold and Dwarves.

GNOME: Guardians of the Earth, Keepers of the Soil, esp. rocks and gems.

GRAIN: (G) Sun

GREENWORLD: The physical world region that is synchronous with Elemental Realms.

GWAI: (AL) Sky

GWAITH: (Q) Shadow

HAL: (SH) Festival day

HARAD: (SY)

HERMETIC MAGICK: An underground Greco-Egyptian mystical tradition.

HISSIE: (Q) Mist

HITH: (S) Mist

HOLED STONE: also Holey Stone, the Druidic Birth Stone or tool of the Earth Element.

HRIVE: (Q) Winter

HWESTA: (Q) Breeze

HYARMEN: (Q) South

IMBAS: (G) Divine inspiration or gnosis; literally "Fire-in-the-Head."

I'RIA: (T) The Source of All Being and Creation

ISH'MAEN: (F) Unseelie Wizard [slur]

ISILYA: (Q) Moon-day or Monday.

ISTAR: (Q) Wizard; pl. *istari*.

JANDA'HAI: (D) Mortal Humans, literally Round-Ears.

JUST-HALVER: also *Geirt Coimitheth*; a spirit feeding on the essence of what one eats.

KALEANAE: (L) Watcher, esp. of the Universe or a plane/dimension.

KALOREN: (A) The bright path or right way.

KANITH: (A) Lunar energies

KEMEN: (Q) Earth Element

KEROTH: (TU) Brother

KH'DEK: (Q) Ice or glass, esp. when used as a magick tool or catalyst.

KIERAN: (TU) Sister

KIRK: (G) from Scottish *Circ*; meaning a sacred sanctuary, esp. a stone circle.

KOBOLD: also kobolda gnoma, the blacksmiths of the Elven-Ffayrie.

KUSANAR: (T) Twilight

KYELA: (SY) Love

LA'AER: (A) Air Element

LAER: (S) Summer

LAIRE: (Q) Summer

LANDS ABOVE: The physical world or world of Humans.

LANDS BENEATH: The Underworld or Otherworld of the Sidhe.

LASSE: (Q) Leaf; pl. *Lassi*.

LAVENDER: Elf Herb

LEOLLYN: (G) The Sun Father, esp. Llew/Lugh of Celtic Mythology.

LES: (G) An herbal medicine bag or "juju pouch" carried by Shamans.

LIA FAIL: (G) Stone of Fate brought to Tara in Ireland from the Otherworld.

LINCHETTO: (IT) Night Elves, a lineage from the Etruscan Kingdom.

LIVEWOOD: *Wizardwood*.

LOR: (A) To shine or shine bright, esp. in relation to knowledge.

LOTESSE: (Q) May

LOTHRON: (S) May

LUMBULE: (Q) Darkness

LUVA: (W) Elvish bow

MACDACHT: (G) Prepubescent childhood

METONIC CYCLE: Great Year, period of 19 years.

MIDDLE EARTH: The physical world of Humans.

MILANA: (T) Forest

MIR: (SY) Jewel

MYHIDR: (AL) A lover who is a Life-Mate but not necessarily a Soul-Mate.

NAIDENACHT: (G) Infancy

NAN: (SY) Valley

NARBELETH: (SY) October

NARIE: (Q) June

NARQUELIE: (Q) October

NARWA: (SY) To remember, like an awakening.

NARWAIN: (S) January

NARVINYE: (Q) January

NEL: (G) Cloud

NIA: (A) Master

NIEVE: (T) A lover who is not a Life-Mate.

NINASTRE: (T) Master of the Woods, esp. Kernunnos or Dagda.

NINUI: (S) February

NISHTAI: (A) Not to walk or follow one's destiny.

NISSA: (SC) A Sylph or Sylve, esp. female.

NOLDO: (Q) High Elf or Danubian Sidhe.

NOLE: (Q) Lore, folklore or knowledge.

NORUI: (S) June

O'FORFAMAR: (SY) Leadership

ONLAY: (G) A charm or spell fixed on a home or specific area.

OR'MN: (A) The Surface World, Middle Earth or world of Humans.

ORNE: (Q) Tree

ORTH: (G) A charm or spell.

OSTARA: (G) also Ostre, Ostera and Easter, *Alban Eiler*, Spring Equinox.

PARMA: (Q) Book

PEHLORA: (A) Water

PERIZADA: (G) Ffayrie-born or Fey-touched.

PHERYLLT: (G) A race of pre-Druidic Dragon priest-kings in Keltia.

PIXIE: (G) Usually defined as female winged sprytes; actually derived from the Scottish Pict-Sidhe.

RAELL: (A) Refuse or trash, esp. energy/habits one wishes to be rid of.

QUENDI: (G) The first-born Elves of Aeurope.

QUENYA: (G) The original language of the *Quendi*; depeicted as "(Q)."

RADE: Times of mass transition of the Seelie Court.

RE'AITAI: (G) Star, esp. the energy current of the SkyFire Element.

RECOGNITION: The innate ability for sensitive Elven-Ffayrie to recognize other ones.

REMEMBRANCERS: Elvish historians and loremasters.

RETHE: (G) March

ROCH: (A) Elven-steed or horse.

ROMEN: (Q) East

SAETH: (SY) Cloak, esp. of invisibility.

SAELR'IR: (A) Spirit of the Forest

SALAMANDER: also *draco salambe*; Elemental Fire-Drakes.

SALAMBE: (GR) The genetic family of Salamanders and Fire-Drakes.

SALAN: (G) Salt, esp. the energy current of the Earth Element.

SATURDAY: Fey-Day

SEAN-SGEAL: (G) A folktale or faery-tale.

SEELIE COURT: The Blessed Court, esp. Elven-Ffayrie of the Sidhe.

SELEK'TAR: (F) A spiritual advisor, usually female.

SENACHIES: (G) Bardic Druids specializing in the Ogham, esp. historical scribes and musicians.

SENDACHT: (G) Old age

SHADOWLAND: also Summerland, realm of the ancestral spirits of the past.

SHAMROCK: also *Trefoil* and *Trifolium*; the four-leaved clover.

SHEA: (G) Fey-touched and/or genius/brilliant.

SHELTIETH: (T) Unseelie, unblessed or dark in polarity.

SHOL: (SY) Elven Breath, like the Dragon's Breath, esp. healing energy.

SIANA: (SY) Yes

SIDHE: (G) pronounced "*shee*"; the High Elves of the Seelie Court, esp. Danubians.

SIDTH-BHRUACH: Silverwand or Ffayriewand, esp. made from the Apple Tree.

SIER: (A) Fire Element

SILPHE: (GR) The genetic family of Sylphs and Sylves, esp. the Sylvanus Folk.

SILVANI: (IT) also Sylvani, a masculine spirit of the woods, esp. an Elf.

SIMULACRA: An imitation or substitute, esp. Human shells in which Elf spirits reside.

SLATAN DRUIEACHD: (G) A Druid's staff.

SLAUGHMAITH: (G) The Good People, esp. the Sidth or Sidhe.

SOLMATH: (G) February

STEMLINE: The straight or middle line used to align Ogham notches.

STONE OF SCONE: Lia Fail or Stone of Destiny.

SYLVA: A treatise on trees or Elvish Forest Magick and wood use.
SYNDARIN: also Sinddarin, a Sylvan Language of the Wood Elves, depicted by Tolkein and designated "(S)" in this catalogue.
SULIME: (Q) March
TAGHAIRM: (G) Necromancy; summoning (talking to) the dead.
TAURE: (SY) also taur, Forest.
TERRESTAI: Everlasting Forest, perhaps a reference to the Universe.
TIR-NAN-OG: (G) A mystic island of perpetual youth, or perhaps a reference to the Otherworld.
THUILE: (SY) Spring
TOR: (A) Tower, lookout tree or tree hideout.
TORLO: (A) Intense strength, brilliance or brilliant light.
TORLORNOS: (A) World Tree or Tree of Life.
TOROTH: (A) Strength of the Oak Tree or immovable Oak.
TRANSIGNATION: An Elemental projects their spirit/consciousness into a mortal body.
TRANSITION: The movement between world and dimensions.
TREE OF LIFE: also Yggdrasil, the metaphoric World Tree.
TREFOIL: also Trifolium, the Shamrock or four-leaved clover.
TROSAD: (G) A ceremonial or ritualistic court for Wizards.
TUAITHBEL: (G) Counterclockwise
TUATHAL: (G) Counterclockwise
TUILE: (Q) Spring
TUESDAY: Elf-Day
UBAID: An ancient proto-Sumerian "Anunnaki" dynastic civilization.
UIAL: (SY) Spring
UNDOME: (Q) Twilight
UNDOMIEL: (Q) Elven-star, esp. a seven-rayed star.
UNICORN: A Creature of Faerie; an icon of innocence, love and beauty.
URIME: (Q) August
URUI: (S) August
VARDA: Queen of Stars; also Anu and Eru, literally "Star Mother."
VASTA: (SY) Awaken
VIRESSE: (Q) April
VIRITH: (S) April
WEDMATH: August
WINTERFILTHE: October
WIZARDWOOD: also *livewood*; that which is removed from the tree by an Elf Wizard.
YEATA: (S) Fire Element
YGGDRASIL: (SC) The World Tree, usually the Ash Tree.

Y TYLWYTH TEG: (G) Name of race residing in Celtic *Caerllen* or Ffayrie-mounds.

ZEISATU: (SY) Consciousness or thoughtforms.

ZHA: (T) The future or what is to come next.

ZIGGURAT: Pyramid-styled buildings used as temples by the ancient Anunnaki.

ZORVAIN: (SY) Mystically charged, esp. with an intention.

[KEY TO ORIGINS: The source of a word is indicated by the letter or letters immediately following each bold entree. They are (A) Abroren; (AL) Alloryne; (D) Drae'sturi; (F) Firefen; (FR) French; (G) Gaelic-Welsh/Celtic; (GR) Greek; (IT) Italian; (L) Lis'tarii; (M) Miaren; (Q) Quenya; (S) Syndarin; (SC) Scandinavian/Norse; (SE) Silver Elves; (SH) Shiri; (SY) Sylvanus Folk; (T) Tyr Tylwyth Teg; and (TU) Tulari.]

Necronomicon: The Anunnaki Bible : 10th Anniversary
   Collector's Edition—LIBER-N,L,G,9+W-M+S *(Hardcover)*

The Complete Anunnaki Bible: A Source Book of Esoteric Archaeology :
   10th Anniversary—LIBER-N,L,G,9+W-M+S *(Paperback)*

Necronomicon: The Anunnaki Bible : 10th Anniversary
   Pocket Edition—*(Abridged Paperback)*

*Gates of the Necronomicon: The Secret Anunnaki Tradition of
   Babylon* : 10th Anniversary Collector's Edition—
   LIBER-50,51/52,R+555 *(Hardcover)*

The Sumerian Legacy: A Guide to Esoteric Archaeology—
   LIBER-50+51/52 *(Paperback)*

*Necronomicon Revelations—Crossing to the Abyss: Nine Gates
   of the Kingdom of Shadows & Simon's Necronomicon*—
   LIBER-R+555 *(Paperback)*

*Necronomicon: The Anunnaki Grimoire: A Manual of Practical
   Babylonian Magick* : 10th Anniversary Collector's Edition—
   LIBER-E,W/Z,M+K *(Hardcover)*

*Practical Babylonian Magic : Invoking the Power of the Sumerian
   Anunnaki*—LIBER-E,W/Z,M+K *(Paperback)*

*The Complete Book of Marduk by Nabu : A Pocket Anunnaki
   Devotional Companion to Babylonian Prayers & Rituals* :
   10th Anniversary Collector's Edition—LIBER-W+Z *(Hardcover)*

*The Maqlu Ritual Book : A Pocket Companion to Babylonian
   Exorcisms, Banishing Rites & Protective Spells* :
   10th Anniversary Collector's Edition—LIBER-M *(Hardcover)*

Necronomicon: The Anunnaki Spellbook : 10th Anniversary
   Pocket Edition—LIBER-W/Z+M *(Abridged Paperback)*

*The Anunnaki Tarot : Consulting the Babylonian Oracle of
   Cosmic Wisdom (Guide Book)*—LIBER-T *(Paperback)*

*Elvenomicon—Secret Traditions of Elves & Faeries : The Book of
   Elven Magick & Druid Lore : 15th Anniversary Collector's
   Edition*—LIBER-D *(Hardcover)*

The Druid's Handbook : Ancient Magick for a New Age
   20th Anniversary Collector's Edition—LIBER-D2 *(Hardcover)*

Draconomicon : The Book of Ancient Dragon Magick :
   25th Anniversary Collector's Edition—LIBER-D3 *(Hardcover)*

NABU—JOSHUA FREE ("Merlyn Stone")
Chief Scribe & Librarian of New Babylon
Bard of the Twelfth Chair at New Forest

JOSHUA FREE
publishing imprint

mardukite.com

Printed in the USA
CPSIA information can be obtained
at www.ICGtesting.com
LVHW091807160923
758409LV00004B/41

9 780578 546209